EDUCATION POLICY PERILS

Education Policy Perils provides educators and those interested in the future of public education with research-based and practical analyses of some of the foremost issues facing public schools today. The collection, written by experienced scholar-practitioners, offers insights that include nuanced descriptions of various challenges facing educators and recommendations for overcoming them with an eye toward more successful policy and better implementation. The authors apply their expertise to a range of issues from international testing to policy challenges related to curriculum on the state and national levels. This volume positions ongoing debates within the wider context of an education landscape struggling to displace junk-science ideology with empirical research. The scope and sequence combined with the expertise of the contributors make this volume a vital resource for educators at all levels during a pivotal time of major changes in education policy.

Christopher H. Tienken is Associate Professor of Education Administration at Seton Hall University, USA.

Carol A. Mullen is Professor of Educational Leadership at Virginia Tech, Blacksburg, USA.

EDUCATION POLICY PERILS

Tackling the Tough Issues

*Edited by Christopher H. Tienken
and Carol A. Mullen*

FOREWORD BY FENWICK W. ENGLISH

KAPPA DELTA PI
INTERNATIONAL HONOR SOCIETY IN EDUCATION

Routledge
Taylor & Francis Group

NEW YORK AND LONDON

First published 2016
by Routledge
711 Third Avenue, New York, NY 10017

and by Routledge
2 Park Square, Milton Park, Abingdon, Oxon, OX14 4RN

Routledge is an imprint of the Taylor & Francis Group, an informa business

© 2016 Kappa Delta Pi

Library of Congress Cataloging-in-Publication Data
Education policy perils : tackling the tough issues / edited by Christopher H. Tienken and Carol A. Mullen.
    pages cm
Includes bibliographical references and index.
1. Education and state—United States.   I. Tienken, Christopher.   II. Mullen, Carol A.
LC89.E28 2015
379.73—dc23   2015021291

ISBN: 978-1-138-89818-9 (hbk)
ISBN: 978-1-138-89819-6 (pbk)
ISBN: 978-1-315-70871-3 (ebk)

Typeset in Bembo
by Keystroke, Station Road, Codsall, Wolverhampton

Printed and bound in the United States of America by Publishers Graphics, LLC on sustainably sourced paper.

DEDICATIONS

Christopher Tienken:
For Gabriella and Francesca—dream out loud. Andate avanti.

Carol Mullen:
To the Living Legend recipients of the National Council of Professors of Educational Administration's Living Legend Award, who are inspiring positive leaders and whose mentoring and collegial friendship keep our flames lit.

CONTENTS

FOREWORD

This compact volume represents a gem in the rich craft of discourse analysis which, as Fairclough (1992) laid out, connects language use to social and cultural processes and the practice of "using language analysis as a method for studying social change" (p. 1).

That we are in a period of profound social and cultural change in public education is attested by the continuing frontal attacks on teacher unions, schools of education, and democratic governance as represented in the tradition of the American school board. Let us not overlook in this era of rapid change the corporatization and privatization of what Bourdieu (1999) called "the left hand" of the state (p. 183). The left hand is represented in public schools and social welfare agencies. These are being cut back or dismantled to the logic of the marketplace. The erasure of the idea of public service as a kind of "professional disinterestedness" based on "militant devotion" (Bourdieu, 1999, p. 184) is happening in our lifetime.

Fairclough (1992) set forth four criteria for linking language analysis to social and cultural change, all of which are an integral part of this coedited book:

- The method would have to be multidimensional in that it would show the relationship between language and the "social properties" of texts to "instances of social practice" (p. 8).
- The method would have to be a multifunctional analysis which contributed to a change in knowledge that would include "beliefs and common sense, social relations, and social identities" (p. 8).
- The method would have to include historical analysis and the idea of intertextuality in which some texts are linked to others in specific ways that then "depend upon and change with social circumstances" (p. 9).

- The method would have to be "critical" in that it should show "connections and causes which are hidden; it also implies intervention, for example providing resources for those who may be disadvantaged through change" (p. 9).

The chapters in *Education Policy Perils: Tackling the Tough Issues* are studded with examples of all four of Fairclough's criteria for connecting linguistic form and content with social and cultural beliefs and practices. The result is a concise, readable, forceful response—a potent source of resistance to the abdication of social justice which we are witnessing in the neoliberal assault on all forms of the left hand of the state in many countries of the world in our times. It would be difficult for me to imagine a timelier and more needed text for all of us deeply engaged in the struggle to retain a vision of the common school for all of the children of all of the people.

Fenwick W. English
R. Wendell Eaves Sr. Distinguished Professor of
Educational Leadership
School of Education
The University of North Carolina at Chapel Hill

References

Bourdieu, P. (1999). The abdication of the state. In P. Bourdieu et al. (Eds.), *The weight of the world: Social suffering in contemporary society* (P. P. Ferguson, Trans.; pp. 181–188). Stanford, CA: Stanford University Press.

Fairclough, N. (1992). *Discourse and social change*. Cambridge, UK: Polity Press.

ACKNOWLEDGMENTS

We are both fortunate to have a long-term, positive relationship with someone very special and talented. We wish to express our gratitude to Kathie-Jo Arnoff, Director of Publications and Managing Editor, *KDP Record,* Kappa Delta Pi (KDP), International Honor Society in Education, for her feedback on the various chapters contained in this coedited book. She is one of the very best editors we have ever known and one of the kindest colleagues with whom we have ever had the pleasure to work. Kathie-Jo also shepherded the contract for this book with Routledge/Taylor & Francis, and she spearheaded the cosponsorship of our book with Kappa Delta Pi.

We thank Routledge/Taylor & Francis and Kappa Delta Pi for their partnership in the formation and sponsorship of this book. With their mutuality and highly responsive publishing timeline, we were provided outstanding managerial assistance.

We also thank the anonymous peer reviewers of our book, who provided keen insights and helpful tips, as well as affirmations that our text exhibits continuity across chapters and has something important to say, and that it will be useful to readers. It was helpful to hear that they thought that each chapter of our book carefully adds a dimension that other chapters do not and that this writing style is critical to making a full picture of national and international comparisons.

INTRODUCTION

Christopher H. Tienken and Carol A. Mullen

Tough issues. To us, these two words best describe the post-No Child Left Behind (NCLB) education policy era for educators and people interested in public education. Issues including curricular standardization, high-stakes testing, college and career readiness, school scandals, international competitiveness, and the corporatization of education grab the mainstream press headlines and draw the attention of policymakers at local, state, national, and international levels. We believe all such issues, and others that are not currently on the media radar but should be, deserve close attention. Among those that should be in the spotlight is the need for equitable and just schools for underserved marginalized student populations and communities committed to the health and well-being of children and youth.

One purpose for this coedited book, titled *Education Policy Perils: Tackling the Tough Issues,* is to provide focused commentary on and analysis of some of the most pressing policy issues facing public school educators and those interested in maintaining a healthy and vibrant public school system. Another purpose is to share insights and provide recommendations from leading scholar-practitioners, particularly from the disciplines of educational leadership and science education, on ways to ponder, navigate, and challenge serious policy issues. Such issues include the commercialization and marketization of public schooling, the standardization of curriculum and assessment, and the internationalization of academic achievement represented by misleading rankings and fueled by policy pressures.

For this collection, we assembled an accomplished group of thought-leaders in education to pierce the veil on some of the most popular and controversial issues in education policymaking. The contributors of each fast-paced and user-friendly chapter describe and analyze an important education reform policy issue of the day. They raise provocative ideas—at times being provocative themselves—essentially exposing what is contentious territory. Contributors also make evidence-informed, practical recommendations for educators and policymakers on how to better approach the policy issues presented so that public education can be improved for all children. Every chapter contains practical information and tips for school practitioners specifically and constituent groups more generally. Each researcher brings national and international education and research experience to the conversation and leverages his or her deep knowledge of the policymaking environment to drill down under the headlines, endeavoring to provide readers with an evidence-based look at what dwells below education's surface.

The volume is separated into two parts, with each part providing at least three research-based practical essays on one of these policy topics:

- Education Leadership in the Current Policy Environment
- Curriculum and Assessment Policy Perils.

Each of seven chapters presents an important policy topic and critical analysis of a pertinent education reform policy issue from the perspective of experienced educators leading the preparation of future school leaders and teachers. Each contributor uses his or her experiential lens to examine the ongoing tensions between ideologically driven education reform policy and empirical research results to provide critical reviews in the form of a laser-like focus on current policy issues and recommendations for education policy and practice.

In the order of the book chapters, coauthors Christopher Lubienski and P. 3. Myers, both of the University of Illinois at Urbana–Champaign, open the volume, challenging the stance that school-choice policies represent an appealing vision for politically engaged parents and communities to cast their lots with educational reformers to change the present conditions of schooling in the United States. They explain the inverted relationship between competition and choice presently found in many education reform policy proposals and the negative implications for school personnel.

In the second chapter, Carol A. Mullen of Virginia Tech takes evidence-based aim at the corporatization of public education. She challenges the corporate network proliferation in the public school sector and sheds light on the rapid erosion of capital. She contends that a major policy problem confronting professional educators in schools and universities is that public education is being abandoned as a public service in the United States. Corporate network proliferation in the public school sector is eroding the capital of these schools. The meaning of formal education becomes distorted where for-profit corporations present themselves as the caretakers of an ethos of public service for the greater good. In this analysis, the public school sector and education policy are conceived of as a network. The connections Mullen traces among markets provide evidence of the neoliberal movement's takeover of public education. She presents a view of a single market wherein one curriculum is adopted, disenfranchising underserved groups by such forces as the momentous financial push by the private sector into the public sector and the influence of foundations over federal policies.

Mariela A. Rodríguez of the University of Texas at San Antonio proposes that leading for social justice is a goal that every school leader must seek to attain in order to make a positive impact in the lives of the children and youth that walk through their school doors. Her goal within Chapter 3 is to present a synthesis of social justice research and theoretical perspectives within an evolving demographic of students such as English learners in U.S. schools. Traditionally marginalized students constitute vulnerable populations that can directly benefit from the practice of social justice leadership in schools.

In the fourth chapter, Thomas Tramaglini, a public school curriculum administrator in New Jersey, and Christopher H. Tienken of Seton Hall University review the evidence of the influence of customized curricula on student achievement in high-poverty high schools. They present results from an original study that supports the practice of proximal curriculum development and calls into question the current policy of mandating one-size-fits-all curriculum standards developed from distal policymaking bodies as a means of improving academic outcomes of students from poverty.

In Chapter 5, Svein Sjøberg of the University of Oslo, Norway, challenges the emergence of the global educational reform movement, where the Organization of Economic Co-operation and Development (OECD), through its Programme for International Student Assessment (PISA) project, has become the key driver. PISA, with its focus on league tables and rankings, influences educational debates and policy in many countries. The OECD, with PISA as the main instrument, is emerging as a kind of global ministry of education, promoting its own standardized curriculum and system of assessment. Providing a detailed analysis of PISA, Sjøberg pushes back on how PISA results are used to legitimize market-driven education and social policies, such as the control of teachers, payment for teachers and principals based on test results, and erosion of the public school system through the privatization and the introduction of more testing regimes.

In Chapter 6, Michael Marder of the University of Texas at Austin tackles the issue of requiring completion of Algebra II for high school graduation. He takes aim at recent policy legislation in the state of Texas that eliminated the requirement that all students complete Algebra II and argues that such policy proposals are short-sighted, actually robbing students of an economically secure future. Marder provides a crisp definition of college and career readiness, and brings clarity to the long-standing issue of how much math is enough math to prepare students for post-secondary life options. Marder presents evidence and argues passionately on behalf of children for policymakers and school administrators to provide a curricular sequence that will lead to maximum post-secondary opportunities.

In the seventh and final chapter, Christopher H. Tienken of Seton Hall University questions the ubiquitous use of standardized test results to drive portions of education accountability policies such as those found in NCLB, the NCLB waivers program, teacher and administrator evaluation programs, high school graduation eligibility, and grade promotion. He demonstrates through scientific study how the results of standardized tests can be predicted, with high levels of accuracy, using community and family demographic factors easily found in U.S. census data. Tienken presents the results of a statewide study conducted in New Jersey in which he predicted the percentage of students scoring proficient or above on the state tests in Grade 5 over a three-year period by using only community and family demographic factors. He offers viable alternatives for policymakers and educators to consider when developing assessment-based education accountability policies.

Whether you are a policy professional, educator, or an interested stakeholder in public education, the chapters in this volume will provide you with evidence-based information and ideas for action. We hope readers will use the information in these chapters to extend and enrich the discussion about education policy at the local, state, national, and international levels. Children do not have a presence in the halls of power or the back rooms where some education policies are made. Adults have a duty to provide a thoughtful presence for them by advocating for policy ideas based on informed professional judgment and demonstrated evidence. In the final analysis, it is the responsibility of all education stakeholders to provide a quality public school experience for future generations. We believe this volume will help in that effort.

We envision various uses for this volume. Professors of education leadership and teacher preparation could use the book as a highly accessible secondary text to complement a more traditional education policy or leadership textbook. The book could be the primary text for an education leadership or teacher leadership course on contemporary issues in education. School administrators might choose to use the text as part of an administrative professional learning community (PLC) or book study as a way to improve their leadership practice and decision-making. We also believe that the book is accessible enough to be informative to noneducators in helping to understand the current education reform policy environment.

Readers are encouraged to contact us with comments and insights about the ideas and content we present. We are also eager to receive suggestions for issues that could be covered in a future edition on education policy. Contact Christopher H. Tienken at christopher.tienken@shu.edu or Carol A. Mullen at camullen@vt.edu.

PART I

Education Leadership in the Current Policy Environment

1

THE RHETORIC AND REALITY OF SCHOOL REFORM: CHOICE, COMPETITION, AND ORGANIZATIONAL INCENTIVES IN MARKET-ORIENTED EDUCATION

Christopher Lubienski
P. S. Myers

UNIVERSITY OF ILLINOIS AT URBANA–CHAMPAIGN

School choice is not a new feature of education in the United States. Yet, since the late 1980s, school choice as education reform policy has helped reshape the administration and character of how educational services are delivered. School choice existed in the postwar era, prior to these changes, with parents of means being able to decide where and with whom their children went to school by way of neighborhood choice. Today, across most states, there is still some mechanism by which parents of varying means can select among different models of schooling. According to the Evergreen Education Group (2014), a digital learning advocacy organization, more than 300,000 students were schooled solely online during the 2013–2014 school year. That organization also reported that during the 2014–2015 academic year, 30 states were expected to have various forms of K–12 schools that operate fully online. The National Center for Education Statistics (2012) estimated that more than 1.7 million students were homeschooled in 2011. Though the online and homeschooled populations represent only a modest number of students, they illustrate the present and increasing options for parents to decide what schooling should look like for their children.

Beyond online schooling and homeschooling, there are a number of alternatives to the assigned neighborhood public school. The other options within the realm of school choice include private schools, magnet schools, charter schools, vouchers, savings accounts, tax credits, deductions, and scholarships (Friedman Foundation for Educational Choice, 2014). Choice also implies a number of administrative or institutional practices that include open enrollment programs, adjustments in admissions policies, creating culturally or linguistically aware schools, or the decentralization of governance, curriculum, assessment, or hiring practices.

Often in educational policy discourse, the forms of schooling are presented as supply-side innovations/interventions away from what is portrayed as the older, bureaucratic catchment-area model. Funding changes, conversely, are often understood as demand-side adjustments. These policies typically tie funding to the student and thus allow the family-cum-consumer some mobility. Similarly, administrative adjustments can impact which students are enabled to attend certain schools in order to generate more movement and demand, while policies that ease entry for new providers into the education market—as is the case with charter schools—can create additional supply (Gaskell, 2002). Most if not all of these policies have come to have wide acceptance and application with policymakers in the United States and elsewhere.

Although school choice and other related issues are and have been important areas of study in departments of public policy, economics, and education policy, there has been little in the way of concerted efforts to involve educational leadership in either the enterprise of cooperative research or the debates around school choice. This is problematic, given that the market logic underlying school-choice policies makes universal assumptions about how schools—and particularly school leaders—will react to competitive incentives placed on them through choice. Because of their unique role in shaping school policy, this chapter seeks to engage educational leadership thinkers and practitioners in the ongoing conversation. Indeed, school and district leaders are central, if only implicitly, in the rhetoric and reality of the "new normal" of school-choice policies. According to Cravens, Goldring, and Peñaloza (2012), these policies have varied effects on what school leaders do within and outside their schools to enhance teaching, learning, and the ability to attract and retain students within their schools.

The latter issue—the enticement of families into schools of choice—is explored in a review of research in the following section of this chapter. Within that section, we consider the often tacit relational proxy of choice for competition. That is, while policies allowing parents to select a school use a rhetoric and visual language of symbols to incite *choice*, what actually drives these policies is the desire for increased *competition* among schools. Following that discussion, the chapter moves into an examination of the inverse relation of choice and competition in a market-like arrangement of schools. Within that section, we highlight the implications of this relationship on school and district leaders.

Finally, we close with a discussion of the meaningfulness of these relationships to school personnel, policymakers, and educational leadership. With school choice being presented using a specific set of messages and symbols, we argue that it is increasingly important that rising principals and school administrators possess a clear view of the landscape of schooling. We hope that this chapter, through a careful progression of extant research, not only clarifies the marketized educational landscape, but also fosters greater connections between educational policy, which seeks to question and formulate present theory, and educational leadership, which deals more readily with the administering of the provision of education.

The Appeals of Choice

School choice is often advanced as an expression of individual freedom. Parents, or "consumers," are "liberated" to select the best educational institution for their child (Feinberg & Lubienski, 2008; Lubienski, 2007b; Lubienski, Weitzel, & Lubienski, 2009). Choice policies give students, parents, and communities freedom from the school to which they are assigned within their district—an assignment usually based on residence. Using the framework of Hirschman (1970), school choice promotes the use of consumer sector style "exit" to address the perceived decline or insufficiencies of a given school so that families can enroll their children in schools thought to be of better quality.

Exit, theoretically, is then akin to Tiebout's (1956) idea of preference expression that has come to be known as "voting with your feet," which is an option that can be made equitably available only to completely mobile populations. Through adopting such market-style mechanisms in the public school sector, it is generally assumed that this arrangement engenders families with a greater sense of agency in shaping children's education and improving their life chances (Bell, 2009).

For reformers, advocacy groups, and proponents in government, school choice offers the promise of greater quality, "including more innovation and responsiveness to consumers, and increased efficiency and overall effectiveness in securing gains in academic achievement" (Lubienski, 2003b, p. 4). Such beliefs are grounded in public choice theory and the presumed benefits of marketization, if not privatization (Lubienski & Lubienski, 2014). Public choice theory asserts that individuals operate largely from their own self-interest, typically best expressed in a businesslike arrangement. This is largely because public bureaucracies cannot be relied upon to operate for the elusive "public good." Bureaucrats, and the bureaucracies they control, are prone to "capture" by special interests that they supposedly regulate (Laffont & Tirole, 1991). According to public-choice logic, this may advance the preferences of interest groups like teachers' unions and other organized policy beneficiaries while failing to meet the needs of myriad other constituencies, such as children, that are less organized but reliant upon the benefits of a well-operating public school system.

Choice allows for the more effective articulation of the interests of these peripheralized groups because "by streamlining these arrangements into a neat consumer ⇒ provider relationship . . . a more business-style conception of the public is less susceptible to internal influences and corruptions" (Lubienski, 2005, p. 467). This newfound ability of consumers to pursue their own preferences within the publicly funded education sector promotes the diversification and decentralization of choice. By allowing schools to diversify in response to choosers' preferences, an atomization of choosers and the subsequent coalescence of "preference clusters" occurs (Lubienski, 2005, p. 467). These groups of consumers will have schools that are more readily able to meet parents' notions of quality, yet, due to the consumer-provider arrangement, are able to exert consumer pressure through dissent and exit (Lubienski, 2006b).

Choice and Competition

While "school choice" is often framed by advocates as the empowerment of families, the policies those advocates propose almost invariably and implicitly involve some level of competition between schools for the choices of the families. Because the ability to choose is essentially moot unless there are substantive differences in a range of alternatives, market logic posits that schools will differentiate themselves—by program or quality (although composition may also be a factor)—in order to attract families and improve the school's competitive advantage in the local education marketplace (Lubienski, 2006a). Indeed, this may mean that schools take measures that effectively put them in the position of choosing students as they establish themselves as exceptional in some regard (Lubienski & Dougherty, 2009).

Yet, some advocates of choice do not discuss this matter outright. This may be because while the idea of "choice" has an inherent appeal, the competition that results from choice can mean that there are winners and losers—something that violates our equity impulse when applied to children. Hypothetically, parents may choose a school that meets their standard of quality and other criteria. When this is presented simply as "choice," it would appear that all children are given a fair opportunity to do well and none are necessarily disadvantaged by the act of choosing. Consumers make choices that may simply be matters of preference, as opposed to differentials in organizational effectiveness—that is, selecting schools on dimensions of programmatic differences instead of distinctions in quality (Lubienski, 2003a). But as schools compete to be chosen, they may recognize competitive incentives to provide parents with incomplete, or "soft" information that shifts the basis of choice away from evidence of school effectiveness toward emotional appeals and group affinity (Lubienski, 2007a). Thus, if parents are choosing schools based on factors other than school effectiveness, this may undercut the driving force market advocates hope to leverage for school improvement (Lubienski, 2007b; Lubienski & Weitzel, 2009).

Another reason for possibly shying away from discussing competition is that the research around the effects of competition in schooling yields mixed—and sometimes detrimental—results. In some studies, competition has been shown to induce some improvement and greater efficiency (Goldhaber & Eide, 2002; Hoxby, 2000). Yet other studies have suggested that competition may induce schools to adopt organizational behaviors with more harmful impacts—for instance, shifting resources away from instruction toward other areas, including marketing (Lubienski, 2005; Ni & Arsen, 2010). In a large-scale study of nationally representative samples of private, charter, and public schools, Lubienski and Lubienski (2014) found that the latter were producing similar or better mathematics results when controlling for demographics across these schools. Moreover, they noted that one of the reasons private and charter schools were underperforming was because in more competitive environments, they often were using their autonomy in ways that were undercutting student outcomes—for instance, by embracing outdated curricula or hiring less effective, uncertified teachers. This "challenges the very basis of the current movement to remake public education based on choice, competition, and autonomy" (Lubienski & Lubienski, 2014, p. 127). Such dynamics might also be evident in student selection, as schools may see opportunities to use their autonomy to avoid certain types of students (Lubienski, Lee, & Gordon, 2013).

While many advocates of competition and choice point to the possibility of better results for minority or impoverished students in schools that compete with one another by design, Frankenberg, Siegel-Hawley, and Wang (2011) found that many metropolitan area charter schools have a percentage of White students that surpasses that of the local public schools; thus minorities are underserved by these charter schools (see also Garcia, 2010). Similarly, Lee and Lubienski (2011) found that there is a trend toward segregation in charter schools in a number of states. Ultimately, what this means is that competition may too often be incentivizing schools to pursue preferred students rather than to develop more effective ways of engaging and educating all students (Lubienski, Gulosino, & Weitzel, 2009). In the following section, we consider some ways that this is happening, as indicated in the research literature.

The Visual and Linguistic Representations of School Competition

As choice and competition increasingly become primary considerations in the education landscape, a set of symbols and marketing strategies employed by schools appears to be emerging. Indeed, for schools to compete, marketing becomes a near inevitability (Lubienski, 2005). For school administrators facing the possibility of a decline in enrollment, particularly to rival schools, consideration of this development and how it might be managed has a pragmatic utility. Cravens et al. (2012) found that while the differences are not statistically significant, school leaders in choice schools (charter, magnet, and private schools) spend more of their time doing public relations-type work, and some charter schools require their teachers to help in student recruitment.

As schools are being placed in the position of attracting students or going out of business, educational and extracurricular activities are reconfigured as potential marketing events: For instance, the school play can be a way to promote the school to potential students (Boldt, 1999; Gilder, 1999; Lubienski, 2006a; Ravitch, 2010). In some cases, schools and districts have hired managers or management companies with no particular expertise in education simply because they better understand how to conceive of schools as firms within a marketplace (Lubienski, 2007a). Of course, the increased need to undertake marketing activities has implications for the preparation of school and district leaders, who must be able to maneuver effectively and ethically through the competitive landscape of school choice.

Although there is a logic that guides the organizational behavior of schools, there are ethical considerations and concerns regarding how these market forces may then impact educational equity. This is made clear in situations where school personnel end up choosing students, as opposed to students choosing schools. In an analysis of enrollment practices in Auckland, New Zealand, schools serving more affluent students were found to be much more likely to employ self-imposed attendance zones that were gerrymandered to avoid areas with greater concentrations of poor and minority students (Lubienski et al., 2013). Moreover, Lubienski, Linick, and York (2012) pointed out that when schools in Washington, DC, sought to market themselves online, charter schools tended to overrepresent images of White and Asian students relative to their actual enrollment to statistically significant degrees. At the same time, public schools were underrepresenting the proportion of Hispanic students in attendance, also to a statistically significant degree.

In sum total, the literature has suggested an incentive on the part of these schools collectively to attract certain populations in order to either retain or enhance their market position. The overrepresentation of Whites and Asian Americans may indicate that certain types of students hold different value for schools in a competitive market. While this work focuses on how schools market themselves, it inherently raises a question regarding the ethics behind the use of racial politics in school competition.

Lubienski (2007b) noted that to "shape a school's status in the marketplace . . . particular types of representation, such as logos, physical plant, dress codes, performance, and school names" are employed. A brief explanation of these different attempts to augment or develop a place within the competitive market of schools follows. (This section relies heavily on Lubienski, 2007b.)

Naming

The use of naming to evoke notions of erudition as well as academic, economic, and ethnic opportunity is an important tool in the competitive landscape of the education sector. Large charter school educational management organizations (EMOs) such as Academica and the Albert Einstein Academies use names that are associated with or connote learnedness and excellence. Charter Management Organizations (CMOs)—including Advantage Schools, Achievement First, Bright Star Schools, Career Success Schools, Lighthouse Academies, and St. HOPE Public Schools—employ names which imply that these networks offer both greater academic and economic opportunities than the traditional public school. Other CMOs—such as Cesar Chavez Public Charter Schools for Public Policy, King-Chavez Neighborhood of Schools, Betty Shabazz International Charter Schools, and the W.E.B. DuBois Consortium of Charter Schools, as well as individual schools such as Sejong Academy of Minnesota, Sheridan Japanese Charter School, and Yinhua Academy—make an overt ethnic and, at times, radical appeal to students and families of color.

Yet, the search for a name that appeals to specific demographics does not end only at schools or networks. Lubienski (2007b) noted:

> The symbolic dimension of school names even affects the labeling of types of schools. Confronted by scattered criticism that charter schools represent a privatizing agenda within public education, many reformers and legislators who support charter schools have chosen school names that seek to allay such concerns.
>
> *(p. 267)*

This naming convention includes the usage of "Community Schools" and "Public School Academies" to officially describe charter schools in Ohio and Michigan, respectively. Other charter advocacy organizations also adopt this approach, emphasizing the public nature of their enterprise: Consider the National Alliance of Public Charter Schools, for example. Note that the intent here is not to delve into the issue of whether or not charter schools are "public" schools (Lubienski, 2001). Indeed, they are typically viewed in a legal sense as public entities that are funded with tax dollars, but managed independent of direct state administration, although critics point to organizational behaviors that distinguish these schools from other public schools.

Buildings

School buildings convey connotations and messages about a school's culture, current positioning, and aspirational position with respect to local hierarchies, as well as notions of value to different constituencies that the school may serve. As Lubienski (2007b) noted, the first public high schools "sought to emulate established academies, colleges, and universities" (p. 268). Indeed, before being remodeled, the United States' second oldest high school, Hartford Public High School, featured cathedral-like spires and a main entrance with three arches.

The significance of the physical plant of a school should not be taken for granted. As Shapiro (2015) wrote:

> The architectural and physical features of learning settings *teach*, as representations of cultural values and understandings that remain with students long after they have left the educational experience.... It is therefore worthwhile to look closely at sets of signification systems as structures that teach and ask questions about the values embedded in learning settings and how they impact learners.
>
> *(p. 8)*

Within the present competitive landscape of schools, the messages coded into the form and function of school buildings may have an even greater meaning.

As many charter schools begin in spaces that were formerly used by district schools, the first message of space is one of finances. Charter schools that are unconstrained by finances to build their own unique buildings convey a message of status. The ornately modern glass and steel exterior of the UNO Soccer Academy in Chicago, completed in 2011, stands out in an economically depressed urban community. This is by design, as the building is meant to speak toward a forward-looking, aspirational culture shift for the largely Latino population that the school serves. The building purposefully does not use any traditional motifs in its angular styling. According to the architect, Juan Moreno, as reported by the local NPR affiliate, UNO CEO Juan Rangel sometimes references Chicago's Loop: "He'll point to it and he'll tell the kids, 'Look, you're not gonna be the custodians of those buildings. You'll be the leaders of those buildings'" (Lutton, 2011). The school is ensconced in soccer culture, as each classroom is named after a country that has hosted the World Cup. Another tacit feature of the building is transparency, as classrooms have glass walls that face out into the corridor and the manicured exterior. The surrounding Gage Park neighborhood is always visible, as are the children (Patton, 2012).

Logos

School symbols, seals, and logos, more than most other signifiers, make a direct appeal to create a brand for schools to retain and attract existent and potential school clientele and constituencies. According to Oswald (2007), "A brand is a system of signs and symbols that engages the consumer in an imaginary/symbolic process that contributes tangible value to a product offering." An example of trying to create a brand that engages historical and cultural symbols can be found at the Newark Charter School:

> The Newark Charter School logo symbolizes our aspirations for our children and their school. The left branch of the symbol, the flame, stands

for knowledge. The right branch, the leaf, stands for the intellectual, social, ethical and physical growth of our students. The center symbol, the diamond, stands for our uniqueness in Delaware (The Diamond State) and the quality of our programs and people.

(Newark Charter School, 2014, paragraph 2)

It is not uncommon for imagery to include plants, leaves, trees, fire, books, schoolhouses, or microscopes when schools attempt to market themselves through the use of logos. The Newark Charter Schools use the diamond as a particularly place-specific reference. Another example of this practice is that many charter schools in the District of Columbia use logos that appear more appropriate for a corporation. These simple yet colorful graphics hint at innovation. Examples of corporate style logos include BASIS Washington, DC, Ingenuity Prep., and District of Columbia International School.

Dress

Semiotician Theo Van Leeuwen (2005) explained, "people use the way they dress to communicate their allegiance to ideas and values, rather than their social class, occupation, and so on" (p. 40). Such allegiance is seen in the dress codes imposed on students and staff alike in schools in competitive environments. Charter schools, and some traditional public schools, place strict controls on what can be worn and when. School uniforms are typically associated with private and religious schools; however, many public and charter schools use school uniforms both to emulate private schooling and as a marketing tool (Lubienski, 2007b). For example, one author of this chapter worked in a charter school that had students wear uniforms or some identifying clothing when they went to visit colleges. Like many other charter schools, the students were required to wear navy blue shirts and khakis at the upper level. The Walton Foundation heavily funded the charter network that the school belonged to, and, whether through coincidence or not, students' attire was quite similar to what employees wore at Wal-Mart (Brewer & Myers, 2015).

Celebrity

In both direct and diffuse methods, celebrity is used to market schools and generally bolster school choice programs. Celebrities have often attempted to use their large amounts of economic and social power to promote learning and market-like schooling agendas. The Soulsville Charter School in Memphis promotes its brand by noting that singer John Legend gave the school $30,000 in August of 2014 (*The Commercial Appeal,* 2014; The Soulsville Charter School, 2014). With school leaders attempting to reshape the Memphis-area schools after the competitive charter landscape of New Orleans (Zubrzycki, 2014),

Legend's donation serves as a point of differentiation within the field of competitors. Harlem Village Academies (HVA, 2014), where Legend serves as the Vice Chairman of the Board, can direct interested parents and students to a YouTube video on Legend's channel of him rehearsing the school song that he wrote with students (Legend, 2011). New York City's choice landscape is competitive for both schools and parents. The HVA YouTube channel (harlemvillage) chronicles visits to the school by President George W. Bush, Bill Cosby, and Legend, and features segments by several network and cable news outlets.

Through repeat exposure, HVA founder Deborah Kenny has attained her own celebrity and frequently discusses education reform on MSNBC's Morning Joe. Retired tennis player Andre Agassi opened a charter school bearing his name in 2001 and has used his celebrity to promote the school and raise substantial funds (Ravitch, 2014). Similarly, retired basketball player and entrepreneur Erving "Magic" Johnson has used his celebrity to help launch a series of schools for "at risk" youth and dropouts (Magic Johnson Bridgescape, 2014). He appears on the front page of the website and has promoted his schools on NBC's Today Show. Less overtly, a number of professional athletes and entertainers are involved with charter schooling, and thus choice and competition, through financial support, board participation, or other forms of advocacy. Examples include singer Alicia Keyes, rapper Pitbull, former basketball player and ESPN personality Jalen Rose, former basketball player turned politician Kevin Johnson, and media personality Oprah Winfrey (Klein, 2014).

School Values

American public schooling espouses and embodies the "values, beliefs, and aspirations" of the middle class (Lubienski, 2007b, p. 270). Lareau (1987) and Labaree (1988) have noted that schools ultimately cater to middle-class ideals as opposed to working-class notions of schooling. Ironically, despite the middle-class orientation of schooling, the present wave of reformers criticizes schooling for being socially and culturally bankrupt. These criticisms are largely put forward as claims of "social engineering, secular humanism, and violence" (Lubienski, 2007b, p. 271).

As a result, schools competing in a quasi-market arrangement seek to differentiate themselves through the use of disciplinary and character-related policies. These schools argue that they are safer and more grounded in common notions of morality than their rivals. Also, schools use "direct and surrogate information about school curricula [so that] parents gain a sense of commitment to academics" (Lubienski, 2007b, p. 271). Given the information asymmetries in the relationship between parents and schools, the employment of programs as signs becomes paramount in attracting and retaining families and students.

This is evident in how schools market their curricular and extracurricular offerings (Lubienski, 2007b):

> Although a comprehensive high school might stress that it offers many curricular (and extracurricular) opportunities for children, a school that highlights only academic images positions itself as an alternative to schools mired in detracking issues, self-esteem enhancement efforts, or equity concerns. Furthermore, the presence of fine arts, foreign language immersion, and technology courses can ... serve as a coded signal that a school will offer the children of ambitious parents many comparative advantages in their academic careers.
>
> *(p. 271)*

The desire to attract and retain desirable students extends across more marketing possibilities; however, school values become an easy way by which class, race, and opportunity preferences can be actively and discursively engaged by schools. In the contest between schools, the overt expression of these values makes their competitive field more evident.

Thus, when schools market themselves so as to note the distant year in which they were established, for instance, an older date can signify appealing values such as tradition, longevity, enduring quality, and prestige, all implying academic excellence and success. On the other hand, in some cases many observers might reasonably read other implications into such a simple bit of information. The date might hearken back to a time when the school was segregated, for instance, or otherwise imply an exclusivity that goes against public education values of accessibility. Inasmuch as some schools recognize the second side of this double-edged sword and use that to shape their pools of potential applicants, this practice can signify that schools are responding to competitive incentives in ways that undercut reformers' stated claims of equitable access.

The Inverted Relationship Between Choice and Competition

Although choice in education quasi-markets is linked to competition, there are empirical studies indicating that choice and competition can lead to problematic outcomes where choice either (a) does not create the desired type of competition or (b) leads to outcomes that undercut the stated goals of reform policies or of public education itself, such as equitable access (Jabbar, 2015; Lubienski, et al., 2009; Lubienski, et al., 2013; Lubienski & Lubienski, 2014). Although accurate information on school choice and competition empowers parents to make the best decisions possible for their child, such information might not always serve the individual school leader well. For instance, armed with better information, parents may opt out of their schools. Yet, as principals and superintendents operate within districts with their own curricular and political agenda, understanding the landscape and logistics of school choice may help to inform how voice and exit are used by other stakeholders to elicit desirable change within those districts. In the previous section, we noted how competition and choice could bring about change with regard to issues such as marketing. In this section, we consider other consequences of school choice and competition, including unforeseen, but not unlikely, outcomes of school-choice policies.

School choice advocates argue that choice and competition lead to greater innovation (Becker, 1999; Manno, Finn, Bierlein, & Vanourek, 1998). Movement across district lines, the entry of additional schools, and funding mechanisms allowing parent-consumers to pick among public and private school options theoretically induce schools to differentiate themselves in order to compete for students and improve their own standing. Schools are encouraged to behave as business-style firms, finding their own competitive advantage. But there is a growing consensus in the research that competition does not cause schools to innovate in the ways that were anticipated. Lubienski (2003a) and Lake (2008) have noted that new schools entering the market tend to offer noninnovative curricular reforms as they seek out a foothold in the competitive landscape.

Notably, traditional forms of curriculum, specifically in elementary schools, may actually underserve students as they pertain to the ability to reason mathematically and express mathematical knowledge (Lubienski & Lubienski, 2014). Curriculum reform, even in independent private schools, can be politically charged and quite difficult (Lubienski, 2003a). Therefore, revisiting the previous examples, many schools do innovate with respect to how and to whom they market themselves. Lubienski (2005) noted that the "apparently unexpected popularity of marketing indicates the existence of corrupted and perverse incentive structures that have the unanticipated potential of short-circuiting reformers' intended objectives of educational innovation and improvement" (p. 480).

Stated differently, marketing may give schools a competitive advantage by attracting a certain type of parent-consumer. Ultimately, however, this marketing disrupts how consumers operate, as information is colored and imperfect. Obviously, there are severe equity implications if choice—purportedly offered as a way to empower underserved groups—instead leads to greater differentials in access to quality schools, as some research has suggested (Rotberg, 2014).

Woessmann and Peterson (2007) contended that equity is a rather new goal for education, finding its roots in the latter half of the 20th century. Since that time, school choice has been argued as a mechanism by which equity in schooling can be achieved. Coons and Sugarman (1973) and others suggested that a well-planned voucher system might lead to equitable outcomes for minorities. To this point, the results have been mixed: Many researchers have maintained that instead of increasing equity, school-choice policies have led to more segregated access and outcomes in schooling (Cobb & Glass, 1999; Garcia, 2010; Krueger & Zhu, 2004; Rotberg, 2014).

Segregation may occur along many different margins; however, the immutable characteristics of ethnicity and gender, along with socio-economic status, are most often discussed in academic journals, governmental reports, and media. A general assumption is that in seeking to be equitable, policies and systems must sacrifice efficiency (Chubb & Moe, 1990). However, this binary is also in need of additional study. With respect to the assumption that equity and efficiency exist as two contested values, Woessmann and Peterson (2007) contended that in order for schools to "challenge students to their highest potential," an "efficient system of education" is needed (p. 22). By this argument, efficiency may well be a hallmark of equity and not a countervailing force.

There is also domestic and international evidence which suggests that as more schools enter into schooling "markets," assuming the student population remains unchanged with these new school offerings, student achievement actually worsens. Though Iatarola, Schwartz, Stiefel, and Chellman (2008) did not make such causal claims, they looked at the small-school reform movement in New York City high schools from 1993 to 2003. At that time, many large schools were being broken up into smaller schools under the assumption that smaller was better and more personalized. Looking at testing data from 1998 and 2003, they found that students in the small schools generally fared worse than their larger school counterparts. Also, small schools entering the district had a more difficult time with issues related to building costs and other costs that have less impact on larger institutions.

Similarly, a study done in the Netherlands (which has had free school choice for all students since the First World War) found that as more schools entered into the municipalities in their sample, student achievement worsened. The authors explained:

> We find a significantly *negative* effect of the number of schools in a municipality on pupils' achievement. A reduction in the number of schools of 10 percent increases test scores on average by 3 percent of a standard deviation. Hence, more school choice (and competition) is—in the setting of primary education in the Netherlands—detrimental for achievement.
>
> *(De Haan, Leuven, & Oosterbeek, 2011, p. 23, emphasis in original)*

Seemingly, it is possible to reach a point where both staffing and supporting all schools become more difficult, resulting in diseconomies of scale for school markets. So even though offering parents more choice makes sense, new schools may find it difficult to enter the market. Presumably, there is the possibility of reaching a partial equilibrium for schools in a market environment, though the nature and effects of such an equilibrium remain contested across academic literature.

Similar arguments center not just on the addition of new entrants into a market, but on families' access to more schooling options. For example, Hoxby (2003) has argued that the exit of a small percentage of students from a district to attend competing charter schools is enough to provoke a strategic organizational response where districts then find ways of becoming more effective, thus improving their academic performance. Other researchers, though, have noted that schools may not respond by directing more resources into instructional efforts, but instead may focus on alternatives such as marketing and other administrative approaches (Arsen & Ni, 2012; Lubienski, 2005).

Along these lines, Lubienski (2001) has argued that the delivery of education, at least up until the current reform movement, can be understood as a public good in that it is publicly funded and nonexclusive. Yet the rise of competition has led to a form of delivery that largely remains publicly funded, but is more rivalrous and exclusive in nature. This is not privatization as it is typically understood—focusing on shifting ownership of entities like schools to private hands—but a formulation of privatization of the delivery of educational provisions that creates firms and atomized actors acting on a specific set of incentives (Lubienski, 2006b). Even as parents compete to get their children into the "best" schools, students from impoverished backgrounds or with special needs are more expensive to educate than students from middle-class or affluent backgrounds. This means that schools can and do compete for certain types of students, recognizing their place within the educational market (Lubienski et al., 2012). Evidence of "creaming" or "skimming" the best students is both found and heavily contested in the present body of educational research (Lacireno-Paquet, Holyoke, Moser, & Henig, 2002).

(Why) Does and Should This Matter?

School marketing instead of curricular innovation, inequitable outcomes, diseconomies of scale in school markets, and privatization all highlight the unintended outcomes of school choice. This is not to say that choice is inherently wrong-minded. Most Americans enjoy a significant amount of choice in their lives, sometimes even to the point of exhaustion (Schwartz, 2004). However, programs of choice and other institutional innovations are driven largely by an economic rationalization from the business world, which is then applied to the educational sphere with the implicit or explicit expectation that the resulting competition will lead to better school choices, operations, and outcomes. This rationale is problematic as it means that certain strategies, tools, and understandings as to how problems are best solved are being leveraged in a field for which they were not designed. Schools and school systems have different goals than those of private sector firms.

In education, both domestically and globally, the logic and tools of firms are applied in an extremely simplistic manner which fails to see educational issues in their full complexity. Other fields—such as sociology, history, political science, educational psychology, and, of course, educational leadership—will undoubtedly continue to offer their unique contributions around education policy arguments and programs. This discourse allows for greater depth in understanding the true scope of problems within education. But the move to impose economic-style analyses and solutions to the problems in education through market mechanisms such as choice and competition represents a serious overreach of a single perspective into a domain that was simply not designed with market-style structures (Kuttner, 1999; Sandel, 2012). In this concluding discussion, we describe in greater depth the implications school choice, competition, and the market-like arrangements in current schooling have for educational leadership.

Being Like a Business

Leadership theorist and psychoanalyst Abraham Zaleznik (2004) constructed a useful frame that draws a distinction between leadership and management. While these ideas come out of the world of business, Zaleznik's idealization of managers is that they are calculated, competent controllers. Leaders, on the other hand, are imaginative and ethically driven. Schools are not businesses, and administrators are not corporate boards, yet how principals' and super-intendents' work might be considered along this continuum of management and leadership is a discussion with which educational leadership is and should remain actively engaged. This engagement becomes especially salient in the present climate of "marketism" in schools—a zealous belief in the power of markets to solve almost all social problems, including those in education (Lubienski & Lubienski, 2014).

In a market-like system, school leaders are required to mind and protect their territories and be expressly responsive to the economic-style signals of dissatisfaction and approval in their local market. These tasks, along with others, constitute the remaking of the principalship. These tasks lie closer to the manager's role and include responsibilities such as market analysis, marketing, and promotional efforts. Other responsibilities more suited to the idea of an entrepreneurial leader require the principal to manage the public face of the school in a more competitive environment and may take additional time away from the task of being the instructional and educational leader for the school. In this market arrangement, future school leaders need to understand the competitive context of their potential places of employ. The administrative imperative becomes to ascertain what they must do in order to effectively maintain or gain a foothold in their local market.

Since the early 2000s, there have been suggestions that schools of educational leadership should copy aspects of business training (Bottoms & O'Neill, 2001), and some business schools are now offering programs of study for prospective educational leaders. These include prestigious publics such as the Darden School of Business, along with the Curry School of Education at the University of Virginia, and noted privates such as the Jesse H. Jones Graduate School of Business at Rice University (Rice University, 2014; University of Virginia, 2014). This shift underscores the changes in the scope of what principals are and do. We cannot, in this chapter, fully address the normative nature of such changes described heretofore. What we can offer is that, at present, economic prescriptions for education, most notably school choice, have produced no significant lasting improvements in education and may have some detrimental impacts. Thus, while changes from administrative toward businesslike thinking may in theory yet yield some positive changes, there should be a wider discussion of what multiple fields of study can contribute in training school leaders.

Implications for Policy

Given the changes in the job of school administrators, which have been partially addressed here, the question for all engaged parties, including policymakers, is what constitutes a good school and district leader. In answering that question, other questions arise. What role should duties that affect the competitiveness of schools play within local area evaluations? How should these responsibilities be weighed in consideration of other duties (e.g., instructional leadership, school improvement)? Should there be any ethical considerations of how schools attempt to compete and market themselves in competition with other schools?

These questions, under older arrangements, might not have mattered much. However, within choice arrangements, they have greater weight. If we are to embrace choice as the driving ethos of schools, then the questions around principals' work, and particularly how they might be expected to compete, should be of the highest interest to policymakers. The consideration of education as a public good further complicates these matters, as competition incentivizes a number of behaviors that might benefit a school, but which may not be socially desirable.

However, the ethical issues may be somewhat clearer. At the local level, administrative policy, which includes school design, education market structure, enrollment policies, and governance, must also be considered in the light of school-choice policy. Such decisions, their meaningfulness, and repercussions must be understood in terms of competitiveness and competition. This means that, like the other areas of choice, educational leadership has the ethical obligation to correct informational asymmetries so that rising administrators might do the same for the families that they serve.

What exactly does it mean to lead a school operating in the market, and of what value is this to students and parents? This chapter begins to address that question, but the question also needs to be addressed through further thoughtful, transdisciplinary research. This work frames the body of research by providing an explication of the literature and the complex questions underlying the nature of choice and competition in education.

References

Arsen, D., & Ni, Y. (2012). The effects of charter school competition on school district resource allocation. *Educational Administration Quarterly, 48*(1), 3–38.

Becker, G. (1999). *Competition.* Paper presented at the Address for the Heritage Foundation 25th Anniversary Leadership for America Lectures, Chicago, IL.

Bell, C. A. (2009). All choices created equal? The role of choice sets in the selection of schools. *Peabody Journal of Education, 84*(2), 191–208.

Boldt, D. (1999). Clinton's school plan misses the mark some ideas hold promise; competition is a better solution. Retrieved from http://articles.philly.com/1999-01-22/news/25490501_1_social-promotions-national-tests-school-district

Bottoms, G., & O'Neill, K. (2001). *Preparing a new breed of school principals: It's time for action.* Atlanta, GA: Southern Regional Education Board.

Brewer, T. J., & Myers, P. S. (2015). How neoliberalism subverts equality and perpetuates poverty in our nation's schools. In S. N. Haymes, M. Vidal de Haymes, & R. J. Miller (Eds.), *The Routledge handbook of poverty in the United States* (pp. 190–198). New York, NY: Routledge.

Chubb, J. E., & Moe, T. M. (1990). *Politics, markets, and America's schools.* Washington, DC: Brookings Institution.

Cobb, C. D., & Glass, G. V. (1999). Ethnic segregation in Arizona charter schools. *Education Policy Analysis Archives, 7*(1), 1–39.

The Commercial Appeal. (2014). John Legend donates $30,000 to Soulsville school. Retrieved from www.commercialappeal.com/news/local-news/john-legend-donates-30000-to-soulsville-school_55339185

Coons, J. E., & Sugarman, S. D. (1973). Vouchers for public schools. *Inequality in Education, 15*, 60–62.

Cravens, X. C., Goldring, E., & Penaloza, R. (2012). Leadership practice in the context of U.S. school choice reform. *Leadership and Policy in Schools, 11*(4), 452–476.

De Haan, M., Leuven, E., & Oosterbeek, H. (2011). *Scale economies can offset the benefits of competition: Evidence from a school consolidation reform in a universal voucher system.* Bonn, Germany: Institute for the Study of Labor.

Evergreen Education Group. (2014). Data and information. Retrieved from www.kpk12.com/states

Feinberg, W., & Lubienski, C. (2008). *School choice policies and outcomes: Empirical and philosophical perspectives.* Albany, NY: State University of New York Press.

Frankenberg, E., Siegel-Hawley, G., & Wang, J. (2011). Choice without equity: Charter school segregation. *Education Policy Analysis Archives, 19*(1), 1–96.

Friedman Foundation for Educational Choice. (2014). *Types of school choice.* Retrieved from www.edchoice.org/School-Choice/Types-of-School-Choice.aspx

Garcia, D. R. (2010). Charter schools challenge traditional notions of segregation. In C. Lubienski & P. C. Weitzel (Eds.), *The charter school experiment: Expectations, evidence, and implications* (pp. 33–50). Cambridge, MA: Harvard Education Press.

Gaskell, J. (2002). School choice and educational leadership: Rethinking the future of public schooling. In K. A. Leithwood & P. Hallinger (Eds.), *Second international handbook of educational leadership and administration* (pp. 915–955). Boston, MA: Kluwer Academic.

Gilder, V. (1999). Want better public education? Support private vouchers. *Imprimis, 28*(9), 5–6.

Goldhaber, D. D., & Eide, E. R. (2002). What do we know (and need to know) about the impact of school choice reforms on disadvantaged students? *Harvard Educational Review, 72*(2), 157–176.

Harlem Village Academies. (2014). Board. Retrieved from http://harlemvillageacademies.org/board

Hirschman, A. O. (1970). *Exit, voice, and loyalty: Responses to decline in firms, organizations, and states.* Cambridge, MA: Harvard University Press.

Hoxby, C. M. (2000). Does competition among public schools benefit students and taxpayers? *American Economic Review, 90*(5), 1209–1238.

Hoxby, C. M. (2003). School choice and school productivity: Could school choice be a tide that lifts all boats? In C. M. Hoxby (Ed.), *The economics of school choice* (pp. 287–341). Chicago, IL: University of Chicago Press.

Iatarola, P., Schwartz, A. E., Stiefel, L., & Chellman, C. C. (2008). Small schools, large districts: Small-school reform and New York City's students. *Teachers College Record, 110*(9), 1837–1878.

Jabbar, H. (2015). *How do school leaders respond to competition? Evidence from New Orleans.* New Orleans, LA: Education Research Alliance.

Klein, R. (2014). How these 15 celebrities are helping shape our future. *The Huffington Post.* Retrieved from www.huffingtonpost.com/2014/03/04/celebrities-open-schools_n_4893141.html

Krueger, A. B., & Zhu, P. (2004). Another look at the New York City school voucher experiment. *American Behavioral Scientist, 47*(5), 658–698.

Kuttner, R. (1999). *Everything for sale: The virtues and limits of markets.* Chicago, IL: University of Chicago Press.

Labaree, D. F. (1988). *The making of an American high school: The credentials market and the Central High School of Philadelphia, 1838–1939.* New Haven, CT: Yale University Press.

Lacireno-Paquet, N., Holyoke, T. T., Moser, M., & Henig, J. R. (2002). Creaming versus cropping: Charter school enrollment practices in response to market incentives. *Educational Evaluation and Policy Analysis, 24*(2), 145–158.

Laffont, J.-J., & Tirole, J. (1991). The politics of government decision-making: A theory of regulatory capture. *The Quarterly Journal of Economics, 106*(4), 1089–1127.

Lake, R. J. (2008). In the eye of the beholder: Charter schools and innovation. *Journal of School Choice, 2*(2), 115–127.

Lareau, A. (1987). Social class differences in family-school relationships: The importance of cultural capital. *Sociology of Education, 60*(2), 73–85.

Lee, J., & Lubienski, C. (2011). Is racial segregation changing in charter schools? *International Journal of Educational Reform, 20*(3), 192–209.

Legend, J. (Producer). (2011). Rehearsing "we rise" with the Harlem Village Academies [Video]. Retrieved from www.youtube.com/watch?v=nMk8GwDnMYg

Lubienski, C. (2001). Redefining "public" education: Charter schools, common schools, and the rhetoric of reform. *Teachers College Record, 103*(4), 634–666.

Lubienski, C. (2003a). Innovation in education markets: Theory and evidence on the impact of competition and choice in charter schools. *American Educational Research Journal, 40*(2), 395–443.

Lubienski, C. (2003b). *School competition and promotion: Substantive and symbolic differentiation in local education markets.* National Center for the Study of Privatization in Education (Occasional paper no. 80). New York, NY: Teachers College.

Lubienski, C. (2005). Public schools in marketized environments: Shifting incentives and unintended consequences of competition-based educational reforms. *American Journal of Education, 111*(4), 464–486.

Lubienski, C. (2006a). Incentives for school diversification: Competition and promotional patterns in local education markets. *Journal of School Choice, 1*(2), 1–31.

Lubienski, C. (2006b). School choice and privatization in education: An alternative analytical framework. *Journal for Critical Education Policy Studies, 4*(1).

Lubienski, C. (2007a). Marketing schools: Consumer goods and competitive incentives for consumer information. *Education and Urban Society, 40*(1), 118–141.

Lubienski, C. (2007b). School competition and the emergence of symbolism in a market environment. In C. F. Kaestle & A. E. Lodewick (Eds.), *To educate a nation: Federal and national strategies of school reform* (pp. 257–280). Lawrence, KS: University Press of Kansas.

Lubienski, C., & Dougherty, J. (2009). Mapping educational opportunity: Spatial analysis and school choices. *American Journal of Education, 115*(4), 485–492.

Lubienski, C., Gulosino, C., & Weitzel, P. (2009). School choice and competitive incentives: Mapping the distribution of educational opportunities across local education markets. *American Journal of Education, 115*(4), 601–647.

Lubienski, C., Lee, J., & Gordon, L. (2013). Self-managing schools and access for disadvantaged students: Organisational behaviour and school admissions. *New Zealand Journal of Educational Studies, 48*(1), 82–98.

Lubienski, C., Linick, M., & York, J. G. (2012). School marketing in the United States: Demographic representations and dilemmas for educational leaders. In I. Oplatka & J. Hemsley-Brown (Eds.), *The management and leadership of educational marketing: Research, practice and applications* (pp. 109–135). Bingley, UK: Emerald.

Lubienski, C., & Lubienski, S. T. (2014). *The public school advantage: Why public schools outperform private schools.* Chicago, IL: University of Chicago Press.

Lubienski, C., & Weitzel, P. (2009). Choice, integration, and educational opportunity: Evidence on competitive incentives for student sorting. *The Journal of Gender, Race & Justice, 12*(2), 351–376.

Lubienski, C., Weitzel, P., & Lubienski, S. T. (2009). Is there a "consensus" on school choice and achievement? Advocacy research and the emerging political economy of knowledge production. *Educational Policy, 23*(1), 161–193.

Lutton, L. (2011). *Hopes for new school shine brightly in its architecture: UNO hopes ultra-modern architecture can inspire kids.* Retrieved from www.wbez.org/story/shiny-charter-school-southwest-side-92058

Magic Johnson Bridgescape. (2014). *Bridging the gap.* Retrieved from http://magicjohnsonbridgescape.com

Manno, B. V., Finn, C. E., Jr., Bierlein, L. A., & Vanourek, G. (1998). How charter schools are different: Lessons and implications from a national study. *Phi Delta Kappan, 79*(7), 488–498.

National Center for Education Statistics. (2012). *Number and percentage distribution of all children ages 5–17 who were homeschooled and homeschooling rate, by selected characteristics: 2011–12.* Washington, DC: Author.

Newark Charter School. (2014). *The meaning of our logo.* Retrieved from http://ncs. charter.k12.de.us/pages/Newark_Charter_School/General_Info/The_Meaning_of_ Our_Logo_and_Ma

Ni, Y., & Arsen, D. (2010). The competitive effects of charter schools on public school districts. In C. Lubienski & P. C. Weitzel (Eds.), *The charter school experiment: Expectations, evidence, and implications* (pp. 93–120). Cambridge, MA: Harvard Education Press.

Oswald, L. R. (2007). Semiotics and strategic brand management. *Semiotix, 8.* Retrieved from http://semioticon.com/sx-old-issues/semiotix8/sem-8-05.html

Patton, L. H. (2012). The story of Chicago's soccer academy. Retrieved from http:// gbdmagazine.com/2012/soccer-academy

Ravitch, D. (2010). The myth of charter schools. *The New York Review of Books.* Retrieved from www.nybooks.com/articles/archives/2010/nov/11/myth-charter-schools

Ravitch, D. (2014). *Why isn't Andre Agassi building tennis camps instead of charter schools?* [Blog]. Retrieved from http://dianeravitch.net/2014/02/18/why-isnt-andre-agassi-building-tennis-camps-instead-of-charter-schools

Rice University. (2014). Rice REEP, Jesse H. Jones Graduate School of Business. Retrieved from http://business.rice.edu/reep.aspx

Rotberg, I. C. (2014). Charter schools and the risk of increased segregation. *Phi Delta Kappan, 95*(5), 26–30.

Sandel, M. J. (2012). *What money can't buy: The moral limits of markets.* New York, NY: Farrar, Straus and Giroux.

Schwartz, B. (2004). *The paradox of choice: Why more is less.* New York, NY: HarperCollins.

Shapiro, B. (2015). Structures that teach: Using a semiotic framework to study the environmental messages of learning settings. *Eco-thinking, 1*(1), 1–13.

The Soulsville Charter School. (2014). *Nine-time GRAMMY-winner John Legend gives support to The Soulsville Charter School.* Retrieved from www.soulsvillecharterschool. org/nine-time-grammy-winner-john-legend-gives-support-to-the-soulsville-charter-school.html

Tiebout, C. M. (1956). A pure theory of local expenditures. *Journal of Political Economy, 64*(5), 416–424.

University of Virginia. (2014). Darden/Curry Partnership for Leaders in Education. Retrieved from www.darden.virginia.edu/darden-curry-ple

Van Leeuwen, T. (2005). *Introducing social semiotics.* New York, NY: Routledge.

Woessmann, L., & Peterson, P. E. (Eds.). (2007). *Schools and the equal opportunity problem.* Cambridge, MA: MIT Press.

Zaleznik, A. (2004). Managers and leaders: Are they different? *Harvard Business Review.*

Zubrzycki, J. (2014). *Charter schools continue to grow in Memphis and Shelby County.* Retrieved from http://tn.chalkbeat.org/2014/04/04/charter-schools-continue-to-grow-in-memphis-and-shelby-county

2

CORPORATE NETWORKS AND THEIR GRIP ON THE PUBLIC SCHOOL SECTOR AND EDUCATION POLICY

Carol A. Mullen

VIRGINIA TECH

> American corporate leadership is an extraordinary, well-financed, determined group of corporate millionaires and billionaires that are financing a self-serving, destructive doctrine on school leaders and public education in America.
>
> *(English, 2014, p. 51)*

Public education in the United States and around the world needs to be defended, as does our right as taxpaying citizens to keep it public (English, 2010, 2014). Who has the moral courage to protect this sector from the dominance of excessively financed networks and affluent advocates from the political right and left? Who has the political capital to take action?

Well-intentioned people are trying to improve public schools in our education policy environment. But they are hampered without support from activists and policy actors. Committed educators and stakeholders are hitting a wall, so to speak: "The only pathways they can see are too often ones prescribed and scripted by others," meaning that they lack the freedom to use their expertise and capacities to develop learner-centered programs (Bogotch & Shields, 2014a, p. 2).

Here I grapple with complexities and nuances involved in the marketization or commodification, also known as the market takeover, of the public education sector in the United States. My intention is to reveal the workings and influence of self-interest groups on the public school sector and education policy. Three questions stem from that intention:

1. What networks and entities are driving current school reform in the United States, and how are they functioning within and affecting the public education enterprise?

2. Whose interests are served by extracting revenues, labor pools, and services from the nation's public school system?
3. What are the implications of the Common Core State Standards (CCSS) (National Governors Association Center for Best Practices & Council of Chief State School Officers [NGA & CCSSO], 2010) for social democracy and social justice in terms of "equality" and "justice" in education?

As a framework for discussion, I use the original concept "Public Education, Inc.," which is a representation of the neoliberal movement's takeover of public education and of the marketization of schooling as a commodity from which profiteers/entrepreneurs benefit economically as well as politically (Mullen, 2015). My writing strategy involves tracing some connections among markets to evoke a bigger picture of these dynamics. Because the markets and their influence are largely invisible, connecting for-profit corporations and their supporting cast of characters is a complicated task. A proliferating number of neoliberal corporations, councils, think-tanks, and sponsors that favor free-market education reforms have co-opted public school rhetoric. By feigning a deep stake in public education and democracy, these entities hide their true intentions of making money and directing education policy.

Take, for example, the propaganda of the money-making lobbyists of the American Legislative Exchange Council (ALEC), who, according to Berliner and Glass (2014), say that they are in the business of improving education by advancing reforms that give parents choice; by making schools more account-able, transparent, and efficient; and by paving the way for youth to become successful adults. ALEC likes charter schools that make money, not public schools (Ravitch, 2013). Prisons and tobacco are business priorities over-shadowing ALEC's marginal interest in education, which ALEC describes with language that echoes public schools' vision statements. ALEC lobbied "politicians to attach free-market reforms to state education laws" (Berliner & Glass, 2014, p. 8). Just as ALEC's members have ventured to turn private prisons into big business by landing severer punishments for criminals, they have turned schools into a marketplace (Berliner & Glass, 2014).

Public Education, Inc. serves as a mechanism for forcing uncomfortable truths to the surface. Aside from serving as a wake-up call to current realities, the concept also provides a medium for equipping educators with the ideologies and evidence needed to claim a greater stake in the corporate appropriation of the public school sector and to take back our public schools and control of them. Public Education, Inc. should elicit a collective moral outcry against the destruction of public education.

The purpose of this conceptual report is to (a) introduce my concept of Public Education, Inc. as a jolt for educators and citizens who want public schools to thrive; (b) outline the parameters and contours of markets and the commodification of school life; (c) summarize CCSS as a policy issue of high relevance today; (d) identify this policy issue in broad terms, giving an over-view of literature in the educational leadership field as well as drawing on curriculum studies, critical studies, and education sociology; (e) address why key stakeholders (e.g., school leaders, teachers, policymakers) should care about the issue; and (f) conclude with a call to action and recommendations for constituents.

Introduction: Public Education, Inc.

Conceptualizing Public Education, Inc. allows me to openly and critically speak to what many public school activists consider a dire situation concerning public schools in the United States. I should first clarify that I do not see all corporations as automatically bad or somehow conspiring against public education. And I do not see entrepreneurial leadership as inherently wrong-headed, especially where those entrepreneurs who seek to turn a profit are not undermining the public school system or higher education institutions. Those who authentically work to achieve social benefits as social entrepreneurs may be making a positive contribution to public education, but this is not my topic. I recognize that many of us in our daily work use the services of corporations and have codependent relationships with them in our roles as customers.

Military–Industrial Complex

In the military industrialization of the 21st century, American society has provided a playbook for Public Education, Inc. by laying the groundwork for public schools to be sold to the highest bidder. The U.S. Department of Defense Education Activity (DoDEA, 2012), under the Office of the Secretary of Defense, adopted the CCSS, as did 43 states and the District of Columbia. The DoDEA, a federally operated school system, operates schools in 12 foreign countries for the children of military families. There is an emphasis on science in addition to language arts and math.

Government agencies like the DoDEA are supported with taxpayers' dollars, yet their neoliberal ideologies and marketing tactics are more like those of the private sector than public service. Taxpaying citizens concerned about the health of public education should want to know and do more. Public education historian Ravitch (2013) explained, "The transfer of public funds to private management and the creation of thousands of deregulated, unsupervised, and unaccountable schools have opened the public coffers to exploitation by large and small entrepreneurs" (p. 4). Abuses of power in the public school sector are a common topic of debate in the education policy domain.

Public Education, Inc. is a by-product of the "military–industrial complex" President Eisenhower (1961) coined in his farewell speech. He alluded to a "compelling" military–industrial need for the nation to "create a permanent armaments industry of vast proportions," arguing against the risks involved in "emergency improvisation of national defense." Yet Eisenhower admitted in his speech that our military spending was completely out of line compared to other priorities: "We annually spend on military security more than the net income of all United States corporations." This admission made a domain comparison between the military world and the corporate world. An alliance. Additionally, he disclosed the high-priority investment of the government in the military and the huge wealth of U.S. corporations.

Eisenhower (1961) also alluded to "misplaced power" and its "total influence" on all sectors of society. Although he did not specify public education or repercussions for schools (or university-based teacher and leader preparatory programs), it seemed presaged. Today's reigning megacorporations—such as Pearson Education and Microsoft—have invaded the public school system with the force of a military campaign. They overpower the agency of schools to serve constituents and communities, and remold them to the self-serving, profiteering interests of the market economy. Consider the insights of this education professor, whose critical take is that Eisenhower's speech

> focuses less on necessary defense and more on generating dollars in the corporate structure by way of developing arms and ammunition not needed, which has grave consequences for public education and its sustainability around democratic values and the common good.
> *(W. A. Kealy, personal communication, October 13, 2014)*

The speaker of these words is a retired senior officer in the military and a vocal Democrat.

Not all readers may be aware of the extent to which the corporate takeover of public schools has been occurring or its historic context, fueling my decision to tackle this topic. Readers may wonder what the moving pieces are, how they fit together, and what the possibilities are for new leadership in the roles of policy actor and advocate. To this end, Bogotch and Shields (2014a) discussed the blindsiding of educators and education leaders who are "often swallowed up by dominant business and governmental interests which today often represent global, corporate, and capitalistic . . . interests gone awry" (p. 2).

As public school activists believe, corporations invade schools, destroying their integrity and the capacity of school people to do their jobs. The military take on this equation is very real, although from another perspective. As James Heintz (2011) of the Political Economy Research Institute explained, heavy investment from the federal government in the military has deprived the nation's schools, robbing them of much-needed improvements in poor infrastructure (e.g., English, 2014; Ravitch, 2013), including horrendous sanitary problems in Michigan schools.

With historical context involving governmental military investments and real costs to public schools, Heintz's (2011) analysis is directed at the financial investment in the military since the 9/11 terrorist attack and the U.S. wars in Afghanistan and Iraq. Total military assets rose significantly starting in that time period to "$1,245 billion ($1.2 trillion) by the end of 2009—an increase of $341 billion" (Heintz, 2011, p. 4). Importantly, he concluded that "if these capital investments were made in U.S. education infrastructure, it would represent an 18.5 percent boost in terms of capital improvements nation-wide" (Heintz, 2011, p. 4). This capital could have footed the facilities bill for improving all makeshift public schools in the country. Without the invest-ment of public assets in schools, the costs of the wars show up as dilapidated facilities in high-poverty areas, compounding the health and safety of the nation's poorest children (Mullen, 2014).

Outside-In Rewiring

In the modern day military–industrial complex, public schools (and colleges and universities) are being rewired from the outside-in by external interest groups. Consider the Broad Foundation, Uncommon Schools, Success Academy, Teach for America—all giant organizations that are run like corporations. Just as we, the taxpaying citizens (e.g., educators and adult students in teacher and leadership preparation programs), are being changed from the outside, we are also being changed from the inside out by colleagues, supervisors, entrepreneurial leaders, and a new crop of neoliberal leaders trained by the corporate giants they quickly come to represent.

Critical awareness among educators, leaders, and professors involves under-standing such prevailing educational dynamics and doing something about them. People we know at work moonlight with marketeers (who sell goods and ser-vices in public schools and advocate for the public school sector to be made into a marketplace, e.g., Gates, 2009) and benefit financially while, importantly, changing the value system of education (Moffett & Newsom, 2014). Yet it is those working in public schools whose jobs are on the line and whose schools are in jeopardy. They are the ones being pressured by accountability policies and measures of student performance. They are the ones being penalized when expectations set by policies fall short (English, 2014; Ravitch, 2013).

It should not escape our notice that we, the taxpaying public, are being conditioned to humanize corporations and see them as valuable education leaders and stakeholders, in effect giving them greater latitude to colonize schools. By not protesting, we are falling prey to the subliminal rewiring of citizens by our highest federal court:

> The U.S. Supreme Court has decreed [that] corporations are people too. And as a person, a corporation has plenty of self-interest in the forms of

revenues and stock prices. Both revenues and profits will benefit from lower taxes—much of which will be spent at the state level financing public education—and cheaper labor costs.

(Berliner & Glass, 2014, p. 6)

Anthropomorphizing corporations by making them out to be benevolent friends and even saviors—in keeping with Gates's (2009) accusatory rhetoric of school failure and messianic messages of corporate intervention—disrupts our ability to spot the bullying tactics that propel market invasions of schools. The hostage-taking of the public education sector should motivate wanting to know how public schools are being exploited for their revenues, services, and cheap labor (Ravitch, 2013).

Zapping School Agency

In the contemporary political scene, as social services become privatized, schools lose their power and agency for protecting the common good. Ian Westbury (2008), a curriculum theorist from Canada, suggested that "the school system is an agency that should exist to support and protect the local service" (p. 3); his concern was that schools break rather than improve that service when school leaders lose sight of this reality. Manipulating standardized test scores is an example of the shortsightedness of school leaders who fear the negative repercussions of poor test outcomes (English, 2014).

Many leading education specialists base their arguments on two premises: (a) There exists a critical mass of influential decision-makers and entities in American society, and (b) there is "misplaced power" (ironically, Eisenhower's own words in 1961) in the erosion of the core mission, common good, local control, and democratic goals of the public education system (e.g., Anyon, 2014; Apple, 2014; Ball, 2012; Barry, 2005; Berliner & Glass, 2014; Bogotch & Shields, 2014b; English, 2010, 2014; Giroux, 2014; Mullen, English, Brindley, Ehrich, & Samier, 2013; Ravitch, 2013; Tienken & Orlich, 2013; Westbury, 2008). Some entrepreneurs—consider the very powerful corporatist Bill Gates (2009)—claim that these are the same ideals that engineer their vision. Supporters of Gates would say that his interventions improve public schools, whereas critics vehemently disagree; social justice proponents have reached boiling point (Bogotch & Shields, 2014b; English, 2014). Ravitch (2012) identified nondemocratic forces tied to the capitalist mindset as think-tanks from the right-wing, wealthy elite—corporations and individuals alike—and legislators who claim that government funding for private enterprise is badly needed. These entities have bought into the myth that America's public schools are hopeless, dismal failures which have dried up state support for public schools. Berliner and Glass (2014) drive home this point:

Modern myths about schools (e.g., private schools offer superior teaching and learning compared with public schools) are likely to be articulated and communicated by organized private interests—by various think-tanks and organizations that stand to gain from widespread belief in the myths.

(p. 7)

Power in the industrial, capitalist market economy of the day is associated with free unregulated markets, competition, and property holdings, not membership in society or good intentions (Bogotch & Shields, 2014a, 2014b). Improving schools is the golden pretense (English, 2011), but in reality money and power are at stake. As English (2014) explained, "The lure of making money is a powerful motivator for these agencies to promote standardization and to take steps to remain in power" (p. xii). Nonetheless, public school defenders are fighting back, even "outing" enemies by name (e.g., English, 2010, 2014; McDermott-McNulty, 2014).

Being Whipped into Shape

Gates (2009), a celebrated hero in this campaign to infiltrate public schools, has insisted that public schools must be subjected to commodification by outsiders—policymakers, companies, and agencies—that are given curricular control. Accordingly, public schools have been bought and sold (English, 2014), and turned into profitable warehouses selling goods and services. With momentum, entrepreneurs rationalize the failure of public schools, paving the way for intervention from outside "experts" and their unchecked conversions. Gates brokered the control of the public school sector by

> promot[ing] unproven school reforms (e.g., high-stakes testing, charter schools, teacher merit pay, the [CCSS]), [intent on] boost[ing] international test scores to reclaim the United States' rightful place at the top of the test results lists—a position we never held.
>
> *(Berliner & Glass, 2014, p. 17)*

Falling prey, high-poverty schools lack the power to take a stand in their own best interests (English, 2014). Many times, these schools have come under mayoral control or the control of mayorally appointed school boards. Democratic values of public education have eroded: "Business values are not appropriate to drive American education," advocates of social justice protest, even though citizens would support "the most efficient use of the taxpayer dollar in the public schools. But that is not an educational core value. . . . Democracy is not efficient and thus, a democratic education is not efficient" (Tienken & Orlich, 2013, p. 42).

Educating poor and minority children and children with disabilities so that they can succeed as contributing members of society is a hallmark of democracy. Markets are ostensibly efficient, making them seductive to stakeholders. School leaders and parents are being misled by Gates's claim that K–12 public schools are simply too expensive to operate, having lost sight of the fact that in a democratic society we do not institutionalize children with disabilities—instead, we support them through better funding in special education (Berliner & Glass, 2014).

Berliner and Glass (2014) confirmed that "modern corporations are beginning to view the public schools as ripe for picking big profits" (p. 6). A functional/instrumental—not educative—role of service provider feeds marketing companies' appetite for operationalizing schools as targets of economic gain (English, 2010, 2014; Ravitch, 2013). William J. Bennett, conservative pundit and former U.S. Secretary of Education (during the Reagan administration) received millions from the U.S. Department of Education under the name K12, Inc., a private company he cofounded (English, 2010). The illusion of being a sponsor of K–12 public education and imitating this system using a company name, but in reality debasing its cherished ideals, serves only to compound the moral bankruptcy Heintz (2011) described.

Megacorporations like Pearson Education are powerhouses, accessing and controlling delivery and evaluation services to the public education sector; their exploitation of the country's public schools is unprecedented. It is challenging to identify all of the influential policy pundits and marketeers, and to unearth their connections to one another. In fact, it has proven exhausting to try and unravel how these networked players manage to mimic the rhetoric of education reform for their own ends. Moreover, it is labor-intensive to assemble the many puzzle pieces, only to realize that the power grid is made of quicksand. We are stuck. The power grid constantly moves. A nimble machine, it extends beyond the federal government to a shadow government operating right under our feet.

Scheming Shadow Governments

Shadow government (also *cryptocracy*) refers to "private individuals who are exercising power behind the scenes, beyond the scrutiny of democratic institutions. . . . The official elected government is in reality subservient to the shadow government who are the true executive power" (Wikipedia, 2014). The shadow government is made up of influential corporations and think-tanks, the elite classes—including the White middle class—and wealthy individuals, for example.

Americans have been primed to think that one government makes decisions for the country and represents our citizenry, when in reality a shadow government (corporate America) is the conduit of its power and influence.

Take, for example, how shadow governments become more powerful and influential in a society where "the White middle and governing classes wish both to reduce the cost of public education to themselves and to find protected privilege for their children and grandchildren in segregated schools" (Berliner & Glass, 2014, p. 5). White middle-class parents have been influencing the fate of urban public schools, hence their very existence.

Parameters and Contours of This Argument

As is likely evident, the focus of this discussion is *not* the curricular or contextual arguments that assess the CCSS, nor is it the content, validity, or effectiveness of the standards. For readers interested in those subjects, critics of the CCSS discuss such important areas as inadequate empirical results (e.g., Berliner & Glass, 2014; Tienken & Orlich, 2013) and insufficient curricular and cultural diversity (e.g., Brass, 2014; McDermott-McNulty, 2014).

Lack of empirical substantiation and diminished local control over curricula are paramount problems. When education policy and standards are delivered top-down, as is happening in the United States, these issues are exacerbated. Tienken (2012) explained that the CCSS initiative does not have empirical backing, yet many educators—not just policymakers—are endorsing it. Further, he attested that curricula should be allowed to flourish at the local level (see Tienken & Orlich, 2013 for an extended explanation).

Similarly, Westbury (2008) insisted that educators in schools and universities are the "*only ones* [emphasis added] with the experience and practical knowledge that is the prerequisite for inventing curricula and pedagogies" (p. 3); hence it is because of the expertise and capacities of curriculum leaders that the demands of students and classrooms alike can be met.

I also do not debate any learning associated with the CCSS. Further, my analysis is not an assessment of the benefits CORE (2013) advocates have claimed, such as enhanced reading and math skills for learners and improved academic standing for schools. (The for-profit corporation known as CORE offers services and products for implementing the CCSS.) This is not a research study of the perceptions of such important constituent groups as parents, teachers, and superintendents. I am also not critiquing the news reports that are incorrectly reporting results and exaggerating the investment of education stakeholders in the CCSS. However, I do present the views of a few school leaders with whom I have interacted, to at least give a sense of their voice.

On the other side of the debate, only peripherally referenced herein, many educators endorse the CCSS, although not necessarily the way it is marketed. These educators approve the way in which the standards were first constructed by corporate interests such as Achieve, Inc., and then reviewed by states and validation panels. There is also perceived buy-in from stakeholders and assumptions of rigor in the development of standards for math and the English language arts (e.g., Darling-Hammond, Wilhoit, & Pittenger, 2014; Jones & King, 2012).

Within those parameters, I return to the discussion of megacorporations with an examination of the facets of their networking influence on public education.

Policy Issue: A Single Market for the CCSS

The CCSS initiative is driven by a school reform network and has led to the creation of a single curriculum, assessment, and instructional resources market. Entrepreneurs with political power are requiring the use of imported tests, services, and products that, at least hypothetically, align with the standards (Brass, 2014; Ravitch, 2013). In a single market,

> the adoption of only one form of curriculum is an example of symbolic power, and it enfranchises some and disenfranchises other groups. . . . It is a myth that any new set of standards that imposes only one type of curriculum will reduce the achievement gap when the gap is built into the system itself.
>
> *(Papa, English, Davidson, Culver, & Brown, 2012, pp. 45–46)*

Wielding "symbolic power," the CCSS initiative is heavily funded, reflecting a momentous financial push by the private sector for implementation in the public sector (Wexler, 2014). An elite network of megacorporations supports the CCSS, which itself "is funded by the richest private foundations in the country," primarily the Gates Foundation and the Broad Foundation (Wexler, 2014, p. 52). Wexler (2014), like other researchers, draws attention to how these foundations have exercised influence over the policies of President Barack Obama and U.S. Secretary of Education Arne Duncan.

Federal Backing Gives Weight

The CCSS is state adopted, but it is misleading to stop right there. Federal weight and nationwide networking were rife during its development. Consider the widespread influence of the Council on Foreign Relations (CFR) Task Force, which actually reworked its stated mission of national security to send the urgent message that U.S. education is not only a dismal failure, but also a national security issue. The Task Force formed a partnership with the federal government and private industry to expand the influence of the CCSS (Blumenfeld, 2012) and spread the military industrialization of the United States. Aligned with the CFR, the U.S. Department of Defense, through its DoDEA field activity branch, colonizes the children of military families on a grand global scale with its strong endorsement and use of the CCSS.

Yet Jones and King (2012) insisted that the CCSS is not a "national curriculum" that violates state and local control of education or places constitutional limits on the federal government's influence over curriculum and pedagogy. Their logic is misleading and dangerous, and so is this demarcation. Those who make this argument invoking constitutional limitations are obscuring how the CCSS works to discipline classroom practice and, moreover, to force radical shifts in the governance of public education in the United States (English, 2014; Papa et al., 2012).

The CCSS did not pop up out of nowhere as a heavily financed policy initiative. The underlying ideologies and practices of corporate accountability and standardization have been inextricably meshed with federal legislation in education that has existed for more than 20 years (Bracken, 2013). As Wexler (2014) explained, policy reform has led to the involvement of the Gates and Broad Foundations, which set in motion the corporate reforms of the CCSS—reforms such as standardized testing; adequate yearly progress (AYP); and CCSS predecessors such as the Elementary and Secondary School Act of 1965 (ESEA, 2003), the No Child Left Behind Act of 2001 (NCLB, 2003), and the Race to the Top (RTTT) Fund.

Ravitch (2013) further documented that "national standards and national assessments created a national marketplace for products" (p. 181). "Equity investors" acted on ideas to make "resources, hardware, and online curricula for the new national [CCSS]. National standards and national assessments created a national marketplace for products" (Ravitch, 2013, p. 181). One consultant (not identified, Ravitch, 2013) predicted that public school officials would be put in the position of wanting to receive assistance from businesses, worrying that if the CCSS tests turned out to be as rigorous as promoted, the students and schools would look bad (Ravitch, 2013). Was this school dynamic an example of backdoor policy manipulation by shadow governments?

Neoliberal Public Enemies

English (2010) "outed" neoliberal public enemies. His work, already a classic, has generated controversy. He ranked Eli Broad as the number one enemy of public education in America, with his multimillion dollar funding and perpetuation of "a top-down corporate takeover of urban school systems" (p. 67). English (2010) stated that the leaders (i.e., noneducators) Broad has promoted are not credible academic educators. Not only do they lack knowledge of the education field, but they also "are beholden to efficiency management tactics and simplistic economic models," and they "discourage innovation and privatize formerly noncommodified public spheres while failing to bring about the dramatic improvements they advertise" (English, 2010, p. 67). In addition, the Broad approach does not offer anything new and keeps its curriculum hidden, as well as its purported experts.

Public enemy number two on English's (2010) list of public enemies is Arne Duncan, whose ideology and practice are driven by the neoliberal agenda that directs the Democratic and Republican parties, with President William "Bill" Clinton and President Obama both endorsing it just as much as any Republican and right-wing think-tanks (e.g., English, 2014; Tienken & Orlich, 2013). Additional enemies, such as former U.S. Assistant Secretary of Education Chester E. Finn Jr., are tied into the neoliberal agenda of commodifying public schools through the CCSS creation, development, and preparation processes. Former U.S. Secretary of Education William J. Bennett has channeled millions of dollars from the U.S. Department of Education through K12, Inc., his private online education company (English, 2010). Note his coopting of "K12."

Further elucidating the marketeers' policy grip in the United States, the most influential agencies in education—the National Governors Association (NGA), Achieve, and CCSSO—are all backers of the CCSS (Bracken, 2013; English, 2014), in addition to the U.S. Department of Education (Wexler, 2014). These networked powerhouses, have been identified by Tienken and Orlich (2013) as having "pushed through the development of the standards" (p. 107). What we got was a prescription for the language arts and math as subjects, with science (and who knows what else) to follow, at the expense of public education's resources more broadly.

It is noteworthy to share some background on the three agencies cited as backers of CCSS, or what many now refer to as the "Common Core":

1. NGA is a trade association that has nothing to do with governors (Bracken, 2013).
2. Achieve, also Achieve, Inc., is "a private contractor" that was created by NGA and quickly completed the "NGA/CCSSO standards-development process" (Tienken & Orlich, 2013, p. 107). Achieve (2008) presents itself as a cutting-edge, empirically grounded think-tank. This is another example of how marketeers are cleverly disguising themselves as legitimate researchers.
3. CCSSO is "one of the organizations that pushed through the development of the [CCSS] standards" that "will form the core curriculum of every public school program, drive another stronger wave of high-stakes testing, and thus become student selection criteria for K–12 programs" such as Title 1 services, gifted and talented programs, and high school course placement (Tienken & Orlich, 2013, p. 107).

Neoliberal Business Networks

Neoliberalism relies heavily on networks as a conduit for penetration of the public school sector. Ball (2012) encouraged empirical researchers to do a "more careful tracing of policy networks that underpin the global expansion of neoliberal ideas" and "descriptions of circulatory systems that connect policy regimes" (pp. 2–3). A deep understanding of the connections among corporate networks and their dynamics will guide educators to empower themselves to take action.

Working in this direction, curriculum professor Morna McDermott-McNulty and literacy professor Michael T. Moore have each documented the Common Core's networks in relation to connections and impact. Moore (as cited in Downey, 2013) concluded, "It is a private club [in which] these people all know each other." McDermott-McNulty's (2013) depiction of the network, shown in Figure 2.1, is thought-provoking.

Figure 2.1 identifies some key players and their connections in today's education policy environment, specifically regarding the overflow of networks supporting the CCSS movement. In my opinion, it is an intriguing instructional exhibition. The reigning neoliberal world view is operationalized as a power grid of brokers dealing not with human beings, their lives and teaching–learning complexities, but with decontextualized services and products rendered transformative for public education.

CCSS Ploys and Bedfellows

Not surprisingly, the states were financially pressured to comply with the CCSS. Wexler (2014) argued that they were indeed "coerced into adopting the standards through federal grants and ... No Child Left Behind waivers" (p. 52; see also Tienken, 2012). From this angle, Jones and King's (2012) viewpoint seems simplistic, not sufficiently attuned to the politics and role of the federal government as a colossal market cooperative.

An NGA brief suggested that the political workings and intentions of governmental marketeers are not even all that covert any more (Nielson, 2014). Consider that the NGA announced that it will use "the bully pulpit" to make states comply with the CCSS-aligned tests (Nielson, 2014, p. 2). Nielson (2014) has rationalized that this action will ensure rigor in the Washington-based bullying tactics that permeate the attitudes and actions of the powerhouse networks—oddly enough, revealing the NGA's machinations while concealing them.

So who is partnering with whom to benefit financially from the CCSS? Wayne Washington (as cited in Downey, 2013) has responded by "outing," among others, a conglomerate network with key players—Achieve, Inc.—which he described as "a Washington, D.C.-based nonprofit group that has been heavily involved in writing the standards, [which] receives funding from corporate titans such as Microsoft, the Bill and Melinda Gates Foundation, Chevron and DuPont." He disclosed the networked connections to administrations and partnerships, as well as Achieve, Inc.'s executives' average salary of $198,916 in 2011 (Washington in Downey, 2013). He continued, saying:

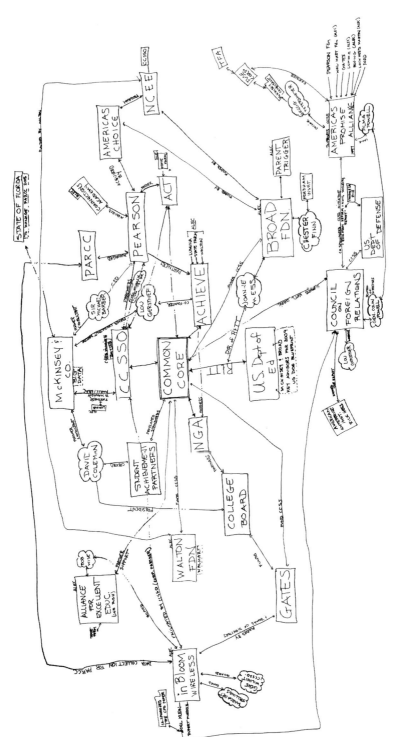

FIGURE 2.1 Who Created Common Core? A Working Flow Chart

McDermott–McNulty (2013) created a hand-drawn illustration to educate her college students about the very real ways neoliberalism has taken over public education. McDermott–McNulty credits Karen Bracken with this remake of her original. Used with permission.

The company's president, former Clinton administration official Michael Cohen, had a salary of $263,800 in 2011. Two national consortia, the Partnership for Assessment of Readiness for College and Careers [PARCC] and Smarter Balanced, having gotten a combined $346 million in federal education grants to create a pair of new standardized tests tied to Common Core.

(Washington in Downey, 2013)

The rich get richer and their shadow governments help them campaign on their own behalf.

Lacking Empirical Evidence

Proliferating changes in the policy reform landscape have come about without proper vetting and testing by school leaders, teachers, and parents (Zhao, 2014). The CCSS was implemented in most states in 2014–2015, with the justification in part being that it is a "godsend" to academically struggling K–12 schools (Tienken, 2012; Wexler, 2014). Tienken (2012) added the crucial perspective that "large social programs" like the CCSS

> should have research to support them prior to being released large-scale on the public. That research should be independent and not created by one or more of the contributors to the program that is released. Neither of those things happened in this case.
>
> *(p. 154)*

These are basic expectations for rigor in curricular programming, long known by education researchers.

Like Brass (2014), whose criticism of the CCSS targets curricular and diversity issues pertaining to reading standards, Tienken (2012) argued that curricular uniformity does not prepare children well—or responsibly:

> It is dangerously naïve and professionally irresponsible to think that one set of standards, based solely on two subjects, can prepare children to access the thousands of college options or even make them attractive to the admissions officers that control access to those options. For example, is it really crucial that all students master the following CCSS English Language Arts standard RI.9-10.7 (CCSSO & NGA, 2010)?
>
> *(p. 154)*

Money-Making Markets

These growing education markets make money hand-over-fist. The incomes of Achieve's executives are but one toxin in this polluted ocean. The resulting education crisis has enabled "state-led" intervention through "the provision of CCSS-based tests (PARCC and Smarter Balanced), prepackaged materials developed by educational publishers, and educational technologies and games" (Brass, 2014, p. 24). In this product-packaged school life, the teacher is being "manufactured" as a consumer of new technologies and is being remodeled to accommodate the tests and services.

In a world of market domination, the teacher who has been classically prepared for the educative role of curriculum maker, or who stays in education because of the independent thinking and professionalism it affords, has been robbed of it. As Papa et al. (2012) attested about the politics involved in education policy and testing, "There is a huge economic interest in the [CCSS] as textbook and other companies stand to gain with a host of prepackaged products ready to sell for the new market created by the new curriculum" (pp. 45–46). Pearson Education has bought McGraw-Hill and numerous other publishing companies, but has had them retain their own names; in a shadow government, a motive for this strategy is to help conceal one's monopoly over public schools (Bracken, 2013).

Private Sector Profits

Networked powerhouse connections across America suggest that conservative and progressive forces have forged partnerships in creating and publicizing the standards (Ball, 2012; Bracken, 2013). Thus, in keeping with the spirit of public education upheld by Papa et al. (2012) and many other public education spokespersons, CCSS is *not* a philanthropic endeavor, despite declarations to that effect. It is disconcerting that "the private sector has developed and established the CCSS with considerable federal support" (Brass, 2014, p. 24), and that is an echoing refrain in the education literature (e.g., English, 2014; Tienken & Orlich, 2013).

Brass's (2014) fiscal breakdown of profitable wins for the private sector animates an undeniable picture of greed:

> The $350 million of federal funding for CCSS-aligned tests represent a small portion of the $4.35 billion in economic stimulus money that the federal department of education has distributed to states, professional organizations, and private businesses to develop and promote the standards and CCSS-aligned tests, services, and products.
>
> *(p. 24)*

Just think about how the federal dollars have been used. Brass (2014) explained that most of it has gone "to subsidize entrepreneurs, testing companies, and the educational technology sector to displace the curricular and pedagogical leadership of elected public representatives—for example, state legislatures, state regents, and local school boards—at the public's expense" (p. 24). However, even while such corporate identifications can be made in addition to establishing interconnections among the market forces, the market conversion of education is neither a smooth nor a transparent operation. Rather, to use a previous metaphor (Mullen, 2013), this mechanistic force consists of many moving parts across corporate structures and within educational systems; it works in and against schools and citizens.

As a single market that is also a reform movement of catalytic proportions, the CCSS has made it possible for for-profit and not-for-profit contractors to make more money doing business with public schools; contractors also benefit from related political opportunities (Brass, 2014; Tienken & Orlich, 2013). Savage, O'Connor, and Brass (2014) have opined that the CCSS movement raises questions about the extent to which today's reforms can be considered public or democratic. The binary between Democratic and Republican ideologies disappears in the neoliberal deconstruction of ideological bleeding brought on by the thirst for money and power (English, 2014; Tienken & Orlich, 2013).

The smoke and mirrors of debates surrounding standards and curriculum taken up by game-changing marketeers such as Bill Gates, Arne Duncan, E. D. Hirsch (founder and chair of the Core Knowledge Foundation), and the Fordham Foundation manage to "work around ideological and legal controversies surrounding a national curriculum" (Brass, 2014, p. 25; see also English, 2014). Brass (2014) wanted educators to know that such disciplinary control of curriculum and instruction limits the democratic jurisdiction of schools.

Thinning of Democracy

The thinning of democracy has been made a hyper-reality by Bill Gates (2009), but I doubt that he would see it that way. His conviction is that the marketization of public schools is a necessary intervention for ensuring a strong democracy in schools and society. His speeches, albeit consisting of generalizations and abbreviated constructions, paradoxically reveal and conceal changes to come.

Gates (2009) himself presents the CCSS as a radical departure from traditional state and local control of public education, as a kind of genesis of school reform on a large scale that is culturally penetrating. Consider that Gates (2009) used the words "for the *first time*" in his foreboding speech, implying that the CCSS represents the rebirth of education:

> Identifying common standards is just the starting point. We'll only know if this effort has succeeded when the curriculum and the tests are aligned

to these standards. . . . Arne Duncan recently announced that $350 million of the stimulus package will be used to create just these kinds of tests.

Gates (2009) also announced that markets would uniformly function top-down for delivery of services and products to schools in the production of better teaching:

> When the tests are aligned with the common standards, the curriculum will line up as well, and it will unleash a powerful market of people providing services for better teaching. For the first time, there will be a large uniform base of customers looking at using products that can help every kid learn and every teacher get better.

Intent on these directions, Gates (2009) has spearheaded the use of the CCSS in reifying standards, disciplining curriculum and teaching, and aligning classroom practice with high-stakes tests. Brass (2014) has assessed these interventions, concluding that they have led to the failure and closing of the most disadvantaged schools in the nation. Advocates of the CCSS assume that alignment of curriculum, pedagogy, and assessment is needed. Brass (2014) has countered that this goal is dangerous, as alignment separates standards from curriculum, making it possible for curriculum and pedagogy to be governed at a distance. Alignment turns curriculum-making into the purview of corporate titans.

CORE and Corporate Control

The corporate titan CORE has wielded its financially draining demands upon schools. The CCSS is big business; just scrutinize the CORE (2013) web pages. Note the expenses associated with its menu of implementation tools (curriculum analysis templates, lesson planning/design templates, and observation rubrics) and add them up. When I asked educator McDermott-McNulty about the CORE based on her firsthand knowledge, she said:

> CORE is a profit-driven vehicle that collects (public) federal, state, and (private) corporate funding to deliver goods and services they advertise as "necessary" to implement education policies (like CCSS) that their education technology industry partners and political beneficiaries lobbied to create in the first place, thus creating a "need" on the one end, and providing the services to fill that manufactured need on the other end.
>
> *(personal communication, September 28, 2014)*

And she added that CORE represents "corporate hijacking of public education at its worst."

Literature Review: Education Policy Networks and the Thinning of Democracy

As further probed in this section, democracy is being thinned by education policy networks propelled by Gates (2009) as well as many neoliberal giants and entities. As market takeover thrives and democracy consequently wanes, the local autonomy of public schools and the democratic learning and preparation of students are adversely affected.

Neoliberalism and Marketization

Sociologist Ball (2012) wrote that neoliberalism values are money, power, and markets, and *neoliberalism* is

> an ideology which promotes markets over the state and regulation and individual advancement/self-interest over common well-being.... Common good and social protection concerns have been given less focus and the market valued over the state, with enhanced market or private sector involvement in the workings of the state.
>
> *(B. Lingard, 2009, p. 18, cited in Ball, 2012, p. 2)*

Curricular and other school practices have been reorganized around a romantic image of free enterprise where the playing field is about capital that can be accumulated and profits made (English, 2014).

Another take on neoliberalism is Wexler's (2014) notion that the reform business enterprise as a collective is undermining struggling children and youth, higher education, and the arts. Apple (2014) went a step farther, asserting that market-based policy reforms are part of the neoliberalist agenda that is breaking schools. Berliner and Glass (2014) and Ravitch (2013) argued that marketeers and policy reformers try to manipulate the public and government into believing that public schools are broken. The persistent language around broken schools has turned public perception sour. This commonly shared belief rationalizes the rapid conversion of public schools into markets that are supposedly in the business of repairing and mending, and without independent, critical agency.

Although I am presenting the takeover of public schools using a critical theoretical lens—integrating the ideas of Fenwick English, Stephen Ball, and Michael Apple, in particular—schools have not literally been "incorporated" like a company. The idea behind my pushback is that schools are being consumed and converted at a rapid rate by free-market-influenced ideas, fed by the sway of neoliberal ideology. Children's lives, teachers' work, and leaders' responsibilities reflect investment opportunities for marketeers and consultants, not only inside the burgeoning education industry, but also within schools and higher education. Schools are looking like the markets controlling them these days, and entrepreneurs disguised as educators promote creeds favoring the greater good while funneling the riches their way.

Corporate Thinning of Democracy

A growing body of literature in education critiques both the ideologies and realities of educational reforms (e.g., Apple, 2011; Mullen, English, et al., 2013; Mullen, Samier, Brindley, English, & Carr, 2013; Tienken & Orlich, 2013). Describing democracies as "thick" or "thin" is social justice language taken from Ball (2012) and Apple (2014) in their analyses of the effect of markets on schools and education policy. Representing only a "thin" segment of public interests, dominant groups are powerful, complex, and invisible in their work, sponsoring "a network of foundations, think-tanks, consultants, entrepreneurs, and corporations" (Ball, 2012, p. xxii).

Ball (2012) attested that "these networks are successful not only because of their connections, money, and ideological sophistication, but also because in many instances state-centric policies are *not* successful or have left a vacuum because of their absence" (p. xxii). An example of the networked marketing reality that Ball (2012) cited is in India, where chains of private schools are overtaking underresourced and overly bureaucratized state schools. Ball (2012) exclaimed that we need to defend a "thickly democratic public sphere" and pave the way for "a radical egalitarian politics of redistribution, recognition, and representation" (p. xxii).

Also convinced that we are witnessing powerful networks of knowledge production in the corruption of public education, Apple (2014) argued that the "'thin' forms of democracy" (p. xx) of markets and consumption practices are outstripping the "thick democracy" (p. 193) of the full participation by citizens (p. xxi). Grounded in his communications with parties in different countries, Apple (2014) sent the "SOS" that perceptions of public education are being distorted and rationalized as wholly and uniformly inadequate to the point of needing private sector intervention:

> Privatization, marketization, competition, choice—these and other similar rhetorical devices are being marshaled to convince the public that what exists in teaching, curricula, evolution, leadership, and so much else is uniformly "bad." They must be replaced with neoliberal, neoconservative, and managerial policies and reorganized around the technologies and ideologies of audit cultures, so that the emphasis is on the constant pro- duction of evidence that one is doing "the right thing."
>
> *(p. xx)*

Nation-states in different countries are overridden with profit-making, and support to this end is not only coming from conservative political parties, Apple

(2011) warned; it is also coming from democratic political parties. Consequently, it is of international importance that education policy trend analysts believe that social gains have regressed in public schooling around the world (e.g., Apple, 2011; Mullen, English, et al., 2013; Mullen, Samier, et al., 2013; Tienken & Orlich, 2013).

Neoliberal networks have found cooperative bedfellows in schools, districts, colleges, universities, and elsewhere. This helps to explain why the corporatization and marketization of public schools has become the new normal. One serious effect is "bankrupting" democracy and its values for advancing the common good (Apple, 2011). Because profits are of paramount importance and people enable the education marketplace to thrive, public schools are constantly being exploited with resources. Just think about how "robotic" curricular circuitry can be seen all around the country with people serving as test-givers, test-takers, consumers, product implementers, and cooperative agents.

To elucidate, the problem is not "contracting or outsourcing to private groups by public schools [as this] has always been commonplace" (Miron, 2008, p. 340). Schools have commonly purchased food from providers, leased buses, and so forth. For about 25 years, though, as policy analyst Miron (2008) explained, "A new form of contracting has occurred, one that involves contracting out the complete operation of public schools to private operators" (p. 340), including student recruitment—a practice Miron considered "controversial." Based on his social policy analysis from 2008, he would likely agree that democracy is thinning even more rapidly than in past years.

Companies are exempt from legal responsibility and can operate without being (fully) seen. Miron's (2008) justifications indicate that for-profit marketeers are not required to adhere to "public laws on transparency [as these] do not cover private companies"; also, school and public officials have become increasingly dependent on the services that private contractors provide. Additionally, evidence is weak for arguing that private companies are more efficient than public schools and have better outcomes: "The only studies that suggest positive performance levels by private contractors are conducted by or commissioned by the private companies themselves" (Miron, 2008, p. 340; e.g., Achieve [a private contractor], 2008).

Giroux's (2014) analysis is of U.S. lobbyists' control of elected representatives and promotion of the interests of megacorporations and the financial sector. The "superrich" buy the policies and laws they need to control the economy. They introduce vast inequality by

> leveraging full use of Americans' wealth and resources—there is more at stake here than legalized corruption, there is the arrogant dismantling of democracy and the production of policies that extend rather than mitigate human suffering, violence, misery, and everyday hardships.
>
> *(Giroux, 2014, p. 7)*

Further, the market has gained "sovereignty" over "democratic governance," Giroux (2014, p. 8) argued. Power-over tactics are "paving the way for models of governance intent on transforming domestic cultures into entrepreneurial agents" (Giroux, 2014, p. 8). Public schools have a different kind of agency (and legacy) than they had in the past, and it is to play second fiddle.

Linguistic Gaming Ploys

Social groups imbue democratic words—*democracy, equality, justice, and freedom*—with meaning. But market campaigns have shaped public perceptions of public schools and the public's limited awareness of what is really happening to the U.S. education system. "Almost 70%" of citizens "favor the idea of charter schools" even though they are "run by private, profit-making companies extracting many millions of dollars of public funding"; moreover, "the only credible studies of charter-school effectiveness show them underperforming traditional public schools" (Berliner & Glass, 2014, pp. 7–8). Being enamored or unquestioning produces blindness.

A new age of colonization seems evident—every which way we turn, the entrepreneurial leadership of neoliberal markets has colonized our public school sector. Democracy gets robbed. Philosopher Habermas (1985) explained that "linguistically mediated interactions" can be "normatively regulated" (p. 2) by groups. The behavior of the social group and its complex activities changes through new sets of "symbolically oriented behaviors" (p. 2), including speech, which sheds light on changing actions and attitudes.

One can see how the use of familiar terms such as *democracy* and *equality* by entrepreneurs may seem confusing and yet strategic. Consider that they are being regulated by them and through networks and interaction that are symbolic, such as game-changing, seductive rhetoric that is as catchy as it is widely advertised and thus instilled (e.g., Achieve, Inc., 2008; CORE, 2013).

Critical educator Apple (2014) explained that this usurpation of the democratic mindset and inherent speech patterns "thins" or weakens the democratic public sphere: "Through long-term and creative ideological work in the media and elsewhere, 'thick' meanings of democracy grounded in full collective participation are replaced with 'thin' understandings where democracy is reduced to choice on a market" (p. xxi). Citizens' participation in education has greatly shifted.

Ball (2012) astutely observed, "Dominant groups attach their policies and practices to the elements of good sense, not only the bad sense of real people's lives" (p. xxii). In this way, they not only mimic the terminology of educators but also use clever word plays that seem reasonable and wise. We should not assume that corporations are mindless—just the opposite.

Language powerfully serves as both an example of commodification and a highly influential phenomenon. Words such as *democracy, equality, justice,* and *freedom* become eviscerated by for-profit markets (Apple, 2011). Words and concepts that are integral to public education's "core" values manipulate our capacity for sense-making and critical reasoning relative to the health of public education. They have taken our "core" and repurposed it.

Thus, megacorporations and other marketeers are using the same words as educators but filling them with their own meanings. "Borrowed" terms include *core, achieve, partnership, assessment, readiness, careers, college,* and *growth.* I think that *achieve* and *achievement* are especially salient in marketing circles and the broadened school–university marketplace.

Take *achieve* or *achievement,* for example. The very concept was coopted when Achieve, Inc. was founded in 1996 at the National Education Summit by governors and business leaders; it is a partner of the Education Trust, Thomas B. Fordham Institute, and National Alliance of Business in the launch of the American Diploma Project. In 2010 the CCSS were released, and Achieve, Inc. partnered with the NGA and CCSSO on the initiative, hiring consultants. Achieve serves as project management partner for the PARCC and manages the state-led development of the K–12 Next Generation Science Standards (released in 2013).

Achieve, Inc. is a network with vigorously growing tendrils. Not only that, it is a shadow government fueled by the standardizing of learning within public schools using tests that ostensibly reflect a common core of English and math knowledge and skills (e.g., Achieve, 2008). But these approaches undercut school agency in curriculum making. Struggling schools in particular are penalized when teachers deemed "incompetent" are removed. Such actions are antithetical to the core value of thoughtfully building human and intellectual capital for a global society (English, 2014; Firestone, 2014).

Importantly, Cuban (2013) criticized megacorporations as failed experiments, largely because they overlook issues of classroom and school context and because they are not, as English (2014) argued, democratic agencies committed to the well-being of children and society. Blinded to understanding school culture and context, business entrepreneurs do not know what is involved in the struggle and success of teachers and children.

CORE is a school reform (like charter schools and hybrid online learning models) that builds upon funding, organization, governance, and curriculum to produce what is deemed to be technology-savvy, prepared graduates. Cuban's (2013) take was that such market reforms are misguided—even wrong-headed. Notably, they underestimate the vital role of context in shaping learning and achievement. Thus, market-driven education policy reforms miss the mark in understanding the milieu in which teachers teach and the everyday complexities they navigate involving the interface between teaching and learning. This interface is informed by challenges surrounding students' socio-demographics and home life, such as lack of support for study and goals.

The thrust of Achieve, Inc. contrasts starkly with the work of John Hattie (2008). Hattie's work on achievement is world-renowned, and his synthesis of more than 800 meta-analyses relating to achievement reflects deep knowledge of the education field. To convey the substance of his findings, he zeroed in on feedback, having found that its use is the single most important influence on student achievement. Achieve, Inc. has produced nothing like Hattie's empirical work.

Firestone (2014) concurred that feedback at the ground level of schools cultivates high-quality teacher performance. He stated that he does not see the CCSS accomplishing this goal: "Teachers need quick, fine-grained feedback that does not encourage gaming the system, and such feedback seems unlikely to come from the state" (p. 105). Feedback, which involves well-honed expertise, is the purview of public school educators. To Firestone, promises from U.S. states of empirical observation to be carried out by data and skilled observers are empty.

Why Care About the CCSS Policy Issue? School Leaders Speak

I have had the opportunity to consult three school leaders in North Carolina to inquire about the implementation of the CCSS in their districts and what types of tools and/or materials they use, as well as their opinions on the CCSS. I could tell from their reactions that the district-level leader and the two principals feel blindsided by this curricular testing machine. Clearly, they are suffering from a range of losses. I could sense that they know that the CCSS has manufactured the appearance of wholehearted buy-in at the grassroots level.

CCSS Standards and Losses

These leaders on the ground level of public schools cited curricular, personnel, and political issues. Regarding the CCSS standards, they specified current cuts in state funding for instructional materials and professional development. The school leaders, referring to the CCSS as the Common Core, also pinpointed losses in teacher positions and teacher-aid hours. They associated these problems with the CCSS, expressing concern over the way in which its implementation had been rushed, implying that they were treated as consumers who were left out of the loop, not as a critical body of stakeholders with proven curriculum expertise.

In regard to these financial, staff, and resource losses, a district leader in North Carolina explained that his public schools

> have newly developed curricula aligned to new standards at the same time the state drastically cut or completely eliminated funding for new

textbooks, instructional materials and supplies, instructional technology, professional development, and cut other areas that resulted in cuts to teacher positions and teacher-assistant hours.

(personal communication, September 17, 2014)

Classroom materials have not been properly vetted and are outdated, according to this same source:

> The math texts we have aren't aligned to the new standards—teachers are photocopying stuff out of different textbooks in order to teach, as well as finding resources online. We recognize that curriculum doesn't equal textbooks, but teachers need vetted content from multiple, high-quality sources, so we have social studies textbooks that don't mention President Obama (now near the end of his second term) and media collections 30 years old or older.
>
> *(personal communication, September 17, 2014)*

A principal of a K–12 school also criticized the politics behind the thrust of the CCSS adoption:

> North Carolina has done a major disservice to the educators and the students. This curriculum was rolled out with little to no thought of what was best for the people it would be impacting. It appears that the only reason the curriculum changed was to hold teachers accountable and to be able to compare our progress to other states. Many of us who are educators have no idea what is coming next. Will we still be using Common Core or won't we? Will we implement Smarter Balance, or won't we? If we don't use Common Core, what will we use? Who is in control of the decisions, the state superintendent or the legislature/governor?
>
> *(personal communication, September 19, 2014)*

Another school principal described the hasty implementation of the CCSS, which did not allow time for educators' reflection and review; hence "if only" laments pepper this statement:

> The whole thing seems to have turned into a political nightmare, and I'm afraid for the students who come to us expecting our very best. If only we could have slowly phased in Common Core. If only teachers and parents would have been given a chance to react to the standards and provide some feedback. We could have implemented pilot curriculum for 2 years and made adjustments at the end of every year. We really missed the opportunity to do something good with the new standards.

And what is scarier is that we have spent very little time reviewing the curriculum changes because everything happened so fast.

(personal communication, September 20, 2014)

To be fair, this same principal made a few positive points about the CCSS launch in North Carolina in regard to coverage of content and student mastery of concepts: "We cover less per grade level and spend more time going deeper into concepts. I also appreciate the fact that many of the standards loop year after year so students have the opportunity to master concepts" (personal communication, September 20, 2014).

Nevertheless, this principal elaborated on the negative impact associated with the politics of the CCSS:

> However, it is difficult to explain all of this to parents. There is such a lack of trust in what we do anymore because of the political cloud surrounding Common Core. Staunch Republican families have been working diligently to end Common Core. When you ask them why, they all quote the lieutenant governor. The federal government wants to monitor and classify our children before they get out of elementary school. Common Core, at its roots, may have a nice foundation. But it is surrounded by such a multitude of issues it's hard to know what is or isn't right with it. This has to be one of the more frustrating things I have had to deal with in my 25 years of service as an educator.

Mistrust, confusion, and frustration are apparent in these responses from veteran leaders. The markets involved in the commodification of their schools, based on their testimonies, include the state of North Carolina, the federal government, and the CCSS engineers.

Conclusions and Implications

In this call to action I address the policy arena, school administrator practice, educational leadership programs, and other constituents. All of these education domains speak to a triple reality: mounting corporate pressures, the erosion of democracy, and social movement building (Anyon, 2014). To public school defenders, I say that we need to band together to urge educators and constituents, importantly policymakers, to work as a collective to create and recreate educational institutions. We need to help the communities that extend beyond our buildings and disciplines to understand the importance of taking action by confronting as well as resisting the commodification of schools, as well as teachers, students, and parents (through such strategies as school choice). We also need accessible communication about the role of competitive markets in knowledge production and education policy.

As educators and school leaders, we can empower ourselves to imagine a different future for public education through consciousness-raising, policy initiatives, and social movements. A tighter connection is needed between school leadership research and the practices of school personnel, but also with advocacy, in that professional staff in school systems have the agency to serve local communities and constituents (Westbury, 2008). The staff who have responsibility for reclaiming their agency include superintendents, school principals, and teachers.

We must take back education by educating ourselves as to the challenge itself and by "resisting and fighting for democracy and keeping public education public" (English, 2014, p. 51). With the CCSS in mind and other policies in the wake, Wexler (2014) cited implications for higher education programs that should be grabbing our attention:

> The new teacher certification reform called edTPA follows the top-down, corporate formula, with the not-so-hidden agenda of disrupting the authority and autonomy of university education programs. In the same spirit of data-driven assessment, the CCSS and corporate views of accountability have made their way into the new certification and licensure process in teacher education. Teacher candidates will be evaluated based on certification tests aligned with the CCSS. Higher education teacher certification programs will be required to teach to the test, readying candidates to be judged by data driven by the Pearson Corporation's tests.
>
> *(p. 55)*

Public school defenders like Wexler (2014) have forecast concerns about the potential of public education to remain a public good. We can bring illumination to this cause by making visible dynamics and connections that illustrate the neoliberal force at work in education.

Market Creep in Education

My construct Public Education, Inc. positions the attacks against public education within a broader societal context. It does not and cannot only refer to the phenomenon of a market takeover of public schools, as universities and colleges are caught in the net. English (2011) described "the movement to standardize leadership and practice" and how this has "created a shift away from the policy of the common good" (p. xi). Standards are "locked into a policy network," he explained, spread widely across such entities as "accreditation agencies, new national professional practice boards . . . and the federal government" (p. xi).

Although it is revolutionary for educators to band together to speak out against the dismantling of public education by marketeers and public policy figures, it is happening with some growing momentum. However, it is sobering to realize that speaking out can actually be silencing (Mullen, 2013). On a day of protest at the American Educational Research Association in 2013 in San Francisco, at which the theme was poverty in schools and communities, there was suppression of free speech and robust intellectual dialogue. Free speech ironically took the nonverbal form of signs, arm-bands, fliers, and protest lines.

I joined the protesters who gathered behind the scenes and outside the banquet room where Arnie Duncan spoke into microphone. Doublespeak—not thoughtful point and counterpoint as is customary in intellectual debate—was reflected in rhetoric that was for and against test-based accountability. After conceding that there are some problems with standardized tests, Duncan said we need better tests. That was his "core" vision.

Some parts of the education community might finally be ready to reclaim public education and defend it against neoliberal assaults that treat it as a consumable commodity that erodes criticality and equity (e.g., English, 2014). Readers who stand against the corporatization, standardization, and privatiz-ation of education will be protesting against the neoliberal message and the mission of influential conservatives who represent and support it. We can take back public education, but there are forces operating within that make this ideal seem overly simplistic and naïve.

Thus, we are being called upon to work against the narrowing of possibilities of what it means to research, know, and learn, and to communicate our understandings so that voices of dissent will not be silenced (see ReclaimAERA, 2013). What forces are destroying institutions and educational values, forging divisions across society?

Internal Market Cooperatives

Consider, for example, the consultants and education researchers in a particular school or discipline. I used the qualification "some parts of the education community" earlier because other parts of the education community would not be ready to reclaim education in the ways that I have been describing. Leaders and educators from schools and universities who are being paid for their work with the CCSS and other standards are internal market cooperatives. There are faculty members and adjuncts, such as seated deans in education colleges and retired district superintendents, some of whom work in higher education institutions, who moonlight with for-profit companies. Pearson Education and CORE are examples of employers who generate the materials for testing, professional development, and training, and deliver the actual training.

If you search corporate and university websites, you will spot educators who sponsor the money-making markets that are draining public school coffers. CCSS beneficiaries and those of other high-stakes tests within these circles stand by the message that these interventions uphold high-quality, rigorous education. From their own work in entrepreneurial leadership comes a new credo of progressivism in the education domain. But they are using their academic positions as reputation magnets for propelling self-interests that support neither the best interests of public schools nor the higher education institutions that employ them and depend on their service.

The policy grip of markets is much tighter and closer to home than Figure 2.1 suggests. That is because there are also researchers, including some leading figures, who conduct consultancy-based studies on the CCSS and other standards. Gone are the empirical distance and critical consciousness that researchers have been trained to develop. Instead, their work is favorably predisposed toward the CCSS. They are themselves representing corporate interests that embolden the shadow government that undergirds education workplaces. Given that "they" are becoming "us," and that our academic culture is being rewired from the outside-in to acquiesce to the new brand of entrepreneurial corporate leadership, it is much more crucial that education as a public service be rescued, kept alive, and cherished.

When internal market cooperatives are visible, can we see them? Ravitch (2010) made the news when she "confessed" to no longer being in favor of market-driven school reforms (e.g., deregulation, private charter schools). Her story of transformation is compelling. It has strong implications for the conversion of internal market cooperatives that often think the way she used to. She changed her mind about the need for a market-based public education system upon recognizing that the very existence of an egalitarian institution that seeks to protect the politically weak, impoverished classes in low-income school communities is threatened by politically powerful corporations, individuals, and classes. She has learned that struggling schools, in particular, are not improved by free-market reforms. And she has come to understand that the buying and selling (i.e., marketization) of education has not brought about a better or more coherent curriculum, and that it, in fact, disrupts this goal.

Ravitch (2010, 2013) also has been worried about the toxicity of past and current federal administrations, citing the high-stakes testing movement and the convergence of private markets that are, in effect, dissolving public school values. Firing teachers and closing schools is a business mindset that, she argues, dismisses the historical reality that schools are community anchors, carrying values, ideals, and traditions from one decade to the next.

Targeting teachers instead of poverty misses the problem, according to Ravitch (2010, 2013). Research shows that poverty is closely associated with the unsatisfactory performance of students (English, Papa, Mullen, & Creighton, 2012; Papa et al., 2012). Fallen by the wayside is the democratic preparation of students who understand the responsibility of citizens in an increasingly diverse global society (Ravitch, 2013).

Not all leading education researchers discuss the corporate market issue and its impact. Darling-Hammond et al. (2014), for example, mentioned major networks involved in the production of the CCSS (particularly CCSSO). Interestingly, coauthors Wilhoit and Pittenger are former directors of CCSSO, the influential body that oversaw the development and adoption of the CCSS. Darling-Hammond directed President Obama's education policy transition team; as a sponsor of the CCSS, she is uniquely positioned to leverage the standards and make their endpoints amenable, in her own words, to college and career readiness. Advocates for the CCSS and its standards and testing turn accountability over to the jurisdiction of private companies; markets, standards, and future readiness are inextricably linked in the norming of a market takeover of education.

The endorsement of CCSS by high-powered, equity-type academics underscores the entrenchment of the standards in high-poverty schools and, moreover, the ingenuity of the neoliberalists in assuming control of public school curriculum by seizing its intellectual and political capital. New education research is being published by reputable presses and, in the case of Darling-Hammond's research, coauthored by powerful market-based reformers (Darling-Hammond, Wilhoit, & Pittenger, 2014).

Referencing the general political context, Ravitch (2013) explained that many "well-meaning" liberals and progressives support market-based reforms, even though these are "antithetical to liberalism and progressivism" (p. 4). She suggested that "good people," and, I add, powerhouse researchers who endeavor to create an equity-minded nation, "are being used by those who have an implacable hostility toward the public sector" (Ravitch, 2013, p. 4).

Neoliberal Damage Assessment

We fund what we value, hence we need to educate one another about the insidious flow of neoliberalism in our daily lives and the information we consume (e.g., English, 2014). Think about how the amount of testing proposed by the U.S. Department of Education connected to national standards is increasing. Testing and standardization are excessive regimes which occupy much daily instructional time and reduce time for nontested subjects (e.g., the arts and humanities). Potentially, standardized tests could be developed for all subjects and given at more grade levels, no matter how far-flung. Pretests and interim tests could potentially be used to measure growth, defined as increases in standardized test scores or "value-added" measures.

And what about the cost of implementing standards and electronically delivering national tests? To offset the enormous expense, expect that funding will be bled from school activities that promote learning in the arts and humanities (English, 2014). Instead of directing all this funding and time to standardized testing, advocates for reform need to redirect the current focus toward poverty (Mullen, 2014; Papa et al., 2012). This money could be spent on meal programs, medical staff, libraries, and facilities to ameliorate the effects of poverty (English et al., 2012; Heintz, 2011; Mullen, 2014; Ravitch, 2010, 2013).

As contributors to this book make clear, we must assess the damage neoliberal solutions (such as more testing and more funding for more testing) impose on public schools. What values will be inculcated upon children and youth? These days, the message is that math, science, and being globally competitive matter most (Zhao, 2014). The arts and humanities—and the pathways they provide for becoming fully engaged, empathetic citizens and leaders—are being lost (Mullen, English, & Kealy, 2014; Wexler, 2014).

Stakeholders in schools can make a difference by advocating against capitalist greed and for a public education that serves all children, everywhere. The vision for transformational leadership has been described by at least a few district superintendents whose struggle within and beyond schools plays out within a contested milieu as they attempt to effect change (e.g., Kelleher & Van der Bogert, 2006).

Organizing for Action

Public school educators—and their constituents and defenders—can build awareness about the effects of neoliberalism and corporate networking on schools by considering these steps:

- Use Figure 2.1 for team building and instructional purposes to educate one another on how the neoliberal power grid functions.
- Identify the sponsors (e.g., publishers, think-tanks) of the curricular materials from your school or district and ask critical questions about who they are. Then make your own connections among the networks they represent and the ways in which your own domain underwrites them.
- Use this book to generate a reading list that gives your team more of an understanding of pertinent education policy issues and the real costs involved for schools, especially for first-generation and low-income students (e.g., English, 2014).
- Conduct seminars/workshops on such topics as neoliberalism and antidemocratic education, education policy and corporate networks, and school empowerment and local control to increase your team's awareness and potency; choose materials to present your rationale. Raise consciousness about such concerns as how programs and people, ideas and language, are being commodified (i.e., marketed, measured, and packaged).
- Discuss how your local control over curriculum and other matters of interest can be increased relative to the level and type of agency you desire, and how your school or district can be more protected from the outside-in and from the inside-out.

- Based on your research and discoveries, make bold assertions about what you and your team have determined as public needs for education and the pathways you think can help move us in that direction.

We need to challenge one another to question the dominant political wisdom. What is our individual and collective responsibility for countering the for-profit, anti-intellectual mindset that damages schools, teachers, students, and families? How do we instead transform education into that which honors the public school mission? Debates like this one put networked policy governance and coalitions under a microscope, and potentially expose the sneak attacks that implicate innocent children and subvert their authentic learning. The spirit of public service needs to survive; education for the common good benefits all children, worldwide.

In this chapter, Public Education, Inc. has served as a device for calling public education stakeholders to attention and action on the current corporatization of public education, which includes all public school districts and higher education institutions—hence the moniker "Inc." Satire has given me leverage for prying open a Pandora's Box of realities and dynamics feeding the greedy corporate machine. A goal is to spark educator and stakeholder consciousness of the corporate siege of public schools and what this means for the schoolhouse.

To education researchers, I am pointing out that some of the literature I reviewed seems to understate the extent to which for-profit corporations and their networked coalitions have invaded public schools. Other current literature reveals how profiteers are much more robustly engaged in symbolic and real forms of power than is generally recognized. And they are waging a forceful, deliberate, and long-term seizure of public education.

Researchers and theorists are indeed identifying aspects of these issues, but sometimes in a moderate way; perhaps because the urgency, magnitude, and impacts of corporate marketization on the public school sector are largely invisible and unknown. There is also a lag in publication, and academics focus on peer-reviewed outlets which lack the immediacy of news media outlets.

A tagline of concern in the published literature is that megacorporations are running public schools in their own best interests. It is as though this subject has until recently been but a sidebar of policy debates, including education research—although there is more research being produced on the interconnections among neoliberalism, corporatization, education policies and standards, and politics in the United States and other countries (e.g., Ball, 2012; English, 2010, 2014; Mullen, English, et al., 2013; Mullen, Samier, et al., 2013; Tienken & Orlich, 2013).

The consequences of market appropriations of education have spurred large-scale social injustice in the United States. Collective action, including protests, can force an activist consciousness to emerge and germinate a new crop of policy actors (English, 2010, 2014). Public Education, Inc. can play a role in stimulating educators and citizens who care about the state of public schools and advancing the common good to stop and mourn the losses, and to think critically and act persuasively.

My intent has been to force the sheer scope of this reality into the light of day. Readers have been given the opportunity to explore issues and create their own connections, and are invited to draw conclusions for themselves.

References

Achieve, Inc. (2008, July 31). *Out of many, one: Toward rigorous common core standards from the ground up.* Washington, DC: Author. Retrieved from www.achieve.org/OutofManyOne

Anyon, J. (2014). *Radical possibilities: Public policy, urban education, and a new social movement* (2nd ed.). New York, NY: Routledge.

Apple, M. W. (2011). Democratic education in neoliberal and neoconservative times. *International Studies in Sociology of Education, 21*(1), 21–31.

Apple, M. W. (2014). *Official knowledge: Democratic education in a conservative age* (3rd ed.). New York, NY: Routledge.

Ball, S. J. (2012). *Global education inc.: New policy networks and the neo-liberal imaginary.* Abingdon, Oxon, UK: Routledge.

Barry, B. (2005). *Why social justice matters.* Cambridge, UK: Polity Press.

Berliner, D. C., & Glass, G. V. (Eds.). (2014). *50 myths & lies that threaten America's public schools: The real crisis in education.* New York, NY: Teachers College Press.

Blumenfeld, S. (2012, July 27). CFR task force calls for education reform. *The New American.* Retrieved from www.thenewamerican.com/reviews/opinion/item/12235-cfr-task-force-calls-for-education-reform

Bogotch, I., & Shields, C. M. (Eds.). (2014a). Introduction: Do promises of social justice trump paradigms of educational leadership? In I. Bogotch & C. M. Shields (Eds.), *International handbook of educational leadership and social (in)justice* (pp. 1–12). Dordrecht, The Netherlands: Springer.

Bogotch, I., & Shields, C. M. (Eds.). (2014b). *International handbook of educational leadership and social (in)justice.* Dordrecht, The Netherlands: Springer.

Bracken, K. (2013, April 18). *Common core: Subversive threat to education.* Presentation at the Chattanooga TEA Party meeting, Chattanooga, TN. Retrieved from www.youtube.com/watch?v=0X0EFeH25bw

Brass, J. (2014). Reading standards as curriculum: The curricular and cultural politics of the common core. *Journal of Curriculum and Pedagogy, 11*(1), 23–25, doi:10.1080/15505170.2014.907551

CORE. (2013). Data charts. Retrieved from www.corelearn.com/Results/Data-Charts.html

Cuban, L. (2013). *Inside the black box of classroom practice: Change without reform in American education.* Cambridge, MA: Harvard Education Press.

Darling-Hammond, L., Wilhoit, G., & Pittenger, L. (2014). Accountability for college and career readiness: Developing a new paradigm. *Education Policy Analysis Archives, 22*(86). Retrieved from http://dx.doi.org/10.14507/epaa.v22n86.2014

Downey, M. (2013, August 25). Common core as a brand name. Who is making money off the new standards? *Atlanta Journal-Constitution.* Retrieved from www.ajc.com/

weblogs/get-schooled/2013/aug/25/common-core-brand-name-who-making-money-new-standa

Eisenhower, D. D. (1961, January 17). *Farewell radio and television address to the American people* (known as the "Military-industrial complex speech"). Washington, DC: White House.

Elementary and Secondary Education Act of 1965. 20 U.S.C.A. § 6301 *et seq.* (West, 2003).

English, F. W. (2010). The ten most wanted enemies of American public education's school leadership. *NCPEA Education Leadership Review, 5*(3).

English, F. W. (2011). (Ed.). *The SAGE handbook of educational leadership: Advances in theory, research, and practice* (2nd ed.). Thousand Oaks, CA: SAGE Publications.

English, F. W. (2014). *Educational leadership in the age of greed: A requiem for res publica.* Ypsilanti, MI: NCPEA Press.

English, F. W., Papa, R., Mullen, C. A., & Creighton, T. (2012). *Educational leadership at 2050: Conjectures, challenges, and promises.* Lanham, MD: Rowman & Littlefield.

Firestone, W. A. (2014). Teacher evaluation policy and conflicting theories of motivation. *Educational Researcher, 43*(2), 100–107.

Gates, B. (2009, July 21). *A bold new vision for education.* Address at the National Conference of State Legislatures, Philadelphia. Retrieved from www.gatesfoundation. org/Media-Center/Speeches/2009/07/Bill-Gates-National-Conference-of-State-Legislatures-NCSL

Giroux, H. A. (2014). *Neoliberalism's war on higher education.* Chicago, IL: Haymarket Books.

Habermas, J. (1985). *The theory of communicative action: Vol. 2. Lifeworld and system: A critique of functionalist reason* (T. McCarthy, Trans.). Boston, MA: Beacon Press.

Hattie, J. (2008). *Visible learning: A synthesis of over 800 meta-analyses relating to achievement.* New York, NY: Routledge.

Heintz, J. (2011, June). *Military assets and public investment.* Providence, RI: Costs of War, Brown University. Retrieved from http://costsofwar.org/sites/default/files/articles/31/attachments/Heintzmilitaryassets.pdf

Jones, A. G., & King, J. E. (2012). The Common Core State Standards: A vital tool for higher education. *Change: The Magazine of Higher Learning, 44*(6), 37–43, doi:10.1080/00091383.2012.706529

Kelleher, P., & Van der Bogert, R. (Eds.). (2006). *Voices for democracy: Struggles and celebrations of transformational leaders.* Yearbook of the National Society for the Study of Education, 105(1). Malden, MA: Blackwell.

McDermott-McNulty, M. (2013, August 25). *Common core developers—a private club you are not in* [Blog post]. Perdido Street School: A blog about public education, politics and schools. Retrieved from http://perdidostreetschool.blogspot.com/2013/08/common-core-developers-private-club-you.html

McDermott-McNulty, M. (2014). "Nothing in common" Common Core. *Journal of Curriculum and Pedagogy, 11*(1), 43-46, doi:10.1080/15505170.2014.908431

Miron, G. J. (2008). The shifting notion of "publicness" in public education. In B. S. Cooper, J. G. Cibulka, & L. D. Fusarelli (Eds.), *Handbook of education politics and policy* (pp. 338–349). New York, NY: Routledge.

Moffett, M., & Newsom, J. (2014, September 30). 3 former UNCG employees charged in moonlighting scandal. *News & Record.* Retrieved from www.news-record.com

Mullen, C. A. (2013). Epilogue: Reclaiming public education. In F. W. English, *Educational leadership in the age of greed: A requiem for res publica* (pp. 60–64). Ypsilanti, MI: NCPEA Press.

Mullen, C. A. (2014). Advocacy for child wellness in high-poverty environments. *Kappa Delta Pi Record, 50*(4), 157–163.

Mullen, C. A. (2015, April). *Corporate network proliferation in the public school sector and rapid erosion of capital.* Paper presented at the Society of Professors of Education meeting, Chicago, IL.

Mullen, C. A., English, F. W., Brindley, S., Ehrich, L. C., & Samier, E. A. (2013). Neoliberal issues in public education [Guest edited 2-volume issue]. *Interchange: A Quarterly Review of Education, 43*(3) & *43*(4), 181–377.

Mullen, C. A., English, F. W., & Kealy, W. A. (2014). *The leadership identity journey: An artful reflection.* Lanham, MD: Rowman & Littlefield.

Mullen, C. A., Samier, E. A., Brindley, S., English, F. W., & Carr. N. K. (2013). An epistemic frame analysis of neoliberal culture and politics in the US, UK, and the UAE. *Interchange: A Quarterly Review of Education, 43*(3), 187–228.

National Governors Association Center for Best Practices & Council of Chief State School Officers. (2010). *Common Core State Standards.* Washington, DC: Author. Retrieved from www.corestandards.org

Nielson, K. (2014, April 3). *Trends in state implementation of the Common Core State Standards: Making the shift to better tests* [Brief]. Washington, DC: National Governors Association. Retrieved from www.nga.org/files/live/sites/NGA/files/pdf/2014/1404NGACCSSAssessments.pdf

No Child Left Behind Act of 2001, 20 U.S.C.A. § 6301 *et seq.* (West, 2003).

Papa, R., English, F. W., Davidson, F., Culver, M., K., & Brown, R. (2012). *Contours of great leadership: The science, art, and wisdom of outstanding practice.* Lanham, MD: Rowman & Littlefield.

Ravitch, D. (2010, March 9). Why I changed my mind about school reform. *The Wall Street Journal,* Opinion. Retrieved from http://online.wsj.com/news/articles/SB100 014240527487048693045751094433053343962?mg=reno64-wsj&url=http%3A%2F%2Fonline.wsj.com%2Farticle%2FSB10001424052748704869304575109443305343962.html

Ravitch, D. (2012, October 30). Missouri public schools under siege [Blog]. Retrieved from dianeravitch.net/2012/10/30/missouri-public-schools-under-siege

Ravitch, D. (2013). *Reign of error: The hoax of the privatization movement and the danger to America's public schools.* New York, NY: Vintage Books.

ReclaimAERA. (2013, May 1). *ReclaimAERA: In defense of research, education, and action for the public good.* Retrieved from http://reclaimaera.wordpress.com

Savage, G. C., O'Connor, K., & Brass, J. (2014). Common Core State Standards: Implications for curriculum, equality and policy. *Journal of Curriculum and Pedagogy, 11*(1), 18–20, doi:10.1080/15505170.2014.908436

Tienken, C. H. (2012). The Common Core State Standards: The emperor is still looking for his clothes. *Kappa Delta Pi Record, 48*(4), 152–155. doi:10.1080/00228958.2012.733928

Tienken, C. H., & Orlich, D. C. (2013). *The school reform landscape: Fraud, myth, and lies.* Lanham, MD: Rowman & Littlefield.

United States Department of Defense Education Activity. (2012, June 5). *DoDEA schools to adopt Common Core State Standards* (Press release). Alexandria, VA: DoDEA. Retrieved from www.dodea.edu/newsroom/pressreleases/06052012.cfm

Westbury, I. (2008). Curriculum in practice. In F. M. Connelly, M. F. He, & J. Phillion (Eds.), *The SAGE handbook of curriculum and instruction* (pp. 1–4). Thousand Oaks, CA: SAGE Publications.

Wexler, A. (2014). Reaching higher? The impact of the Common Core State Standards on the visual arts, poverty, and disabilities. *Arts Education Policy Review, 115*(2), 52–61, doi:10.1080/10632913.2014.883897

Wikipedia: The Free Encyclopedia. (2014). Shadow government (conspiracy). Retrieved from http://en.wikipedia.org/wiki/Shadow_government_%28conspiracy%29

Zhao, Y. (2014). *Who's afraid of the big bad dragon? Why China has the best (and worst) education system in the world.* San Francisco, CA: Jossey-Bass.

3

LEADING IN A SOCIALLY JUST MANNER: PREPARING PRINCIPALS WITH A POLICY PERSPECTIVE

Mariela A. Rodríguez

UNIVERSITY OF TEXAS AT SAN ANTONIO

Nationally, student diversity is increasing. According to the U.S. Census Bureau (2015), more than 20% of the school-age population in the country speak a language other than English at home. Specifically, populations of English learners (ELs) whose first language is Spanish have steadily increased in southwestern states (Arriaza, 2003; National Center for Education Statistics, 2014). Other states, such as South Carolina, Kentucky, and Nevada, had some of the fastest growing EL populations in the 2000–2010 decade (Horsford & Sampson, 2013).

Given this increase in ELs across the United States, university-based principal preparation programs must integrate bilingual education leadership research into their required programs of study. Making preparation programs in educational administration relevant to the job demands of leaders in schools serving diverse students is key (Riehl, 2000). Making the content of preparation programs relevant to the demographic context in which leaders will serve is necessary to effectively prepare prospective leaders for positions in schools that are often deemed low-performing by state standards and rarely attract the quality leaders necessary to support successful change (Darling-Hammond, Meyerson, LaPointe, & Orr, 2010; Hess & Kelly, 2007). School leaders must make every effort to promote high-quality teaching and learning in every school. This vision will create educational settings in which students could develop their skills beyond state accountability measures that focus on a single snapshot of performance on a standardized test. Such restrictive educational policies come to the forefront when the discussion turns to traditionally marginalized groups of students like those learning English as a second language (Gándara & Hopkins, 2010; Menken & García, 2010).

This chapter highlights the important role of the principal in the development of inclusive bilingual education programs for ELs. Such programs are additive in nature, because a goal of the curriculum is to build on ELs' native language while introducing English. These types of programs are the opposite of subtractive programs whose outcome is typically the loss of ELs' native language, which is replaced by English language acquisition. These latter programs exist due to various policy implications stemming from rigid accountability measures that mandate testing for student achievement in English (García & Kleifgen, 2010). The political landscape in the United States related to immigrants who speak languages other than English is mirrored in schools (Bartlett & García, 2011). This reality makes it relevant for school leaders to be political advocates for English learners in their schools by providing them a safe learning environment that is nurturing while being academically rigorous.

The cohort model discussed here is a result of collaborative planning among program faculty to meet the challenge of preparing school leaders who will promote the aforementioned environments for ELs through actions that reflect social justice ideologies in their schools (Cambron-McCabe & McCarthy, 2005). Such leaders have only the highest expectations for the children and maintain a "capabilities approach to leadership" (Larson & Murtadha, 2002, p. 155). Principals who espouse this approach support curriculum and instruction that is aligned to the goals of language development for ELs. These principals allocate resources to effectively sustain bilingual education programs that meet accountability standards without losing students' home language (García & Frede, 2010; Salomone, 2010).

For school leaders to demonstrate support for ELs, it is imperative that principal preparation programs incorporate culturally relevant initiatives within their training components (Reyes, 2006; Suttmiller & González, 2006). Such well-prepared leaders are needed in public education, and especially in schools with large numbers of ELs. In these schools, meeting the academic and social needs of these underrepresented students supports the basic tenets of social justice, particularly in regard to how students acquire English through bilingual education programs that value both the native language of ELs as well as the English language (Theoharis & O'Toole, 2011). This type of commitment to student learning would demonstrate that principals were working toward less restrictive language policies that do not devalue students' home languages, but rather see them as an asset for language transfer (Valdés, 2001). The role of the principal in encouraging such practices in schools is relevant to the future academic outcomes of ELs.

Current research literature identifies relevant content that would inform school administrators as to their leadership roles in schools with significant numbers of ELs. While literature regarding effective leadership practices for traditionally high-achieving, high-poverty schools has been addressed (Lyman

& Villani, 2004; Reyes, Scribner, & Scribner, 1999), there remains a dearth in school leadership research concerning the crucial role of instructional leadership for the success of ELs and the specific roles and responsibilities of the principal (Fierro & Rodríguez, 2006). In this vein, the literature surrounding social justice leadership must be explored so that it can become a seminal point of discussion in leadership preparation.

Literature Review

Bilingual education programs for educating English learners in schools are based on language policies that reflect political contexts in which the acquisition of English trumps the maintenance of home language for ELs (Tollefson, 2013). In researching language practices in Arizona schools, Moore (2014) learned that schooling practices were highly influenced by the political movements of the day, particularly the "English-only" initiative that voters in that state had supported. Such discriminatory beliefs toward immigrant students showed that the hegemony of English in the United States was evident in school matters related to the academic instruction of ELs. Thus it is important for principals to be aware of the negative consequences of practices that label and stigmatize students (Menken, 2008). In so doing, principals can then make concerted efforts to resist derogatory influences and instead focus on equity-building reforms that will help ELs to make linguistic and academic gains (Menken, Kleyn, & Chae, 2012).

The awareness that principals will gain is reminiscent of what renowned critical educator Paulo Freire (1970) called "conscientization." He discussed how educators had to reflect on and critically analyze social contexts. Then, he argued, individuals must take action. Such action supports social justice for all (Sernak, 2008). Now consider the meaning of social justice in educational leadership. Theoharis (2007) comes to the forefront regarding the work of such leaders in school contexts through his research study of principals who led effective efforts for all students in their schools. The study participants, selected because they are leaders who are advocates, included principals who demonstrated a commitment to fair and ethical decisions related to students. Such educators understand the value of empowering students to achieve their potential in learning environments that facilitate such development. In his book, Theoharis (2009) discussed the ways in which principals sought equity-building in their schools as a manner of initiating reform. These efforts helped to sustain a school culture that was inclusive of all students in all programs. The needs of students, both academic and social, were met through collaborative efforts among administrators, teachers, parents, and other stakeholders.

Various researchers have called attention to social justice as a key component in principal preparation programs (Brunner, Hammel, & Miller, 2003; Furman, 2012). The research looked at the development of leaders through coursework and field experiences from a social justice perspective. A call for action was brought forward by well-known scholars in educational leadership who proposed educating leaders for social justice (McKenzie et al., 2008). Leading for social justice is something that can be taught through experiential learning and research. In learning how to be advocates for change, school leaders can facilitate efforts in their schools that will improve the social and academic outcomes of students. Research by DeMatthews and Mawhinney (2014) supported the need to help future school leaders learn how to be effective stewards of social justice, because that capacity would assist them in their daily work in schools.

Likewise Capper, Theoharis, and Sebastian (2006) provided one of the earliest frameworks for preparing educational leaders for social justice. In their model, they described seven key aspects of social justice leadership to be incorporated within leadership preparation programs, and how these aspects were not only related, but also intertwined. The seven aspects were: (a) emotional safety for risk taking, (b) curriculum, (c) pedagogy, (d) assessment, (e) critical consciousness, (f) knowledge, and (g) skills (p. 220).

A cross-case analysis of three social justice-oriented preparation programs was performed by Rodríguez, Chambers, González, and Scheurich (2010), who identified critical elements such as cohort models, critical consciousness embedded in course offerings, and social justice socialization of faculty. The authors affirmed that such elements were cornerstones of leadership preparation programs seeking to revamp their curriculum.

Social justice approaches demand more from principal preparation programs to make them more relevant in today's context (Jean-Marie, Normore, & Brooks, 2009; Tucker, Young, & Koschoreck, 2012). This chapter focuses on social justice related to principal preparation regarding the education of students who are linguistically diverse. School leaders serving as advocates for ELs can demonstrate informed decision-making by knowing the characteristics of effective bilingual education programs, communicating with parents, and extending the accountability rhetoric to include equitable programs for these learners (Rivera et al., 2010; Scanlan & López, 2012). The preparation of such leaders is vital for the long-term success of ELs and their future levels of educational attainment. This, in turn, will benefit society as a whole through the contributions that ELs will make both socially and in their careers.

The Site: A Hispanic-Serving Institution

This public, four-year, Hispanic-serving institution is in an urban city about 200 miles northwest of the U.S.–Mexico border. The university has a designated service area that includes 12 school districts within one county: six urban districts and another six districts that constitute both urban and rural demographics. The three largest school districts range in size from 56,000 to more than 71,000 students. Due to demographic changes, the city is home to several ethnic populations, and almost all of the elementary schools in these districts offer transitional bilingual programs, dual language education programs, or ESL programs to meet the needs of a culturally and linguistically diverse student body (Texas Administrative Code, 2012).

Program Description

Currently, the principal preparation program at this university consists of a 36-hour master's degree in Educational Leadership that includes requirements for principal certification in Texas. Traditional course offerings such as school law, finance, and supervision are required in addition to coursework in curriculum and human relations. These courses help to prepare school principals for the demands of the role.

Yet, within the required coursework, there is no offering of specific courses on leadership for bilingual education programs. Given the context described earlier, there is a critical need for principals to be effectively trained to lead bilingual education programs (Menken & Solorza, in press). Bilingual education theory and practice have been taught as part of a three-credit special programs administration course within the master's degree program. To expand the leadership pipeline, the faculty recruited experienced teachers who worked with ELs on a daily basis. The intent was for educators who already espoused advocacy for linguistically diverse students to facilitate more effective practices for this group of students once the teachers became school leaders in decision-making roles. Such decisions would directly impact ELs through bilingual program development and resource allocations for such programs (Alanís & Rodríguez, 2008; Rodríguez & Alanís, 2011). The course offerings were tailored to the cohort by making the curriculum and assignments relevant to working with ELs in urban settings. A primary goal was to help extend the leadership development of bilingual education teachers who already demonstrated socially just practices in their classrooms.

Promising Practices of the Program

A faculty-initiated pilot program consisted of a cohort of 23 students seeking principal certification. Prerequisites for selection and participation within this cohort included having earned a master's degree in bicultural/bilingual education. The recruitment approach involved "tapping" graduates who had completed the required master's degree in bilingual education and grooming them for leadership in various districts within the university's service area.

The model of delivery of educational leadership coursework for this cohort differed significantly from that of the traditional principal certification program. Students enrolled in two courses per semester that were delivered through a team-teaching model. Students came to campus only once a week for an extended evening in which the two courses were integrated. This timeline served as an incentive for teachers with demanding schedules to be able to complete requirements within a flexible approach.

The team-teaching approach provided faculty members with opportunities to prepare seamless course offerings that highlighted their respective areas of expertise. This model also allowed for students to make stronger connections across course content. Practical, field-based learning experiences and an internship that extended throughout coursework (rather than just as a capstone) were additional components of this delivery model. The model allowed for collaborative interactions among students from various schools so they could learn from one another (Darling-Hammond et al., 2010). Faculty members created opportunities for students to engage in reflection about how they could merge their expertise in bilingual education with the leadership skills they were learning through the certification program.

Conclusions

At the end of the two-year period, all 23 cohort members successfully completed the principal preparation program geared to extending the social justice and advocacy practices of bilingual teachers. Graduates of this educational leadership and policy studies program applied for leadership positions within the 12 districts located within the city and additional districts located in surrounding communities. In their new roles, these advocates of bilingual education will be able to demonstrate support for ELs in their schools through additive bilingual education practices (Rodríguez, González, & Garza, 2013).

The importance of making preparation programs in educational administration relevant to the job demands of school administrators should be of specific concern to faculty, primarily those charged with preparing school leaders to serve ELs (Scanlan & López, 2015). Given the evolving demographic representation of students in the United States, those institutions seeking change must consider these themes as an integral part of school leadership preparation.

Policy Relevance and Implications

As national policy perspectives lean toward restrictive language policies for ELs, it is imperative for school leaders to advocate for practices that support them (Gándara & Hopkins, 2010). Darder (2012) discussed how culture and power in today's classrooms are prevalent factors that affect the instruction of bicultural students. Thus, principals who believe in socially just initiatives for traditionally marginalized students must have the professional development and experience to carry out such initiatives effectively (Jensen & Sawyer, 2013).

The perspective taken by Orelus (2014) regarding language diversity in schools stems from his research surrounding the disappearance of certain languages through colonization. Such work is an example of the power of language in society and, thus, in schools. National and state-level policies related to language, particularly second language learning, are often influenced by misinformed prejudices (Rios-Aguilar, González Canché, & Sabetghadam, 2012). Instead educators must focus on considerations such as those described by Callahan and Gándara (2014), who have deemed bilingualism as advantageous in current and future labor markets. The time has come to establish principal preparation programs with opportunities for the development of policy awareness and critique for the leaders of tomorrow's schools. Only then can leaders make effective contributions toward the education of ELs and all students.

References

Alanís, I., & Rodríguez, M. A. 2008). Sustaining a dual language immersion program: Features of success. *Journal of Latinos and Education, 7*(4), 305–319.

Arriaza, G. (2003). Schools, social capital and children of color. *Race, Ethnicity and Education, 6*(1), 71–94.

Bartlett, L., & García, O. (2011). *Additive schooling in subtractive times: Bilingual education and Dominican immigrant youth in the Heights.* Nashville, TN: Vanderbilt University Press.

Brunner, C. C., Hammel, K., & Miller, M. D. (2003). Transforming leadership preparation for social justice: Dissatisfaction, inspiration, and rebirth—An exemplar. In F. C. Lunenburg and C. S. Carr (Eds.), *Shaping the future: Policy, partnerships, and emerging perspectives* (pp. 70–84). Lanham, MD: Scarecrow Education.

Callahan, R. M., & Gándara, P. C. (2014). *The bilingual advantage: Language, literacy, and the US labor market.* Buffalo, NY: Multilingual Matters.

Cambron-McCabe, N., & McCarthy, M. M. (2005). Educating school leaders for social justice. *Educational Policy, 19*(1), 201–222.

Capper, C. A., Theoharis, G., & Sebastian, J. (2006). Toward a framework for preparing leaders for social justice. *Journal of Educational Administration, 44*(3), 209–224.

Darder, A. (2012). *Culture and power in the classroom: Educational foundations for the schooling of bicultural students* (20th anniv. ed.). Boulder, CO: Paradigm Publishers.

Darling-Hammond, L, Meyerson, D., LaPointe, M., & Orr, M. T. (2010). *Preparing principals for a changing world: Lessons from effective school leadership programs.* San Francisco, CA: Jossey-Bass.

DeMatthews, D., & Mawhinney, H. (2014). Social justice leadership and inclusion: Exploring challenges in an urban district struggling to address inequities. *Educational Administration Quarterly, 50*(5), 844–881.

Fierro, E., & Rodríguez, M. A. (2006). Leadership for bilingual education: Reflections on social justice. *Journal of School Leadership, 16*(2), 182–196.

Freire, P. (1970). Cultural action and conscientization. *Harvard Educational Review, 40*(3), 452–477.

Furman, G. (2012). Social justice leadership as praxis: Developing capacities through preparation programs. *Educational Administration Quarterly, 48*(2), 191–229.

Gándara, P., & Hopkins, M. (2010). *Forbidden language: English learners and restrictive language policies*. New York, NY: Teachers College Press.

García, E. E., & Frede, E. C. (Eds.). (2010). *Young English language learners: Current research and emerging directions for practice and policy*. New York, NY: Teachers College Press.

García, O., & Kleifgen, J. A. (2010). *Educating emergent bilinguals: Policies, programs, and practices for English language learners*. New York, NY: Teachers College Press.

Hess, F. M., & Kelly, A. P. (2007). Learning to lead: What gets taught in principal-preparation programs. *Teachers College Record, 109*(1), 244–274.

Horsford, S. D., & Sampson, C. (2013). High-ELL-growth states: Expanding funding equity and opportunity for English language learners. *Voices in Urban Education, 37*, 47–54.

Jean-Marie, G., Normore, A. H., & Brooks, J. S. (2009). Leadership for social justice: Preparing 21st century school leaders for a new social order. *Journal of Research on Leadership Education, 4*(1), 1–31.

Jensen, B., & Sawyer, A. (2013). *Regarding educación: Mexican-American schooling, immigration, and bi-national improvement*. New York, NY: Teachers College Press.

Larson, C. L., & Murtadha, K. (2002). Leadership for social justice. In J. Murphy (Ed.), *The educational leadership challenge: Redefining leadership for the 21st century.* (pp. 134–161). Chicago, IL: University of Chicago Press.

Lyman, L. L., & Villani, C. J. (2004). *Best leadership practices for high-poverty schools*. Lanham, MD: Scarecrow Education.

McKenzie, K. B., Christman, D. E., Hernandez, F., Fierro, E., Capper, C. A., Dantley, M., & Scheurich, J. J. (2008). From the field: A proposal for educating leaders for social justice. *Educational Administration Quarterly, 44*(1), 111–138.

Menken, K. (2008). *English learners left behind: Standardized testing as language policy*. Buffalo, NY: Multilingual Matters.

Menken, K., & García, O. (Eds.). (2010). *Negotiating language policies in schools: Educators as policymakers*. New York, NY: Routledge.

Menken, K., Kleyn, T., & Chae, N. (2012). Spotlight on "long-term English language learners": Characteristics and prior schooling experiences of an invisible population. *International Multilingual Research Journal, 6*(2), 121–142.

Menken, K., & Solorza, C. (in press). Principals as linchpins in bilingual education: The need for prepared school leaders. *International Journal of Bilingual Education and Bilingualism*. doi:10.1080/13670050.2014.937390

Moore, S. C. K. (Ed.). (2014). *Language policy processes and consequences: Arizona case studies*. Tonawanda, NY: Multilingual Matters.

National Center for Education Statistics. (2014). *English language learners*. Washington, DC: U.S. Department of Education. Retrieved from https://nces.ed.gov/programs/coe/indicator_cgf.asp

Orelus, P. W. (Ed.). (2014). *Affirming language diversity in schools and society: Beyond linguistic apartheid*. New York, NY: Routledge.

Reyes, A. (2006). Reculturing principals as leaders for cultural and linguistic diversity. In K. Téllez & H. C. Waxman (Eds.), *Preparing quality educators for English language learners: Research, policy, and practice* (pp. 145–165). Mahwah, NJ: Erlbaum.

Reyes, P., Scribner, J. D., & Scribner, A. P. (Eds.). (1999). *Lessons from high-performing Hispanic schools: Creating learning communities*. New York, NY: Teachers College Press.

Riehl, C. J. (2000). The principal's role in creating inclusive schools for diverse students: A review of normative, empirical, and critical literature on the practice of educational administration. *Review of Educational Research, 70*(1), 55–81.

Rios-Aguilar, C., González Canché, M. S., & Sabetghadam, S. (2012). Evaluating the impact of restrictive language policies: The Arizona 4-hour English language development block. *Language Policy, 11*(1), 47–80.

Rivera, M. O., Francis, D. J., Fernandez, M., Moughamian, A. C., Lesaux, N. K., & Jergensen, J. (2010). *Effective practices for English language learners: Principals from five states speak.* Portsmouth, NH: Center on Instruction, RMC Research Corporation.

Rodríguez, M. A., & Alanís, I. (2011). Negotiating linguistic and cultural identity: One borderlander's leadership initiative. *International Journal of Leadership in Education: Theory and Practice, 14*(1), 103–117.

Rodríguez, M. A., Chambers, T. V., González, M. L., & Scheurich, J. J. (2010). A cross-case analysis of three social justice-oriented education programs. *Journal of Research on Leadership Education, 5*(3.5), 138–153.

Rodríguez, M. A., González, M. L., & Garza, E., Jr. (2013). Meeting the needs of Hispanic students in public schools: Implications for principal preparation. In B. Gastic, & R. R. Verdugo. (Eds.), *The education of the Hispanic population: Selected essays* (pp. 187–200). Charlotte, NC: Information Age Publishing.

Salomone, R. C. (2010). *True American: Language, identity, and the education of immigrant children.* Cambridge, MA: Harvard University Press.

Scanlan, M., & López, F. (2012). ¡Vamos! How school leaders promote equity and excellence for bilingual students. *Educational Administration Quarterly, 48*(4), 583–625.

Scanlan, M., & López, F. A. (2015). *Leadership for culturally and linguistically responsive schools.* New York, NY: Routledge.

Sernak, K. S. (2008). School reform and Freire's methodology of conscientization. In A. H. Normore (Ed.), *Leadership for social justice: Promoting equity and excellence through inquiry and reflective practice* (pp. 115–149). Charlotte, NC: Information Age Publishing.

Suttmiller, E. F., & González, M. L. (2006). Successful school leadership for English language learners. In K. Téllez & H. C. Waxman (Eds.), *Preparing quality educators for English language learners: Research, policy, and practice* (pp. 167–188). Mahwah, NJ: Erlbaum.

Texas Administrative Code. (2012). Chapter 89. Adaptations for special populations: Subchapter BB. Commissioner's rules concerning state plan for educating English language learners. Retrieved from http://ritter.tea.state.tx.us/rules/tac/chapter089/ch089bb.html

Theoharis, G. (2007). Social justice educational leaders and resistance: Toward a theory of social justice leadership. *Educational Administration Quarterly, 43*(2), 221–258.

Theoharis, G. (2009). *The school leaders our children deserve: Seven keys to equity, social justice, and school reform.* New York, NY: Teachers College Press.

Theoharis, G., & O'Toole, J. (2011). Leading inclusive ELL: Social justice leadership for English language learners. *Educational Administration Quarterly, 47*(4), 646–688.

Tollefson, J. W. (Ed.). (2013). *Language policies in education: Critical issues.* New York, NY: Routledge.

Tucker, P. D., Young, M. D., & Koschoreck, J. W. (2012). Leading research-based change in educational leadership preparation: An introduction. *Journal of Research on Leadership Education, 7*(2), 155–171.

U.S. Census Bureau. (2015). *State and county quick facts.* Washington, DC: U.S. Department of Commerce. Retrieved from http://quickfacts.census.gov/qfd/states/00000.html

Valdés, G. (2001). *Learning and not learning English: Latino students in American schools.* New York, NY: Teachers College Press.

PART II

Curriculum and Assessment Policy Perils

4

CUSTOMIZED CURRICULUM AND HIGH ACHIEVEMENT IN HIGH-POVERTY SCHOOLS

Thomas Tramaglini

KEANSBURG (NJ) SCHOOL DISTRICT & RUTGERS,
THE STATE UNIVERSITY OF NEW JERSEY

Christopher H. Tienken

SETON HALL UNIVERSITY

The Soviet Union's launch of the Sputnik I satellite on October 4, 1957, and the corresponding Soviet and Chinese propaganda campaigns trumpeting the virtues of superior communist education systems, inadvertently triggered one strand of the modern movement to standardize public school curriculum and assessment in the United States (Bracey, 2009; Tienken & Orlich, 2013). The purported failure of American public education to win the race to space was amplified during the ensuing decades by groups of anti-public school policymakers and pundits. They used different means to project a message of school system failure. Nonempirical government reports, legislation, think-tank literature, and lists of unfounded failures of the public school system conveyed the message that standardized curriculum standards and standardized testing programs provide the best means to ensure global economic superiority and national security for the United States.

The large-scale standardization of curriculum and assessment at the national level took a large leap forward with the passage of the No Child Left Behind Act of 2001 (NCLB, 2003). In 2009, the National Governors Association for Best Practices (NGA), in collaboration with the Council of Chief State School Officers (CCSSO), introduced the Common Core State Standards (CCSS) for mathematics and English language arts. The national curriculum standards movement evolved further in 2010 when 45 U.S. states voluntarily adopted this set of common curriculum standards for grades K–12 mathematics and English language arts. One advertised mission of the common core was to:

provide a consistent, clear understanding of what students are expected to learn, so teachers and parents know what they need to do to help them. The standards are designed to be robust and relevant to the real world, reflecting the knowledge and skills that our young people need for success in college and careers. With American students fully prepared for the future, our communities will be best positioned to compete successfully in the global economy.

(NGA & CCSSO, 2010, p. 1)

Nationally standardized curricula standards initiatives are being propagated not only in the United States. Other English-speaking countries that once had decentralized systems of public education—such as Australia, New Zealand, and the United Kingdom—have, or are in the process of imposing, national curriculum standards, standardized testing, and narrow student achievement targets. Standardization and centralization of curriculum standards appears to be an international movement.

Distal and Proximal Curriculum

The widespread adoption of the CCSS by education bureaucrats in the United States signifies an education policy shift toward a national curriculum based on goals developed distally from the student by corporations and for-profit consultants such as Student Achievement Partners and Achieve, Inc. (Porter, McMaken, Hwang, & Yang, 2011). The CCSS represents America's policy shift away from local curriculum development and customization toward centralized curriculum planning. Some scholars have referred to this shift as the Stalinization of education (Baines, 2011).

However, a body of research on the influence of curriculum quality on student achievement suggests that if students are to succeed academically in the 21st century, policymakers and school personnel should pursue the development of a customized set of standards and corresponding curriculum at the local level, in close proximity to the student. Advocates of local curriculum development urge educators and stakeholders at the local level to deliberate, develop, customize, and evaluate the curriculum to better meet the needs of the students who experience it (Zhao, 2012).

Wang, Haertal, and Walberg (1993) investigated various factors that influenced student achievement on traditional standardized assessments. The researchers identified a pattern of influence among the hundreds of empirical articles, book chapters, books, and peer-reviewed reports: The closer or more proximal the independent variables were to the student (e.g., student characteristics, home environment, classroom instruction, curriculum), the stronger the influence was on student achievement compared to variables located distally to the student (e.g., legislation, state/national policies).

Proximal curriculum design and development, customized to meet the needs of the students who must experience it, does not automatically beget better academic achievement. But proximal curriculum development and design, found in the classical curriculum literature, are components of a quality curriculum associated with higher student achievement and better outcomes on socio-civic measures such as indicators of citizenship (e.g., Aikin, 1942; Giles, McCutchen, & Zechiel, 1942; Tyler, 1949; Wrightstone, 1935).

Policy Problem

High school principals in the United States face a legislated mandate to improve student achievement on state-mandated standardized tests such as the Partnership for Assessment of Readiness for College and Careers (PARCC) and the Smarter Balanced Assessment Consortium (SBAC), especially in communities ravaged by poverty where levels of achievement are furthest away from state and federally prescribed proficiency levels. However, since the inception of the George W. Bush administration's NCLB curriculum and assessment standardization law and the Barack Obama administration's Race to the Top (RTTT) and NCLB waiver programs, little empirical research has examined the relationship between state curriculum standards customized at the local level and the achievement on state standardized tests of high school students who attend schools that serve poor communities. Given the accelerating policy trajectory in the United States of developing and mandating the use of distal curriculum standards and one-size-fits-all achievement expectations, studies that explore the relationship between local curriculum development and student achievement have the potential to influence and inform education policymaking, especially in the accountability arena.

The classical empirical literature and more recent studies on curriculum design and development suggest that a locally customized curriculum is associated with higher student academic achievement on multiple measures (e.g., Finkelstein, Hanson, Huang, Hirschman, & Huang, 2010; Hmelo-Silver, 2004; Tyler, 1949). Specifically, curriculum that is developed, deliberated, and customized at the local level to meet the social, emotional, and cognitive needs of the students in a specific school or town appears to provide a link to higher student achievement as measured by standardized tests and alternative forms of assessment (Aikin, 1942; Strobel & van Barneveld, 2009; Wang, Haertel, & Walberg, 1993; Wirkala & Kuhn, 2011).

Our purpose for this nonexperimental, correlational, explanatory study was to determine the strength of relationship between the degree of curriculum customization in high schools serving New Jersey's poorest youth and student achievement on the New Jersey high school exit exam in mathematics and language arts administered in Grade 11. We guided the study with an overarching policy question: What relationships exist between the degree of

(a) customized curriculum design, (b) curriculum development, and (c) forces that influence curriculum at the local level, and student achievement in mathematics and language arts in the state-mandated high school exam?

Theoretical Perspectives and Literature

Results from recent and classic research support a customized curriculum as one factor necessary to improve student achievement, especially when used as a proximal variable. The theoretical framework for curriculum customization rests upon three domains: (a) curriculum design, (b) curriculum development, and (c) forces that influence curriculum (e.g., Aikin, 1942; Giles, McCutchen, & Zechiel, 1942; Hlebowitsh, 1987; Presseisen, 1985; Smith & Tyler, 1942; Tanner & Tanner, 1975, 2007; Tyler, 1949; Wrightstone, 1935). The domains are grounded in previous research on the progressivist curriculum paradigm and have a history of improving student achievement; yet little is known about their influence during the standards-based era since the inception of NCLB and now with the advent of the nationalized common core curriculum.

The Curriculum Paradigm

Tanner and Tanner (1975) synthesized nearly 100 years of empirical research connecting curriculum and various characteristics of schools, including student achievement, and reported that a quality curriculum, deliberated, designed, and customized at the local level is an important variable. Results from empirical research such as the Eight-Year Study and other classic studies support the curriculum paradigm (Aikin, 1942; Dewey, 1899; Giles, McCutchen, & Zechiel, 1942; Smith & Tyler, 1942; Taba, 1962; Wrightstone, 1935; Wrightstone, Rechetnick, McCall, & Loftus, 1939).

The curriculum paradigm synthesized by Tanner and Tanner (1988, 2007) suggested that four principles can guide curriculum design and development: A curriculum should (a) acknowledge the nature of the learner as an active constructor of meaning who brings prior experiences to the learning situation; (b) be organized as a fusion of subject-matter knowledge and personal experience; (c) acknowledge that students develop cognitively and socially in stages, not finite periods of time; and (d) be sensitive to social forces and developed in a democratic manner (Dewey, 1902, 1938; Tanner & Tanner, 2007; Tyler, 1949; Wrightstone et al., 1939).

Although a few researchers have argued against the validity of a curriculum paradigm (Barrow, 1984; Hirsch, 1998; Jickling, 1988), Tanner and Tanner (1975, 2007) urged that the paradigm for how curriculum should be designed and developed should continue to be debated, and serve as a guide in that debate by focusing attention on what is known empirically about curriculum customization. Tanner and Tanner (1975) likened the paradigm to a compass, in that it guides decision-making about curriculum, instruction, and program development.

Curriculum Content and Design

Customized curriculum includes articulated and coordinated content at the local level, aligned to the curriculum paradigm (Tanner & Tanner, 1975, 2007). Curriculum content should be designed using the curriculum paradigm as a guide for attaining local goals while acknowledging that children develop cognitive, socially, and morally at different paces and stages (e.g., Erikson, 1968; Kohlberg, 1970; Piaget, 1950, 1970). Curriculum should be designed so that knowledge is organized and presented as a fusion of the subject-area disciplines and personal experience of the students who must experience the content (Dewey, 1902, 1938; Parkay, 2000). The design of a curriculum can help to connect the content of the curriculum to the students through the use of problems, projects, or activities relevant to students.

Results from several classic experimental and quasi-experimental studies that involved tens of thousands of children in various environmental contexts have demonstrated that when curriculum design and development were customized to balance student needs and experiences, content knowledge, and external priorities in a progressive manner, student success (e.g., student cognitive, social, and emotional growth) was more likely to occur. Results from studies such as the Eight-Year Study, the New York City Experiment, and the Wrightstone Study suggested superior academic and socio-civic results on traditional measures and alternative assessments (e.g., Aikin, 1942; Jersild, Thorndike, Goldman, Wrightstone, & Loftus, 1941; Wrightstone, 1935). Results also indicated that customized curricula focus on a balance between student needs and societal needs (Anderson & Krathwohl, 2001; Bloom, 1956, 1976). Other researchers provided more current examples of practices that embrace aspects of the curriculum customization and the connection to higher student achievement (Marzano, Pickering, & Pollock, 2001; Pease & Kuhn, 2011; Walker & Leary, 2009; Zhao, 2009).

An overarching theme found in the literature is that curricula customized to student needs have goals that balance organizational outcomes, such as increased student achievement and socio-civic development, with students' personal needs and experiences (Dewey, 1899; English & Steffy, 2001; Tyler, 1949). Contrarily, when locally customized curricular goals, objectives, and activities are absent or subjugated to distal bureaucratic mandates, attention can shift from customizing curriculum to meet the needs of local students, to standardizing curriculum, instruction, and assessment to meet the needs of distant and abstract policy proposals and mandates (e.g., Linn, 2003). The conception of the learner as an active constructor of meaning who brings prior experiences to the learning situation can become replaced by a more passive view of the learner as someone who absorbs a set of facts and skills.

The results from Au's (2007) meta-synthesis of 49 qualitative studies suggest that distally developed state and federal curricula initiatives affect teaching and learning negatively. He suggested that high-stakes assessments and standardized curriculum changed the goals of schools and teachers, as well as curricular goals, by narrowing content to the material most likely to be tested by the distally developed assessment. Curriculum became a static object from which teachers transmitted facts and processes found on the mandated statewide assessments.

Other findings suggested that deviating from the guiding design principles of the curriculum paradigm fragmented the curriculum and instruction in schools, and led to gaps in learning from grade to grade (English & Steffy, 2001). The myopic focus on distal goals can limit the degree of customization on the part of school personnel for fear of not attaining state or federally mandated levels of performance.

Curriculum Development

A customized curriculum resembles a dynamic system in which development is an ongoing, democratic process that supports teaching and student learning at the local level because the process of development begins with local needs (Dewey, 1899; English & Steffy, 2001; Tyler, 1949). Tanner and Tanner (2007) posited that high school principals and school district administrators must continuously develop curricula with stakeholders to build on previous curricular work and to meet the demands of children and society. An ongoing system of local curriculum development allows school community members to focus on various organizational needs, including raising student achievement and fostering growth of the affective domain.

The participants in the Eight-Year Study underscored the efficacy of the proximal curriculum development process (Aikin, 1942). In that quasi-experimental study, high school personnel in the 30 participating school districts were given the flexibility to develop their curricula and programs in nonstandardized ways. School administrators, teachers, parents, and other stakeholders worked toward shared goals by developing systems for curriculum development, instruction, and assessment that aligned with the curriculum paradigm.

A locally controlled, democratic process of curriculum development promoted involvement by teachers and other stakeholders in the process of customizing curricula for the students who experienced it. As demonstrated in the Eight-Year Study, customization of curriculum is more likely to occur when curriculum design and development occur in a democratic environment. When they have input, teachers have more opportunities to scaffold and extend topics as well as connect topics to authentic and interesting scenarios and socially conscious problems (Aiken, 1942; Kliebard, 2004; Tyler, 1949).

The Argument for Keeping It Local

The process of customized curriculum development can promote changes in culture and belief systems in schools. In a meta-analysis of 69 schools, Marzano, Waters, and McNulty (2005) expanded on teacher collective efficacy research conducted by Goddard, Hoy, and Woolfolk Hoy (2000) and found that effective education personnel collaborate to build communities that have purpose. The process of customizing curricula to meet the needs of students in a specific school provides opportunities for collegial discussion and the reimagining of the school vision. Utilizing "envisionment" building strategies (Applebee, Langer, Nystrand, & Gamoran, 2003, p. 685) allows school leaders and teachers to work together in common activities to achieve a common goal in the name of students.

Empirical evidence also suggests that when school personnel use a distally developed or prepackaged curriculum without customizing, or use only the distally developed state standards as a substitute for customized curricula, student achievement can increase at slower than expected rates, or even decrease. For example, Langer (2001) found that high school personnel that resisted democratic curricular customization to meet the needs of their students in a standards-based environment had lower student proficiency on standardized tests than school personnel that embraced local curricular customization. In the study, schools were unable to meet the needs of state and federal mandates and reforms with a stagnant curriculum that was not customized by the teacher. Scores from the National Assessment of Education Progress (NAEP) have suggested slower growth during the NCLB era than in the years prior (Tienken & Orlich, 2013). Furthermore, the achievement gap between Blacks and Whites, and Hispanics and Whites, narrowed at a slower pace during NCLB than in the years prior.

Similarly, some researchers described the misuse of textbooks as having a standardizing effect on curriculum and instruction (Tanner, 1999). In cases in which textbooks took the place of locally customized curriculum standards, objectives, and activities, there were negative influences on student achievement (Wilson, Peterson, Ball, & Cohen, 1996). It seems as if standardization of curriculum standards and objectives leads to lower achievement unless educators customize them for their students.

Methodology

We used a correlational, cross-sectional, explanatory design (Johnson, 2001). Correlational research explores the relationships among two or more variables.

The quality of a correlational design depends on the depth and rationale of the constructs that guide the research design. We sought to identify statistically significant ($p \leq .05$) relationships between three independent variables of curriculum quality grounded in previous research and high school student achievement on the New Jersey high school exit exam in high schools that serve the poorest communities in New Jersey. The three characteristics of a customized curriculum identified in the literature related to curriculum design, curriculum development, and forces that influence curriculum.

We used simultaneous multiple regression (SMR) analysis to identify relationships among characteristics of curriculum quality represented from survey responses of curriculum practices and student achievement as measured by results from statewide annual tests of mathematics and language arts. We chose SMR over other forms of regression, such as logistic regression or discriminant analysis, because (a) we sought to explain the influence of customized curriculum, not compare groups against one another; (b) the data were continuous, not dichotomous; and (c) our research questions were associative in nature (Cohen, Cohen, West, and Aiken, 2003; Green, Camilli, & Elmore, 2006). Correlational designs seek to identify associations and influence among variables. However, one important advantage of using a correlational design for this study was that it allowed us to study existing conditions with intact groups.

Data Collection: Census

To secure as large a data set as possible, we collected data by census. Census data collection occurs when researchers attempt to collect data from the entire population. We targeted all New Jersey high school principals who worked in schools located in A, B, and CD District Factor Groups (DFGs). School districts in New Jersey are categorized in alphabetical groups A–J, with A districts located in the state's poorest communities and J districts located in the wealthiest communities. Categories A, B, and CD represent school districts located in the poorest communities in the state, many of them in urban centers.

New Jersey Department of Education (NJDOE, n.d.) personnel developed DFGs in the mid-1970s, in part to make school funding decisions and to compare student performance on statewide assessments across school districts with similar demographics and socio-economic characteristics. The method used to determine which DFG a school district is classified into derives from six variables related to socio-economic status (NJDOE, n.d.): (a) percent of adults with no high school diploma, (b) percent of adults with some college education, (c) occupational status, (d) unemployment rate, (e) percent of individuals in poverty, and (f) median family income.

To determine the public high schools available for data collection in our target sample of DFG categories A, B, and CD, we first downloaded all high school-level assessment data from the NJDOE (2009) assessment database into a data set. We sorted the data by DFG and identified 324 high schools in New Jersey across all DFG categories (Grades 9–12, nonvocational, noncharter). Then we disaggregated the number of high schools and students in each district factor group. There were 49 high schools in the A District Factor Group, 39 in the B District Factor Group, and 29 high schools in the CD District Factor Group, for a total of 117. In 2009, the number of students in each of the lowest socio-economic groupings ranged from 8,292 to 12,175 (n = 29,393). The sample represents 31.3% of all students in the state who took the 2009 New Jersey High School Proficiency Assessment (HSPA).

We chose to survey principals instead of central office administrators, teachers, or curriculum supervisors, because in New Jersey the principal is the person ultimately held responsible for student achievement and teaching in the school building by state-mandated accountability policies. The principal is responsible for the curriculum delivery and monitors the curriculum that is delivered. The principal approves professional development activities, including curriculum-writing activities. Thus, the principal is statutorily mandated to know the current status of curriculum and instruction operations.

Some might posit that teachers would have been a better target population for our survey. We argue that teachers would not have had the big picture understanding of the underlying process of curriculum design, curriculum development, and forces that influence curriculum because they are not statutorily responsible for the operation of the school. In New Jersey, it is the principal who is held accountable for all the education processes that take place within his or her building.

Instrumentation

We used data from two sources: (a) student achievement data for language arts and mathematics from the HSPA, and (b) a curriculum customization survey. We received permission to use and adapt a curriculum development and design survey instrument constructed by Tanner and Tanner (2007) from the authors and from Pearson, their publisher. Survey research allows researchers to describe the perceptions of various stakeholders associated with the study (Berends, 2006).

Survey Design

The curriculum survey was adapted from Tanner and Tanner's (2007) Best Practice Checklist for Curriculum Improvement and School Renewal. Twenty-six of the 119 questions in the checklist were selected initially because they related to the research from the review of the literature describing curriculum customization. The other 93 questions did not relate specifically. Next, we filtered questions to meet two other criteria: the questions needed to reflect administratively mutable factors of curriculum customization, and the questions needed to reflect factors of curriculum quality that were related to high schools.

Pilot Study

We completed a pilot study to validate the survey instrument and to determine the reliability of the question subsets. During the winter of 2008, a survey consisting of 50 questions (24 on curriculum quality and 26 on external forces that affect curriculum design) was administered to 15 participants, who were principals with advanced degrees in the education sector. We administered the surveys with an online survey tool. Each participant in the pilot study also completed a feedback form with various questions on matters such as the amount of time it took to complete the survey, wording of the questions, quality of questions and responses, depth of questions and responses, and readability.

We eliminated and revised questions to be more concise, as suggested. The final survey contained 21 questions within three subscales related to curriculum quality: (a) curriculum design, (b) curriculum development, and (c) forces that influence curriculum.

Reliability

Reliability is a measure to determine the reproducibility of the survey data (Litwin, 1995). We used Cronbach's (1951) alpha test of internal consistency to check the reliability of the revised survey. Minimum alphas of at least 0.70 or higher are considered reliable measurements (Nunnally & Bernstein, 1994). The alpha coefficient for curriculum design was 0.835; curriculum development, 0.859; and forces that influence curriculum, 0.804.

Variables

Curriculum customization was measured via responses from the curriculum customization survey. The survey included 21 questions within three subsets of questions. Curriculum quality was measured with eight questions, followed by six questions focused on curriculum development. The last subset included seven questions focused on external forces on curriculum that can influence achievement. All of the questions in each of the three subsets were placed on a 4-point interval agreement scale (strong evidence, some evidence, little or no evidence, evidence to the contrary). Each question was scored from 1 to 4, where 1 represented a low or poor score and 4 an excellent or high score. We chose to keep an even number of indicators to decrease response bias, ease fatigue, and force respondents to make a judgment.

Independent Variables

We used the percentage of free lunch and reduced lunch eligibility at the school level as an independent variable indicator of student socio-economic status because of the empirical evidence that ties eligibility to ultimate student achievement when measured by standardized tests. Eligibility for free/reduced lunch relates to U.S. poverty guidelines. The percentages for free/reduced lunch eligibility in each school appear on the NJDOE website.

We are aware of the potential weaknesses of relying solely on combined free/reduced lunch status as the primary indicator of a student's complete economic status (Harwell & LeBeau, 2010). Free/reduced lunch status is a blunt indicator of socio-economic status, and we know that there exist meaningful differences between being eligible for free lunch and being eligible for reduced lunch. The differences influence student achievement. For example, data from the National Assessment of Education Progress (NAEP) for math and language arts results for Grades 4 and 8 showed that students eligible for free/reduced lunch scored significantly ($p < .05$) lower statistically than students not eligible for free/reduced lunch (Tienken & Orlich, 2013).

The free lunch category captures more of the deleterious effects that poverty has on standardized test achievement than the reduced lunch category. However, states do not often separate lunch eligibility into the two distinct reporting categories on their state report cards and instead report achievement as one category: free/reduced lunch. This masks some of the negative influences of poverty, because the scores for students eligible for free lunch would be even lower than those in the category known as free/reduced lunch. The combined free/reduced lunch category does not allow for deep exploration of the effects of poverty because reduced lunch classification includes students whose family income is up to $39,220, nearly twice the poverty level.

We believe that the influence of socio-economic status on student achievement when measured as a combination of free/reduced lunch eligibility is more conservative than if we were able to break out the percentage of students eligible for free lunch and the separate percentage of students eligible for reduced lunch in each school. Therefore we believe our final analysis underreports the actual influence of poverty on the test results. This is a limitation of the study and a limitation of the way that state education personnel report their data.

We also included the percentage of students with disabilities as an independent variable, because historically students with disabilities score lower on standardized tests than their nondisabled peers. Thus, we wanted to control for a factor that can influence achievement within our models.

Dependent Variables

The High School Proficiency Assessment (HSPA) is the statewide high school exit assessment that measures student achievement at the high school level in

New Jersey. All first-time Grade 11 students take the HSPA, and all students in New Jersey must pass the HSPA to graduate from high school and receive a standard high school diploma.

The 2009 HSPA contained three sections, of which two (language arts literacy and mathematics) were used to construct the dependent variables. The language arts literacy assessment of the HSPA contained assessment items to gauge content mastery in reading and writing. The reading section consisted of two passages (narrative and persuasive). The passages varied in length from 2,100 words in the narrative text to 3,300 words in the persuasive text (NJDOE, 2009). Both passages contained 10 multiple-choice questions and two open-ended questions. In addition to the reading questions, there were two writing prompts: one picture prompt and one speculative prompt. Both writing responses were scored on the 6-point New Jersey Holistic Scoring Rubric (NJDOE, 2009). Overall, the language arts literacy assessment was worth 54 raw score points (NJDOE, 2009).

The mathematics assessment of the HSPA measured student achievement on four mathematics content standards. A total of 30 multiple-choice and six open-ended questions (48 total points) assessed students' knowledge of mathematics in number and numerical operations, geometry and measurement, patterns and algebra, and data analysis, probability, and discrete mathematics (NJDOE, 2009). Within each of these content areas there were strands focusing on specific subsets of mathematics, such as geometric properties and coordinate geometry.

The statisticians contracted by NJDOE personnel converted raw, scale scores that ranged from 100 to a possible total score of 300. The state personnel classified students who scored below 200 (100–199) as partially proficient. Students who achieved a scale score of 200–249 were considered proficient, and any scale score of 250–300 was advanced proficient.

Data Collection

To collect the survey data on curriculum quality, we conducted a census of the school principals from the high schools in the DFG categories A, B, and CD in New Jersey ($n = 117$). The first survey attempt yielded 24 participants. After two weeks, we sent a follow-up email to those who did not respond initially. We also called school administrators directly to solicit participation. The follow-up attempt yielded 30 additional participants. We sent another round of email and made more phone calls as part of our third follow-up round and yielded 18 more surveys for a total of 72. We accepted only complete surveys and thus had to drop one that provided only partial responses.

We ended the data collection process with a total of 71 complete data sets and a 61% response rate. To achieve generalizability to the population of 117 high schools at the 95% confidence interval with a margin of error of 5%, we needed a final sample size of 87. Although our sample size is not large enough to generalize to all high schools located in poorer communities, it satisfies the 95% confidence interval with a margin of error of approximately 7% (Krejcie & Morgan, 1970).

Missing Data

We used maximum likelihood estimation to obtain estimates of model parameters (Allison, 2002). The goal of maximum likelihood estimation (MLE) is to identify the population parameter values most likely to have produced a particular sample of data (Peugh & Enders, 2004). The MLE method can be used in conjunction with other statistical analysis such as regression analysis, and it yields estimates based on the model of fit that most likely represents the data presented in the data set.

Also, because we used only complete survey responses and the NJDOE had complete achievement data for the 71 high schools whose principals answered the survey, the concern about missing data was minimized. As mentioned earlier, before we conducted our analysis, we eliminated one high school from the analysis because of incomplete responses on the survey. That respondent answered fewer than half the survey questions. The final sample contained 98.6% of the responding high school leaders, and each response was complete with no missing data.

Data Analysis

The initial step in the data analysis was to extract descriptive statistics, and organize and summarize the characteristics of the sample and variables involved in the study (Slavin, 2007). The descriptive analysis investigated the frequencies (sample, independent, and dependent variables), the measures of central tendency (mean, median, mode), measures of variability (variance and standard deviation), and measures of normality (skewness). Following the descriptive analysis, we used multiple regression analysis to test the hypothesis identified in this study (curriculum quality). The overarching hypothesis was that curriculum quality would not have a statistically significant influence on achievement.

SMR typically has several assumptions that had to be met to allow us to reasonably interpret the regression results (Keith, 2006, p. 186). In both of our regression models of best fit, the dependent continuous variables were linear functions of the independent variables for language arts literacy and mathematics, and the data were normally distributed. Each variable of curriculum associated with curriculum customization was drawn independently from the assessment coefficients. Subsequently, the variance of the error (homoscedasticity) in each SMR model was not a function of any of the results from the New Jersey

HSPA for language arts literacy or mathematics. We then checked the data to ensure they met other assumptions for conducting simultaneous multiple regression. The relationships between predictor and dependent variables were linear, as demonstrated by scatterplots; the residuals were distributed normally and not related to the predictor variables; and the final data sets were not abnormally skewed beyond reasonable limits of +/− 1.000. The initial language arts data set had a slight negative skew that we accounted for through a statistical procedure described in a later section.

Statistical Power Analysis

Statistical power analyses can be done before or after data collection. Prior to data collection, a priori, the main purpose of conducting a power analysis is to determine the appropriate sample size for rejecting a null hypothesis if the null hypothesis is false. After data collection, post hoc, the main purpose of conducting a power analysis is to determine the chances of having correctly rejected a false null hypothesis, provided a sample of a certain size, a certain coefficient of determination or R^2, and a certain p value such as .01 or .05 for rejecting the null hypothesis. Cohen (1988) suggested the adequate statistical power coefficient should be .80 or above. A series of power analyses conducted after the data collection (post hoc) with the formula $P = 2 \times (1 - \Phi(z))$, using an online power calculator G-Power, indicated power levels of .80 and higher for all multiple regression models.

Using the work of Field (2013), we conducted a secondary analysis of sample size power for verifying a minimum acceptable sample size for simultaneous multiple regression. Field stated,

> If your aim is to test the overall fit of the model: (1) if you expect to find a large effect [R^2 > .26] then a sample of 77 will always suffice (with up to 20 predictors) and if there are fewer predictors then you can afford to have a smaller sample; (2) if you're expecting a medium effect, . . . you should always have a sample size above 55, and with six or fewer predictors you'll be fine with a sample of 100; . . . but the take-home message is that if you're looking for medium to large effects, sample sizes don't need to be massive, regardless of how many predictors you have.
>
> (p. 313)

We included three to five predictors in a model and were seeking to find large effects. Hence, the sample size we used (n = 71) provided enough power to identify an effect size of at least .80 at the 95% confidence interval when our models included three variables. The power was somewhat decreased in our larger models, which simply means it was more difficult for the smaller effect sizes to be identified. In our case, this could mean that some of our effects are underreported due to small samples.

Limitations

One limitation of this study was the use of correlation research, which describes relationships, not cause. Correlation between two variables does not necessarily imply that one causes the other (Slavin, 2007). Another limitation was that although the active variables included in this study are important parts of high schools in New Jersey, other variables might also influence student achievement. The design does not account for all factors that could influence achievement but does include important factors such as socio-economic status and percentage of students with disabilities.

The sample size in some of our larger models is also a potential limitation because the sample sizes might not permit us to identify effect sizes less than 0.50. Thus, our models might have underreported some of the positive effects of curriculum customization.

The reliability of New Jersey statewide assessment results in mathematics and language arts literacy has been rarely documented. Nonetheless, researchers have suggested that reliability coefficients remain higher than 0.70 for the full test (Nunnally & Bernstein, 1994; Streiner, 2003). The technical manuals for the HSPA indicate that some individual domain clusters do not have high reliability coefficients (NJDOE, 2006), but the full tests in language arts and mathematics have coefficients that exceed 0.80.

Results

The mean enrollment for the sample was 1,200 students, with a standard deviation of 686.5. The large standard deviation indicates variation in the student populations in the high schools in the sample. Enrollment sizes varied widely within each DFG with standard deviations between 528.6 and 724.4. Schools in DFG B were somewhat smaller on average than schools in the other DFGs, with somewhat less variability in size. Approximately half of the students (50.3%) in the sample were eligible for free/reduced-price lunch. Nearly 16.5% of the students in the sample were eligible for special education services.

Considering the first group, 32 high schools were located in the lowest socio-economic category, DFG A. Their mean student enrollment was 1,213 students, with a standard deviation of 724.4. Among schools in DFG A, the mean percent of students eligible for free/reduced lunch was 69.3. In the next group, 16 high school principals responded to the survey from the B district factor grouping. The mean enrollment size in the sample of high schools was nearly the same at 1,104 students, with a standard deviation of 528.6. Forty-one percent of the students in DFG B were eligible for free/reduced lunch. In the

TABLE 4.1 Variable List

Variable name	Variable description	Range
Achievement assessment		
HSPALAL	Language arts literacy	158.40–242.10
HSPAMAT	Mathematics	161.50–242.50
Curriculum customization		
CURRDES	Curriculum design	13.00–32.00
CURRDEV	Curriculum development	10.00–26.00
CURRFOR	Curriculum forces	12.00–33.00
Other variables		
PCTFARL	Percentage free/reduced lunch	18.60–92.70
SPECED	Percentage special education	2.00–29.00

last group, 23 high school principals responded from the CD district factor grouping. Among the 23 high schools in the CD group, the mean student enrollment was 1,248, with a standard deviation of 748.6, and 30.2% of the students were eligible for free/reduced-price lunch.

Variables

The variable list in Table 4.1 includes names, descriptions, and ranges for the dependent variables (a) HSPA language arts and (b) HSPA math, and independent variables. The three independent variables listed under curriculum customization are (a) curriculum design, (b) curriculum development, and (c) curriculum forces. Two additional variables, (a) special education and (b) free/reduced lunch are listed under other variables.

The mean student enrollment in the sample of 71 lower socio-economic high schools was 1,199.85 students, and the standard deviation was 686.53 students. The mean scale scores for HSPA achievement in language arts literacy (HSPALAL) and mathematics (HSPAMAT) differed, at 212.53 to 204.77 respectively. The variances of the data were similar, with language arts literacy having a standard deviation of 14.67 and mathematics 15.41.

Curriculum customization had three subcategories, for which the data collected through the survey instrument yielded a complete set of data for the 71 high schools. For the first subcategory, there were 32.00 possible points associated with curriculum design. The mean of the responses was 24.66, and the variance was 4.99. Curriculum development had a total of 26.00 possible points associated with the subcategory. The mean response was 19.00 and the variance was 3.64. The mean for the curriculum forces variable was 22.82 out of a total of 33.00 points possible, with a standard deviation of 5.82

TABLE 4.2 Description of Variables

Variable name	n	Mean	SD
Achievement assessment			
HSPALAL	71	212.53	14.67
HSPAMAT	71	204.77	15.41
Curriculum customization			
CURRDES	71	24.66	4.99
CURRDEV	71	19.00	3.64
CURRFOR	71	22.82	5.82
Other variables			
PCTFARL	71	50.35	21.26
SPECED	71	16.50	5.06

(see Table 4.2). The mean percentage of students with special needs for the sample was 16.50, and the mean percentage of students eligible for free/reduced lunch in the high school sample was 50.35, with a standard deviation of 21.26.

Survey Reliability

We conducted another reliability analysis, post hoc, to check score reliability. Internal consistency for each of the subscales for curriculum quality remained high. The Cronbach's alpha coefficient for curriculum design was 0.890; curriculum development, 0.829; and forces that influence curriculum, 0.873. The internal consistency exceeded the minimum Cronbach's alpha of at least 0.70 or higher in all areas, and thus the survey can be said to have produced reliable measurements (Nunnally & Bernstein, 1994).

Correlations and Regressions

To explain the relationships between high school student achievement (New Jersey HSPA) and the three curriculum variables, we utilized SMR in two separate models—one for language arts literacy and one for mathematics. After our data set was prepared for analysis, we independently regressed (SMR) New Jersey HSPA scores for language arts literacy and mathematics with index variables for curriculum design (CURRDES), curriculum development (CURRDEV), and forces that influence curriculum (CURRFOR). We also included the percentage of students eligible for free/reduced lunch (PCTFARL) and the percentage of students eligible for special education services (SPECED) as control variables. Therefore, the dependent variable—the average school-level scale score on the NJHSPA in language arts literacy/math—is a combination of the constant

$$(b_0) + b_1\text{CURRDES} + b_2\text{CURRDEV} + b_3\text{CURRFOR} + b_4\text{PCTFARL} + b_5\text{SPECED}$$

Findings

The correlation coefficients for curriculum design ($r = .41$, $p < .01$) and curriculum development ($r = .35$, $p < .01$) were statistically significantly and moderately correlated to language arts achievement, and curriculum forces was statistically significantly negative ($r = -.15$, $p < .05$). The results for the curriculum variables were not unexpected. As suggested in the extant literature, curriculum design and development are a proxy for customization and have a history of having a positive influence on student achievement. Curriculum forces are external pressures with a history of lowering achievement. Things such as a heavy focus on standardized testing and using the textbook as a proxy for the curriculum create negative forces on achievement.

As anticipated, based on a review of the literature, the Pearson correlation coefficient for free/reduced lunch was statistically significant ($p < .01$), negative, and strong ($r = .61$), whereas the percentage of students receiving special education services was not (see Table 4.3). Our findings fit within the existing literature on influence of poverty status on student achievement (e.g., Sirin, 2005).

HSPA Language Arts Literacy Regression Analyses

First we tested data assumptions for regression by examining the normal probability plots or the residuals and scatter diagrams of residuals versus the

TABLE 4.3 Correlations for HSPA Language Arts Literacy and Curriculum Customization ($n = 71$)

Variable	1	2	3	4	5
HSPALAL	.41**	.35**	−.15*	−.61**	−.10
1. CURRDES					
2. CURRDEV					
3. CURRFOR					
4. PCTFARL					
5. SPECED					

Note: Sig. *$p < .05$; **$p < .01$

TABLE 4.4 Multiple Regression Analysis Summary for Curriculum Customization and HSPALAL (n = 71)

Predictors	B	SE B	β	t	Sig.
CURRDES	.817	.285	.331	−4.363	.005
CURRFOR	−.588	.221	−.277	2.871	.010
PCTFARL	−.263	.060	−.454	−4.363	.000
SPECED	−.071	.088	−.074	−.813	.419
Constant	221.570	8.172	27.110		

predicted residuals. Our initial tests indicated that the HSPALAL dependent variable had a negative skew of −1.177, just above the acceptable limits of + or − 1.000.

Upon closer inspection of the data, we observed an outlier score of 158.40, which was three standard deviations below the mean language arts scale score in the sample. In this case we used the Winsorizing procedure to substitute the outlier score with a score of 173, which was one standard deviation higher (Field, 2013). A score of 173 was just 2 points away from the next highest value, 175, which was not an outlier in our data set. After Winsorizing the HSPALAL data, we inspected for skewness again, and the amount of skewness was reduced to −0.786, within acceptable limits less than + or − 1.000.

Next, we ran our first simultaneous regression model. The predictors accounted for 48% (R^2 = .477, Adjusted R^2 = .437, p < .01) of the variance on language arts literacy scores. This is considered a large effect size (Cohen, 1988). However, the variables curriculum design and curriculum development exhibited multicolinearity above 2.000. Therefore, we chose to run additional models in which we removed either design or development. Our model of best fit included four variables, one of which was curriculum design.

Our model statistically and significantly predicted HSPALAL scale scores F (4, 66) = 14.09 p < .001. R^2 for our model was .46, suggesting that the model accounted for 46% of the variance. The adjusted R^2 was .43. Table 4.4 displays the unstandardized regression coefficients (B), intercept (constant), and the standardized regression coefficients (β).

HSPA Mathematics Regression Analyses

We tested assumptions of the HSPAMAT data by examining the normal probability plots and scatter diagrams of residuals versus the predicted residuals. Our initial tests indicated the HSPAMAT math dependent variable had a slight negative skew of −0.402, within acceptable limits of + or − 1.000.

TABLE 4.5 Correlations for HSPA Mathematics and Curriculum Customization ($n = 71$)

Variable	1	2	3	4	5
HSPAMAT	.43★★	.36★★	−.10	−.61★★	−.11
1. CURRDES					
2. CURRDEV					
3. CURRFOR					
4. PCTFARL					
5. SPECED					

Note: Sig. ★p < .05; ★★p < .01

The Pearson correlation for curriculum design and mathematics achievement on the HSPA was statistically significant at .43 ($p < .05$). Curriculum development demonstrated a statistically significant positive relationship to HSPAMAT at .36 ($p < .05$). Free/reduced lunch was statistically significantly correlated at .61 ($p < .01$). No statistically significant relationship was found, however, between the forces that influence curriculum or percentage of students eligible for special education services and HSPA mathematics achievement (see Table 4.5).

As with the HSPALAL regression model, curriculum design and curriculum development exhibited a high degree of multicolinearity within the initial HSPAMAT model. Therefore, we ran a second model with only curriculum design to eliminate the multicolinearity. Table 4.6 describes the multiple regression model of best fit with four variables, excluding curriculum development. Our model statistically significantly predicted HSPAMAT scale scores $F (4, 66) = 21.77$ $p < .001$. R^2 for our model was .569, suggesting that the model accounted for 57% of the variance. The adjusted R^2 was .543.

TABLE 4.6 Multiple Regression Analysis Summary: Curriculum Customization and HSPA Mathematics ($n = 71$)

Predictors	B	SE B	β	t	Sig.
CURRDES	.899	.320	−.291	2.826	.006
CURRFOR	−.805	.250	−.304	−3.266	.002
PCTFARL	−.346	.070	−.477	−5.131	.000
SPECED	−.925	.250	−.304	−3.742	.000
Constant	233.590	10.007			

Implications

The results suggest that high school students performed better when school personnel designed and used a curriculum customized at the local level, when controlling for student socio-economic status as measured by free/reduced lunch eligibility. This finding, along with the extant literature, suggests that one-size-fits-all curriculum standards might not work for every student. In other words, the exclusive use of distally developed curriculum standards without customization at the local level might influence lower student achievement on state standardized tests.

The findings suggest that school personnel from higher-performing, high-poverty high schools customized their state-mandated content standards to better meet the needs of their learners more than school personnel from lower-performing, high-poverty high schools. The findings from this and other studies suggest that high school administrators should consider curriculum customization as a viable method for improving student achievement and meeting the academic needs of more students.

The more school personnel redesign state-mandated curriculum to meet the needs of their students through the use of activity-based problems and projects, the better their students performed on state tests. Of course, the redesign can go only so far when there are high-stakes tests involved. Some things from the mandated curriculum must always remain.

The forces of curriculum were negatively correlated with student achievement. This indicates that personnel in lower socio-economic high schools who taught to the state test and did not customize the state-mandated curriculum standards from their state education agency had lower student achievement.

These two findings also call into question the practice of state education bureaucrats mandating the use of model state curricula for low-performing schools serving children from poverty (NJDOE, 2014). The results reported in the existing literature and findings from this study suggest that student achievement of students from poverty is higher in the New Jersey high school exit exam in mathematics and language arts in schools where personnel customized the curriculum more, whereas achievement was lower in schools that did not customize. The New Jersey model curriculum is an amateurish, noncustomized simple list of objectives and superficial recommendations of how to make low-level mathematics and language arts connections. The model is in direct opposition to the research on curriculum customization and is an example of standardization, not customization.

Implications for Educators

Recent standardization reform movements, specifically the adoption of CCSS and high-stakes standardized testing programs by a majority of the states, suggest that the arrows in the reform quiver used to influence student achievement and educators' teaching and leadership behaviors are distal in nature, developed far from the student. The findings from our study associated with the clusters of curriculum customization and student achievement were practically significant, suggesting that high school educators in New Jersey, and perhaps in other states, might want to reflect upon their approaches to distal curriculum-making and testing. At a minimum, high school leaders should consult the existing literature, theories, and results from this study to consider customizing the curriculum at the local level for the students who are mandated to accept it.

High school leaders in schools serving lower socio-economic areas might consider the importance of both curriculum design and curriculum development with regard to achievement. We recommend three introductory practices, each predicated on the curriculum paradigm and the idea that teachers should be actively involved in the design and development of curricula, for school administrators to consider implementing with their teachers: (a) vertical articulation and horizontal coordination of curriculum, (b) scaffolded learning activities to meet the various developmental needs of students, and (c) problem-based and project-based activity invention conventions with teachers to help design customized local activities that address the cognitive, social, and emotional needs of students (Bullough & Kridel, 2003; Department of the Interior, 1918; Tanner & Tanner, 2007; Wrightstone et al., 1939).

Vertical articulation is a practice in which teachers from various grade levels, for example Grades 9–12, meet to examine and discuss the vertical curriculum alignment for their subject areas. The articulation meetings should be facilitated to provide a professional structure and focus. Some purposes of vertical articulation are to (a) review curricula for consistent progressions of skills and knowledge; (b) determine skills and knowledge that need to be scaffolded so that students can learn within their zone of proximal development (Vygotsky, 1978); (c) review evidence and information about techniques that aid student connection to content and areas in which students struggle to make meaningful connections; and (d) create and revise problem-based, project-based, and scenario-based activities.

Activities and objectives should be scaffolded to meet the various cognitive and social readiness levels of the students mandated to complete them. Therefore, local curriculum should include objectives that are pliable enough to represent various levels of complexity or that allow for activities to be differentiated by readiness complexity. Educators at the local level could design open-ended activities and student outcome products that are naturally differentiated by readiness and create tiered learning objectives, and include both in the written, customized district curriculum documents. In this way teachers need only refer to the local curriculum document for ideas on how to teach within their students' zone of proximal development (Vygotsky, 1978).

The development of problem-, project-, and scenario-based activities should focus on creating teaching and learning situations in which the students are active constructors of meaning and have the opportunity to use their content knowledge and skills in authentic situations (Tanner and Tanner, 2007; Zhao, 2012). Current events and issues that pique the interest and passion of students should be used as the context for these types of activities (Dewey, 1938; Tienken & Orlich, 2013). Professional development sessions, faculty meetings, department meetings, and other appropriate times can be used for activity invention conventions. All activities should become part of the school district's approved curriculum and should be easily accessible to teachers and parents.

Because policymakers and bureaucrats seem unwilling or unable to change course, school administrators must stop waiting for superman to change the policy landscape. They must make changes within the spheres of influence in which they operate. That is, use the basic ideas we provided to institute curriculum development as an ongoing process, where the design and development of the curriculum are the central foci of school operations.

Implications for Policy

Clearly, education reform policy is not moving in the same direction as the extant empirical literature, theories, and our results. The policy trend is for greater centralization and standardization of curriculum standards and development. Some states, such as New Jersey and New York, have issued model curriculum, model activities, and model assessments for districts. We suggest that policymakers switch course and allow for greater customization of curriculum standards at the local level. Clearly state legislatures have the constitutional power to guide education. We are simply recommending that they act to return a balance between local control and state mandates.

We do believe a middle ground can be reached in which state-mandated standards can coexist with locally developed standards, objectives, and activities. We believe, given the extant literature and our results, that state-mandated standards should not be allowed to constitute the majority of the standards in a local district curriculum. School personnel should be allowed to pick and choose standards that they find helpful from the state, but then have the freedom to add their own and customize design and development at the local level.

In the end, proximal curriculum development has a demonstrated, superior track record of raising student achievement on many different measures. It is the local diversity and customization that helps to meet the needs of the unique student populations served at district and school levels. That diversity should be seen as a strength and something to develop and capitalize upon, instead of something to standardize and homogenize.

References

Aikin, W. M. (1942). *The story of the eight-year study with conclusions and recommendations.* New York, NY: Harper & Brothers.

Allison, P. D. (2002). *Missing data.* Thousand Oaks, CA: Sage.

Anderson, L. W., & Krathwohl, D. R. (Eds.). (2001). *A taxonomy for learning, teaching, and assessing: A revision of Bloom's taxonomy of educational objectives.* New York, NY: Longman.

Applebee, A. N., Langer, J. A., Nystrand, M., & Gamoran, A. (2003). Discussion-based approaches to developing understanding: Classroom instruction and student performance in middle and high school English. *American Educational Research Journal, 40*(3), 685–730.

Au, W. (2007). High-stakes testing and curriculum control: A qualitative metasynthesis. *Educational Researcher, 36*(5), 258–267.

Baines, L. (2011). Stalinizing American education. *Teachers College Record.* Retrieved from www.tcrecord.org (ID Number: 16545)

Barrow, R. (1984). *Giving teaching back to teachers. A critical introduction to curriculum theory.* Totowa, NJ: Barnes & Noble.

Berends, M. (2006). Survey methods in educational research. In J. L. Green, G. Camilli, & P. B. Elmore (Eds.), *Handbook of complementary methods in education research* (pp. 623–640). Mahwah, NJ: Erlbaum.

Bloom, B. S. (Ed.). (1956). *Taxonomy of educational objectives: Book 1: Cognitive domain.* White Plains, NY: Longman.

Bloom, B. S. (1976). *Human characteristics and school learning.* New York, NY: McGraw-Hill.

Bracey, G. W. (2009). U.S. school performance, through a glass darkly (again). *Phi Delta Kappan, 90*(5), 386–387.

Bullough, R. V., & Kridel, C. (2003). Adolescent needs, curriculum and the eight-year study. *Journal of Curriculum Studies, 35*(2), 151–169.

Cohen, J. (1988). *Statistical power analysis for the behavioral sciences* (2nd ed.). Mahwah, NJ: Erlbaum.

Cohen, J., Cohen, P., West, S. G., & Aiken, L. S. (2003). *Applied multiple regression/correlation analysis for the behavioral sciences* (3rd ed.). Mahwah, NJ: Erlbaum.

Cronbach, L. J. (1951). Coefficient alpha and the internal structure of tests. *Psychometrika, 16*(3), 297–334.

Department of the Interior. (1918). *Cardinal principles of secondary education: A report of the Commission on the Reorganization of Secondary Education, appointed by the National Education Association.* Washington, DC: Bureau of Education.

Dewey, J. (1899). *The school and society.* Chicago, IL: University of Chicago Press.

Dewey, J. (1902). *The child and the curriculum.* Chicago, IL: University of Chicago Press.

Dewey, J. (1938). *Experience and education.* New York, NY: Macmillan.

English, F., & Steffy, B. (2001). *Deep curriculum alignment: Creating a level playing field for all children on high-stakes tests of educational accountability.* Lanham, MD: Scarecrow Press.

Erikson, E. H. (1968). *Identity: Youth in crisis.* New York, NY: Norton.

Field, A. (2013). *Discovering statistics using IBM SPSS statistics* (4th ed.). Thousand Oaks, CA: Sage.

Finkelstein, N., Hanson, T., Huang, C.-W., Hirschman, B., & Huang, M. (2010). *Effects of problem based economics on high school economics instruction: Final report.* (NCEE 2010-4002). Washington, DC: National Center for Education Evaluation and Regional Assistance, Institute of Education Sciences, U.S. Department of Education.

Giles, H. H., McCutchen, S. P., & Zechiel, A. N. (1942). *Exploring the curriculum: The work of the thirty schools from the viewpoint of curriculum consultants.* New York, NY: Harper & Brothers.

Goddard, R. D., Hoy, W. K., & Woolfolk Hoy, A. (2000). Collective teacher efficacy: Its meaning, measure, and impact on student achievement. *American Educational Research Journal, 37*(2), 479–507.

Green, J. L., Camilli, G., & Elmore, P. B. (Eds.). (2006). *Handbook of complementary methods in education research.* Mahwah, NJ: Erlbaum.

Harwell, M., & LeBeau, B. (2010). Student eligibility for a free lunch as an SES measure in education research. *Educational Researcher, 39*(2), 120–131.

Hirsch, E. D., Jr. (1998). Why general knowledge should be a goal of education in a democracy. *Common Knowledge, 11*(1/2), 1, 14–16.

Hlebowitsh, P. S. (1987). *Purpose and change in American educational policymaking and practice* (Unpublished doctoral dissertation). Rutgers, The State University of New Jersey, New Brunswick, NJ.

Hmelo-Silver, C. E. (2004). Problem-based learning: What and how do students learn? *Educational Psychology Review, 16*(3), 235–266.

Jersild, A. T., Thorndike, R. L., Goldman, B., Wrightstone, J., & Loftus, J. J. (1941). A further comparison of pupils in "activity" and "non-activity" schools. *Journal of Experimental Education, 9*(4), 303–309.

Jickling, B. (1988). Paradigms in curriculum development: Critical comments on the work of Tanner and Tanner. *Interchange, 19*(2), 41–49.

Johnson, B. (2001). Toward a new classification of nonexperimental quantitative research. *Educational Researcher, 30*(2), 3–13.

Keith, T. Z. (2006). *Multiple regression and beyond.* Boston, MA: Pearson.

Kliebard, H. M. (2004). *The struggle for the American curriculum: 1893–1958* (3rd ed.). New York, NY: RoutledgeFalmer.

Kohlberg, L. (1970). Education for justice. In J. M. Gustafson (Ed.), *Moral education* (pp. 57–65). Cambridge, MA: Harvard University Press.

Krejcie, R. V., & Morgan, D. W. (1970). Determining sample size for research activities. *Educational and Psychological Measurement, 30*(3), 607–610.

Langer, J. A. (2001). Beating the odds: Teaching middle and high school students to read and write well. *American Educational Research Journal, 38*(4), 837–880.

Linn, R. L. (2003). Accountability: Responsibility and reasonable expectations. *Educational Researcher, 32*(7), 3–13.

Litwin, M. S. (1995). *How to measure survey reliability and validity.* Thousand Oaks, CA: Sage.

Marzano, R. J., Pickering, D. J., & Pollock, J. E. (2001). *Classroom instruction that works: Research-based strategies for increasing student achievement.* Alexandria, VA: Association for Supervision and Curriculum Development.

Marzano, R. J., Waters, T., & McNulty, B. A. (2005). *School leadership that works: From research to results.* Alexandria, VA: Association for Supervision and Curriculum Development.

National Governors Association Center for Best Practices & Council of Chief State School Officers. (2010). *Common Core State Standards.* Washington, DC: Authors.

New Jersey Department of Education. (2006). High school proficiency assessment, spring 2006. Trenton, NJ: Author.

New Jersey Department of Education. (2009). High school proficiency assessment, 2008 state summary [Data file]. Trenton, NJ: Author. Retrieved from www.nj.gov/education/schools/achievement/2009/hspa

New Jersey Department of Education. (2014). Model curriculum mathematics. Trenton, NJ: Author. Retrieved from www.state.nj.us/education/modelcurriculum/math

New Jersey Department of Education. (n.d.). District factor groups. Retrieved from www.state.nj.us/education/schools/achievement/dfg.htm

No Child Left Behind Act of 2001, 20 U.S.C.A. § 6301 *et seq.* (West, 2003).

Nunnally, J. C., & Bernstein, I. H. (1994). *Psychometric theory* (3rd ed.). New York, NY: McGraw-Hill.

Parkay, F. W. (2000). Perspectives on curriculum criteria: Past and present. In F. W. Parkay & G. Hass (Eds.), *Curriculum planning: A contemporary approach* (7th ed., pp. 305–313). Boston, MA: Allyn & Bacon.

Pease, M. A., & Kuhn, D. (2011). Experimental analysis of the effective components of problem-based learning. *Science Education, 95*(1), 57–86.

Peugh, J. L., & Enders, C. K. (2004). Missing data in educational research: A review of reporting practices and suggestions for improvement. *Review of Educational Research, 74*(4), 525–556.

Piaget, J. (1950). *The psychology of intelligence* (M. Piercy & D. E. Berlyne, Trans.). New York, NY: Routledge & Kegan Paul.

Piaget, J. (1970). *Science of education and the psychology of the child* (D. Coltman, Trans.). New York, NY: Orion.

Porter, A., McMaken, J., Hwang, J., & Yang, R. (2011). Assessing the common core standards: Opportunities for improving measures of instruction. *Educational Researcher, 40*(4), 186–188. doi:10.3102/0013189X11410232

Presseisen, B. Z. (1985). *Unlearned lessons: Current and past reforms for school improvement.* Philadelphia, PA: Farmer Press.

Sirin, S. R. (2005). Socioeconomic status and academic achievement: A meta-analytic review of research. *Review of Educational Research, 75*(3), 417–453.

Slavin, R. E. (2007). *Educational research in an age of accountability.* Boston, MA: Pearson.

Smith, E. R., & Tyler, R. W. (1942). *Appraising and reporting student progress.* New York, NY: Harper & Brothers.

Streiner, D. L. (2003). Starting at the beginning: An introduction to coefficient alpha and internal consistency. *Journal of Personality Assessment, 80*(1), 99–103.

Strobel, J., & van Barneveld, A. (2009). When is PBL more effective? A meta-synthesis of meta-analyses comparing PBL to conventional classrooms. *The Interdisciplinary Journal of Problem-Based Learning, 3*(1), 44–58.

Taba, H. (1962). *Curriculum development, theory and practice.* New York, NY: Harcourt, Brace, & World.

Tanner, D. (1999). The textbook controversies. In M. Early & K. J. Rehage (Eds.), *Issues in curriculum: Selected essays from NSSE yearbooks* (pp. 115–140). Chicago, IL: University of Chicago Press.

Tanner, D., & Tanner, L. (1975). *Curriculum development: Theory into practice.* New York, NY: MacMillan.

Tanner, D., & Tanner, L. (2007). *Curriculum development: Theory into practice* (4th ed.). Upper Saddle River, NJ: Pearson.

Tanner, L., & Tanner, D. (1988). The emergence of a paradigm in the curriculum field: A reply to Jickling. *Interchange, 19*(2), 50–58.

Tienken, C. H., & Orlich, D. C. (2013). *The school reform landscape: Fraud, myth, and lies.* Lanham, MD: Rowman & Littlefield.

Tyler, R. W. (1949). *Basic principles of curriculum and instruction.* Chicago, IL: University of Chicago Press.

Vygotsky, L. S. (1978). *Mind in society: The development of higher psychological processes* (M. Cole, Ed.). Cambridge, MA: Harvard University Press.

Walker, A., & Leary, H. (2009). A problem-based learning meta analysis: Differences across problem types, implementation types, disciplines, and assessment levels. *The Interdisciplinary Journal of Problem-Based Learning, 3*(1), 12–43.

Wang, M. C., Haertel, G. D., & Walberg, H. J. (1993). Toward a knowledge base for school learning. *Review of Educational Research, 63*(3), 249–294.

Wilson, S. M., Peterson, P. L., Ball, D. L., & Cohen, D. K. (1996). Learning by all. *Phi Delta Kappan, 77*(7), 468–477.

Wirkala, C., & Kuhn, D. (2011). Problem-based learning in K−12 education: Is it effective and how does it achieve its effects? *American Educational Research Journal, 48*(5), 1157–1186.

Wrightstone, J. W. (1935). *Appraisal of newer practices in selected public schools.* New York, NY: Teachers College Press.

Wrightstone, J. W., Rechetnick, J., McCall, W. A., & Loftus, J. J. (1939). Measuring social performance factors in activity and control schools of New York city. New York, NY: *Teachers College Record, 40*(5), 423–432.

Zhao, Y. (2009). *Catching up or leading the way: American education in the age of globalization.* Alexandria, VA: Association for Supervision and Curriculum Development.

Zhao, Y. (2012). *World class learners: Educating creative and entrepreneurial students.* Thousand Oaks, CA: Corwin.

5

OECD, PISA, AND GLOBALIZATION: THE INFLUENCE OF THE INTERNATIONAL ASSESSMENT REGIME

Svein Sjøberg

UNIVERSITY OF OSLO

Beginning in the mid-1990s, the Organisation for Economic Co-operation and Development (OECD) started creating the Programme for International Student Assessment, now well known as PISA. Since the first publication of PISA rankings in 2001, based on the testing that took place in 2000, the results have become a global gold standard for educational quality. Although the political and educational importance of PISA varies from one country to another, the results often set the scene for public debate on the quality of education for the more than 65 countries and cities that participate in the test. PISA performance tables are widely published in mass media and also used by politicians and education policymakers. In many countries, educational reforms are launched in direct response to PISA results. The testing takes place every three years; including the results from PISA 2012 testing (OECD, 2014), we now have data from five rounds of PISA.

The intentions of PISA are related to the overall political aims of the OECD and the underlying commitment to a competitive global free-market economy. PISA was constructed and intended for the 30+ industrialized and wealthy OECD countries, but a similar number of countries and economies have subsequently joined. When the most recent PISA results were presented, OECD (2014) claimed to have participation from 90% of the global economy. For educators, this may seem a surprising way of reporting student participation; but it indicates the focus of the PISA project: economics. The economic focus might also account for the extreme importance that is now attributed to PISA rankings. It seems common sense that high scores on PISA reading, mathematics, and science are predictors for the country's future economic competitiveness. Bad rankings from PISA are thought to be ominous signals for the economic future of a country.

I will return to the crucial point of interpreting rankings toward the end of this chapter.

Tables of country rankings on PISA scores are often taken at face value, not only in the media, but also by policymakers and politicians. The PISA undertaking is a well-funded multinational techno-scientific machine—undoubtedly the world's largest empirical study of schools and education. Recent estimates suggest that the annual cost, without adding the expense of involving half a million students and tens of thousands of schools and their teachers, is approximately 80 million Euro (Maslen, 2013). Given its size and importance, PISA has to be understood not just as a study of student learning, but also as a social phenomenon in a wider political, social, and cultural context (Lundgren, 2011).

PISA rankings create panic and discomfort among policymakers in practically all countries, including the high-scoring ones (Alexander, 2012). The discomfort produces an urge for politicians and bureaucrats to do *something* to rectify the situation that they believe the results describe. However, because PISA does not tell much about cause and effect, creative educational reforms that are not at all empirically founded are introduced, often overnight.

This chapter will raise many important questions about the PISA project, focused on two critical arguments with implications for education policy-making. The first argument relates to the PISA project itself and is that basic structural problems are inherent in the PISA undertaking and, hence, cannot be *fixed*. I will argue that it is impossible to construct a test that can be used across countries and cultures to assess the quality of learning in real life situations with authentic texts. Problems arise when the intentions of the PISA framework are translated into concrete test items to be used in a great variety of languages, cultures, and countries. The requirement of "fair testing" implies by necessity that local, current, and topical issues must be excluded if items are to transfer objectively across cultures, languages, and customs. This runs against most current thinking in science education, where "science in context" and "localized curricula" are ideals promoted by UNESCO and many educators, as well as in national curricula.

My second argument relates to some of the rather intriguing results that emerge from analyses of PISA data. It seems that pupils in high-scoring countries also develop the most negative attitudes toward the subjects on which they are tested. It also seems that PISA scores are unrelated to educational resources, funding, class size, and similar factors. PISA scores also seem to be negatively related to the use of active teaching methods, inquiry-based instruction, and computer technology. PISA scores seem to function like a kind of IQ test on school systems. A most complex issue is reduced to simple numbers that may be ranked with high accuracy. But, as with IQ scores, there are serious concerns about the validity of the PISA scores. Whether one believes in the goals and results of PISA, such issues need to be discussed.

One positive aspect of PISA is that it has brought schools and education to the forefront in the media and in political debates internationally, and even more so nationally in many countries. However, the PISA results seem to be accepted at face value, and there are few critical voices. The focus of this chapter, therefore, will be on the especially problematic sides of PISA testing.

What Does PISA Claim to Measure?

The emerging picture of what PISA tests measure is in many ways confusing. In some places, the PISA authors claim that the tests do *not* measure school knowledge or competencies acquired at schools; but in other places, they state that the tests actually do measure the quality of the nations' school systems. Let us consider some details.

The overall aims of PISA had already been stated in 1999, before the first PISA testing took place in 2000:

> How well are young adults prepared to meet the challenges of the future? Are they able to analyse, reason and communicate their ideas effectively? Do they have the capacity to continue learning throughout life? Parents, students, the public and those who run education systems need to know.
>
> *(OECD, 1999, p. 7)*

Those exact words have been repeated in practically all PISA reports from the OECD during the more than 15 years since then. One can hardly object to ambitions like these. It would be great if PISA really did answer these questions, as the authors have claimed. In other reports, however, the authors are more modest. They emphasize that PISA scores do not actually provide measures of the quality of education systems, but rather the collective results of the school, home, and social environments.

PISA is rather explicit that the tests do *not* measure quality according to national school curricula, but measure based on the definitions and framework made by the OECD-appointed PISA experts (OECD, 2006a). The PISA framework clearly states that the knowledge and skills tested by PISA "are defined not primarily in terms of a common denominator of national school curricula but in terms of what skills are deemed to be essential for future life" (OECD, 2006a, p. 11). In essence, the PISA creators are claiming that they have identified the critical skills necessary for future life, for all humans on the planet. The same framework also states that tests exclude elements that are specific to a country's school curriculum.

So, although PISA states that it does not test knowledge acquired in schools and that it does not test according to national curricula, the PISA results are interpreted by OECD officials and policymakers around the globe as valid measures of the quality of national school systems, and the PISA reports are chock-full of policy recommendations regarding schools (Loveless, 2009).

The Politics of the OECD PISA Project

OECD is an organization for the highly industrialized and economically developed nations. The mandate of the organization lies in the name: Organisation for Economic Co-operation and Development. The home site (www.oecd.org) is explicit about the OECD's mission. Its aim is, above all, to promote policies and set standards for economic development in a global, competitive, free-market economy. One should remember that the E in OECD stands for Economic, not Educational. But education is certainly a driving force in economic development and national competitiveness, and has therefore become an important element of the OECD's concerns and policy advice.

The mandate of the OECD also explains why the PISA subjects are reading, mathematics, and science. According to OECD officials, these subjects are seen to be key elements for competitiveness in a world economy driven by science and technological development. But this selection of subjects also carries an implicit message about what is considered to be important in schools and in the development of young people. One should note the domains that are *not* included when PISA measures the quality of schools: the humanities, social sciences, ethics, foreign languages, history, geography, and physical education. One might also note that PISA does not address attributes that are central in many countries' official purposes of education, such as equity, empathy, solidarity, curiosity and engagement, and care for the environment. In public and political debates, statements about the agreed (and legally binding) purposes of the school system are often forgotten or ignored when the quality of the school is based on PISA scores and rankings.

It is interesting to note that in the PISA 2012 testing, a new component was added: "financial literacy" (OECD, 2013a). Of course the addition was as a consequence of the free-market economic mandate and priorities of the OECD. This module was included in the testing by some 40 countries.

The OECD is often very clear about the economic purposes of PISA and the competitive, international nature of the PISA rankings:

> In a global economy, the yardstick for success is no longer improvement by national standards alone, but how education systems perform internationally. The OECD has taken up that challenge by developing PISA, the Programme for International Student Assessment, which evaluates the quality, equity and efficiency of school systems in some 70 countries that, together, make up nine-tenths of the world economy.
>
> *(OECD, 2010a, p. 3)*

There seems to be a contradiction here regarding the structural nature of PISA and what the authors claim to measure. On the one hand, the OECD claims that PISA does not measure quality according to school curricula, or even the knowledge acquired at school. On the other hand, the OECD claims that it does evaluate "the quality, equity and efficiency of school systems." As mentioned, it is also interesting that the overall importance of PISA is defined in terms of the fraction of the world economy tested, rather than in terms of the fraction of the world's population, further indicating its structural focus on competitive economics, not comprehensive education.

The competitive economic perspective is also at the forefront when PISA results are presented to the public. At the PISA 2006 Release Conference in Washington, DC, on December 4, 2007, a portion of the invitation read as follows:

Losing Our Edge: Are American Students Unprepared for the Global Economy?

The lessons learned from the PISA results . . . can, and should, be used to inform U.S. education policy so that our students graduate . . . ready to compete, thrive, and lead in the global economy of the twenty-first century.

(Alliance for Excellent Education, 2007)

The political, economic, and indeed normative use of PISA by the OECD is also very clear. The OECD makes regular economic reports to many countries, with advice on future policy. My own country—Norway—is an example. In the Economic Survey report to Norway in 2008, OECD experts gave the following general advice: Norway should increase differences in salaries, reduce public spending, increase the rate of unemployment, reduce the level of sick leave salaries, and reduce pensions for people with disabilities (OECD, 2008). This advice was given just before the financial crisis.

This particular OECD report to Norway had the education system as the focus. With PISA data as input for its calculations, OECD gave advice on how to make Norwegian schools better. The operational definition of a "better school" was a school that is "cost-effective," that is, could give more PISA points per dollar spent on education. The very definition of a good school thereby ignored the national priorities set for our school system. The OECD educational advice was that Norwegian schools could become better by closing smaller schools, increasing class size, introducing more testing, publishing results at school (and teacher) level, and basing teacher payments on achieved test results. The report ended with a clear warning: "Higher spending on schools will have no effect" (OECD, 2008).

The essence of this "expert advice" was that Norway should become a different kind of country—hardly objective, neutral, scientific advice. In fact, Norway is not the only country to receive this kind of advice. PISA creates country-specific reports for all participating OECD countries.

National Policies Based on PISA: Examples

Though the attention given to PISA results in national media varies between countries, in most countries it is formidable and has increased after several rounds of PISA testing (Breakspear, 2012). In Norway, the results from both PISA 2000 and PISA 2003 made the newspaper headlines. Our then Minister of Education Kristin Clemet (2001–2005), representing the conservative party Høyre, commented on the PISA 2000 results, which were released a few months after she had taken office: "Norway is a school loser, now it is well documented. It is like coming home from the Winter Olympics without a gold medal" (which, of course, for Norway would have been a most unthinkable disaster!). She even added, "And this time we cannot even claim that the Finnish participants have been doped!"—a reference to a recent cross-country championship (*Aftenposten,* January 2001, as translated by author).

The warlike headlines in all the Norwegian newspapers told residents that "Norway is a school loser." The headlines, however, were misleading: Norway's scores were actually close to the OECD average in the three test domains in PISA 2000 and PISA 2003. With the media's help, however, the results from PISA shaped the public image of the quality of our school system, not only in regard to the aspects that had in fact been studied, but also for more or less all other aspects of school. It became common wisdom that Norwegian schools in general were poor quality and that Norwegian classrooms were among the noisiest in the world, although noise levels had barely been studied in PISA. The media presented tabloid-like and oversimplified rankings. Unfortunately, the public as well as politicians accepted these skewed generalities as objective scientific truths about our education system. There was little critical public debate, and the researchers behind the PISA study did nothing to modify the false impression and remind the public about the limitations of the study and the fact that Norway in reality ranked among the middle of the OECD countries. In sum, PISA created a public image of the quality of Norwegian schooling that was unjustified and detrimental to the long-term health of the education system and the country itself. Surveys among Norwegian teachers have since shown that they consider the effects of the PISA project as a serious detriment to their daily work.

PISA has not only shaped the public image of Norwegian schools, but has also served to legitimize potentially harmful school reforms. Under Minister of Education Clemet, a series of educational reforms was introduced in Norway. Most of those reforms referenced international testing, mainly PISA, as justification. In 2005, there was a change in government, and shortly afterward Clemet's Secretary of State Helge Ole Bergesen (2006) published a book in which he presented the "inside story" on the reforms made while they were in power. A key feature of the book was the many references to large-scale achievement studies. Bergesen (2006) explicitly stated that these studies provided the main arguments and rationale for curricular as well as other school reforms. Under the heading "The PISA Shock," he confirmed the key role of PISA:

> With the [publication of the] PISA results, the scene was set for a national battle over knowledge in our schools.... For those of us who had just taken over the political power in the Ministry of Education and Research, the PISA results provided a "flying start."
>
> *(Bergesen, 2006, pp. 41–42, author's translation)*

In these memoirs, Bergesen (2006) also described how the Ministry deliberately created an atmosphere of panic and urgency, and how all resistance was successfully characterized as unscientific and ideological.

When the next PISA round showed a small fall in Norway's test scores, the ground was prepared for a major school reform, to be called The Knowledge Promotion. All political parties were on board. Later, in the 2009 parliamentary election campaign, the prime ministerial candidate (who was to be Prime Minister for the same party from 2013) had the following main message, even with a personal signature in the leading Norwegian newspaper:

> I, Erna Solberg, herewith guarantee that if we [i.e., Høyre, the moderate/ conservative party] form the Government after the election, we can promise more PISA points.
>
> *(Aftenposten, March 27, 2009, author's translation)*

It is most interesting that this statement was made shortly after the Norwegian Parliament unanimously passed a new law setting out the foundational values for Norwegian schools. During the election campaign, no reference was made to the key words in this law (e.g., equity, solidarity, empathy, concern for the environment). It is also notable that the red/green Labour-dominated Norwegian government that took office in 2005 followed more or less the same policy.

In the many white papers on schools that were presented from the government to the parliament in the years 2001 to 2013, references to the PISA project and "OECD experts" steadily increased, and by 2013 they appeared on nearly every page. There is no doubt that the major reforms of Norwegian schools over the last decade have been strongly influenced by the OECD, with PISA as the main instrument. These reforms are also characterized as examples of New

Public Management (Møller & Skedsmo, 2013). Among many reforms, we have established a high-stakes national testing system whose categories are more or less adapted from the PISA framework. The new national curriculum is also strongly influenced by the language and categories in the PISA framework.

In sum, international rankings, in particular PISA, are seen as the ultimate measure of the total quality of the Norwegian school system, and new reforms were introduced in response to the perceived challenge. Most reforms on curriculum, national testing, accountability, and transparency also follow the policy advice that emerged from the PISA studies. More private schooling, free choice of schools, and the growth of private consultancies for testing and reporting also are current trends that respond to the panic in the wake of PISA rankings.

In the autumn of 2014, Norwegian teachers went on strike—not for higher salaries, but in response to more external control of their working hours and other working conditions. The underlying cause of the conflict was the growing demand for more testing, reporting, and control of teachers' work, which had been triggered by the "PISA shock." Similar developments have occurred in other countries, including our neighbouring countries Denmark and Sweden. It is noteworthy, however, that all these "solutions" to the perceived crisis are more or less the opposite of what our Nordic neighbour and declared "PISA winner," Finland, is doing.

Germany had a similar PISA shock. The results from the first PISA round placed Germany below the OECD average. This became an important issue in the German election the following year, and the perceived bad results also led to major initiatives to promote the quality of science and mathematics education. The German national institute for science education, IPN (Institut für die Pädagogik der Naturwissenschaften), received large grants to improve the quality of science education. IPN also had the contract to run PISA in Germany. From the perspective of science education, one may say that bad results are good news, much the same way that the Sputnik shock was good news for science and mathematics educators in the Western world. The influence of PISA in Germany went even further, with the country's later introduction of national standards for science education (Steffen & Hößle, 2014).

The OECD readily boasts about the influence of PISA. An official working paper reviewed the policy impacts and the normative effects of PISA. With obvious pride, the report stated:

> PISA has been adopted as an almost global standard, and is now used in over 65 countries and economies.... PISA has become accepted as a reliable instrument for benchmarking student performance worldwide, and [the] PISA results have had an influence on policy reform in the majority of participating countries/economies.
>
> *(Breakspear, 2012, pp. 4–5)*

This report reviewed literature as well as results from the OECD's own questionnaires, and provided a ranking of the impact that PISA had on all OECD countries. The report noted that even "high-performing countries such as Korea and Japan have enacted reforms in response to a large range of PISA results" (Breakspear, 2012, p. 12).

Interestingly, the United States ranks 28th on the PISA listing based on the scoring of "informing policy-making process," with PISA's influence classified as "moderate" (Breakspear, 2012, p. 14). Rutkowski (2014) argued that PISA's rather limited impact on American schools may be the main reason why the federal government and OECD are eager to introduce PISA-based Test for Schools in the United States. That move could get PISA closer to the decision-makers in the U.S. education system and thereby increase its normative power.

PISA, Free-market Thinking, and Globalization

My point so far has been to argue that PISA should be seen and understood in a wider political context. The two key elements here are free-market thinking and globalization. In regard to free-market thinking, the PISA project, organized by the OECD, can be seen as part of a current international policy trend, where concepts and ideas from the market economy are used in the education sector. The term New Public Management is used to describe this market-driven philosophy, which is supposed to make the public sector more efficient. Words like *quality, efficiency, transparency, accountability,* and *value for money* are among those used to describe these policy reforms in many public sectors. Public services such as schools and higher education, culture, and healthcare are all being invaded by market terms.

Other public sectors are experiencing the same trend. Services such as policing, security, postal delivery, transportation, water supply, household garbage handling, and sewage and waste water management all come under attack in the name of efficiency and value. Traditional public services are increasingly subjected to competitive bids from private actors. Outsourcing of key public services, a process that is eased by new regulations on international trade, is increasingly going to multinational companies. Most major international trade agreements now include provisions for privatizing public sectors. This trend toward marketization and privatization characterizes developments in several countries. And the education sector is at the forefront, with the OECD and its PISA project as an efficient tool (Meyer & Benavot, 2013).

The other, and related, political/economical perspective that pervades PISA is that of globalization. The economy is becoming globalized, large multinational corporations are important actors, and the workforce has to be flexible and moveable. Nations and multinational corporations compete in a common market. Hence, the thinking goes, there is a need for common standards in education, common systems for exams, degrees, and qualifications. Such tendencies to standardize education processes operate within units such as the European Union, an example being the Bologna process and its introduction of a common degree system in higher education. In key areas, the OECD is playing an increasingly important role by developing and monitoring common standards, indicators, and measures (Grek, 2009).

This PISA-inspired process represents a political pressure to standardize, harmonize, and universalize national institutions such as a country's school system, and to promote competition on the global educational scene. While most science educators argue for context-based teaching and localized curricula, the pressure from the PISA project is in the opposite direction. A driving force behind these reforms is often the use of indicators—quantifiable and measurable standards that can be used for calculations (Popkewitz, 2011). PISA test scores and rankings are ideal for this purpose, whether or not that usage was intended by the PISA researchers.

Universally Valid "Real Life" Indicators?

A fundamental premise for the PISA project is that it is indeed possible to "measure" the quality of a country's education using indicators that are common to all countries despite differences in things that affect school outcomes such as social structure, traditions, culture, natural conditions, ways of living, and access to free public education. As noted, PISA claims to measure how well the young generation is prepared to meet the challenges of tomorrow's world (OECD, 2007). Such an ambition assumes that the challenges of tomorrow's world are already known and more or less identical for young people across countries and cultures. It assumes one universal conception of success and a universal set of necessary skills.

Although life in many countries does have some similarities, one can hardly assume that the 15-year-olds in the United States, Japan, Turkey, Mexico, and Norway are preparing for the same challenges, careers, and economies, or that they need identical life skills and competencies. It is also important to remind ourselves that the PISA academic framework and its test are meant for the relatively rich and modernized OECD countries. When this instrument is used as a benchmark standard in the 30+ non-OECD member countries that take part in PISA, the mismatch between the PISA test and the needs of the youth in those nations becomes even more obvious.

One should also remember that the target population of the PISA testing is the whole age cohort of 15-year-olds. This is, in most countries, toward the end of what in most countries is comprehensive school. The great majority of these young people have to face realities that are local and national. Only a minority of them will operate in a global, international marketplace.

All countries have their own school and education systems based on national decisions set most often by democratically elected governments and institutions.

National traditions and deliberations have resulted in foundational legal statements about the overall purposes of the school, the level or levels of government with jurisdiction and influence over public schooling, and more concrete details such as time allocations for school subjects, aims, objectives and curricula, and exam structure. These traditions are often at the heart of the nation's identity, and the set of such laws and regulations is the mandate that society has given to the schools, the teachers, and all who work to improve the quality of a nation's schools.

OECD officials, however, explicitly claim that the PISA academic framework does not relate to any national school system because what they measure does not fit any one country's school system. In reality, the framework is made up of sets of perceived universal, presumably culture-free, curricula as decided by the OECD and its experts. The rather explicit goal of the OECD with its PISA project is to be an agent of change in the education system in the participating countries. In this respect, one may say that PISA is a success story (Lawn & Grek, 2012). The international test movement, in particular PISA, leads to policy convergence across nations. However, this goal is detrimental to the expression of educational values within countries and to cultural identity and diversity in general.

Steps Toward the PISA Test

The process of developing the PISA ambitions into the actual test items the students get has several stages, each with serious obstacles that require many decisions. The first step from intention to test is the selection of the knowledge domains (or school subjects) that should be included. The OECD chose three domains (or "literacies") for the PISA testing: reading (in the mother tongue), mathematics, and science. Though these are important and basic subjects, one should keep in mind that most subject-area domains are not included in PISA, nor are the three domains in their entirety.

Of course, one test, even a test like PISA, cannot assess all possible school subjects; but by selecting some subjects and ignoring others, PISA implicitly sends a message to the public as well as politicians about what is important for schools and future life. The actual choice of reading, science, and mathematics also reflects the basic purpose of OECD: the concern for economic competitiveness in a global, high-tech market economy. As mentioned, when PISA extended its repertoire in 2012, the added domain was "financial literacy" (OECD, 2013a).

The PISA Framework

The next step in the process of developing the actual PISA test is to create a testing framework, in reality a curriculum. Here is where the measurement and curriculum experts come in. The key institutions that win the competitive bid, and the selected subject-matter specialists, are in charge of a lengthy process to develop the framework. The people selected for this purpose are well-known international experts in their fields, often among the most respected and accomplished in the world. But, of course, they work within the frames decided by PISA as a project, and they must all be fluent in English, which is the dominating language in all deliberations and working documents. In addition to the subject-matter specialists, psychometricians play a key role in the whole process.

Most scholars will probably find the PISA frameworks developed by these expert groups to be most interesting, with ideas, perspectives, and subject-matter detail that is of very high quality (e.g., OECD, 2013a). Rather than models to be copied, these documents could be used as sources for inspiration to make national curricula and to stimulate the debate over educational priorities. The problem is, however, that this framework now serves as a normative international, universal curriculum, and a framework for an international testing regime.

Item Selection and Test Construction

The next step is to "operationalize" the frameworks—that is, to use the frameworks for the development and selection of test items, and for the construction of the PISA tests as a whole. For more detail on the technicalities in this complicated process, readers are encouraged to access the more than 400-page technical reports for each test (e.g., OECD, 2009a, for the PISA 2006 testing). However, some elements in the process are as follows. Each PISA country (OECD countries only) is invited to submit test items that fit the framework and are based on authentic texts for real-life situations. Through a complicated process involving initial screening and selection, national and international piloting, prefield trials, main field trial round, and psychometric analysis, that involve many actors and subcommittees and many meetings for negotiations and debate, the final series of test items is decided. The complexity of this one stage in the process is apparent from the following extract from the technical report:

> These analyses . . . included the standard ConQuest® item analysis (item fit, item discrimination, item difficulty, distracter analysis, mean ability, and point-biserial correlations by coding category, item omission rates, and so on), as well as analyses of gender-by-item interactions and item-by-country interactions. On the basis of these critical measurement statistics, about 40 new items were removed from the pool of items that would be considered for the main study.
>
> *(OECD 2009a, p. 41)*

A logical consequence of wanting to make a fair international test is that an item cannot be used if it behaves in an unfair fashion. While this is a sensible argument from a statistical, psychometric point of view, it also means that items close to the real life contexts of some countries but not others have to be removed. The principles for exclusions are described as follows:

> The main reasons for assessing units as unsuitable were lack of context, inappropriate context, cultural bias, curriculum dependence, just school science and including content that was deemed to be too advanced.
>
> *(OECD, 2009a, p. 34)*

This section of the technical manual clearly states that units (items) that relate to issues considered "inappropriate" (controversial in a particular country), have a "cultural bias" (positive or negative), or are close to the school curriculum (in some countries but not in others) were excluded. The statement also explicitly states that "just school science" should be excluded. This is, again, a clear statement that PISA does not measure knowledge or issues related to school curricula. Based on these criteria, it seems somewhat strange that such a test is used to judge the quality of science taught at school in each country. In the final science literacy test, for example, Norwegian students will find nothing about the key elements of the Norwegian economy. They will not find questions on topics such as oil and gas in arctic conditions on the continental shelf, aquaculture and fish farming, and hydroelectric power plants. Neither will they find anything about current topical issues and conflicts regarding the conservation of nature, current political conflicts between nature conservation (e.g., wild wolves) and sheep farming, snow, skiing or skating, the Northern Lights (a main focus of research of the university in Tromsø), or the challenges of an arctic climate. Students in other countries, of course, are also not likely to find questions relating to their own culture, nature, history, or current national challenges.

In reality, the test items in the final science test are decontextualized, or the context is contrived or historical. This cleansing of culture and context does not occur because of nefarious intentions built into the testing framework, but because of statistical necessity and concern for "fairness." The decontextualized and contrived nature of the assessments runs contrary to all recommendations by science educators as well as by many national goals of promoting a science curriculum that is relevant, interesting, and context-based.

Item Texts, Language, and Translation

A further set of complications arises in relation to item texts, language, and translation. Most PISA items are based on rather lengthy texts that constitute the stem, called the "stimulus." The intention is positive: namely, to present real, authentic texts and real life situations. But this contrived realistic format—in particular, the length and complication of the stimulus text—also makes the PISA items different from most tests that are commonly used in mathematics and science (also in TIMSS, the other large-scale study of science and mathematics achievement). This format is, of course, a deliberate choice by PISA specialists, and it reaffirms that PISA does not really test subject-matter school knowledge from school curricula.

It is often claimed that many PISA items are to a large degree testing reading skills rather than science and mathematics competencies. The strong correlations between the test results on the reading, mathematics, and science assessments lend support to such a claim. The fact that PISA items in later PISA versions have become shorter may indicate that this critique has been taken seriously and has led to a reduction in the heavy load on reading skills.

A robust finding in PISA, as well as other kinds of reading tests such as PIRLS (Progress in International Reading Literacy Study), is that girls outperform boys in reading in all countries. More surprising is that the gender difference in the PISA science and mathematics scores favors girls more than most other kinds of tests. This unusual gender pattern may, at least partially, be explained by the heavy reading load in many PISA items and the strong correlation between reading achievement on PISA and achievement on the mathematics and science sections. PISA test scores show a gender pattern in science and mathematics that is different from the TIMSS results in many of the same countries, as well as other tests such as national exams. It is also interesting that the PISA gender pattern differs when the students answer questions on a computer-based questionnaire, as they do in the so-called Computer-Based Assessment in Science (CBAS) version. In the computer-based test, the boys actually outperform the girls in science (OECD, 2010b). This is an indication that the context and the mode of data collection also influence the results to a significant degree, which is important to recognize as PISA migrates to an entirely computer-based format.

The authentic texts that constitute the stimulus in each item originate in a certain situation in one of the OECD countries and in the language of that country. This text is then translated into the two official PISA languages before being submitted for consideration. If accepted, the item is then translated into the language of each of the participating PISA countries. This translation process follows very strict rules and detailed instructions (e.g., OECD, 2009a).

This translation process raises many questions. Thorough analysis of the PISA reading test items has been carried out by Arffman (2007) and discussed in journal papers. Arffman (2010) provided a detailed text-analytical study of the translation from English to Finnish of three PISA items as an example of how both meaning and context change in the translation. Her study reveals in detail many critical dimensions in this process. One of her conclusions, based on translation theory and on a review of results from earlier empirical studies, is that one can never arrive at what may be called "equivalence of translation." For example, neither poetry nor good prose can be translated according to a formalized set of rules—a fact that all good translators will acknowledge. Something is always lost, or meaning is modified in translation.

Yet even where the quality rules should have been followed, seemingly nonstandard translations appear. There seems to be a lack of empirical studies looking into this important aspect of PISA (and also TIMMS and PIRLS) testing. The key role played by these texts in PISA makes such scrutiny very important.

A thorough cross-national check of translations requires the cooperation of researchers from many countries with considerable linguistic skills as well as subject-matter knowledge. Some languages, however, lend themselves to rather easy comparisons, even for nonlinguists. The three Scandinavian languages Swedish, Danish, and Norwegian, for example, are very similar—more like dialects, in fact, in part with a common literary tradition. A simple demonstration uses the translation of a single item about cloning from English into these three languages. Since its release in the 2006 test, this item about cloning the sheep Dolly has become a well-known example (OECD, 2009b). The stem text of the original, in English, is reproduced in Figure 5.1.

Based on this English (and the French) original, the three Scandinavian texts (now available from the national PISA website) were translated, presumably according to the detailed rules and instructions given by PISA. The most striking and immediate observation is that the three Scandinavian texts become strange and clumsy. Equally important is the fact that the resulting three versions are quite different from one another, and they have all changed the original meaning in some dramatic ways:

- The Swedish, Danish, and Norwegian texts changed the word "nucleus" to "cell nucleus," thereby providing the hint that the "small piece" in Question 2 is indeed a cell.
- While the English (and Swedish) texts stated that he removed "the material that would have determined sheep 2 characteristics," the Danish text stated, "he removed the genetic material," thereby changing the meaning in the sentence as well as introducing a science concept that does not appear in the original.
- In the Norwegian version, "all material is removed from the egg-cell" makes the sentence more or less meaningless.
- The Danish text altered Question 1 and asked, "Which sheep is Dolly a copy of?" In Danish, the word "identical" was considered problematic, which is indeed true. The Danish version is also more in line with the title of the item: "A copying machine for living things." This way of talking and writing about cloning is actually never used in any Nordic language, and probably not in other languages either.

S128: Cloning

Read the newspaper article and answer the questions that follow.

A copying machine for living beings?

Without any doubt, if there had been elections for the animal of the year 1997, Dolly would have been the winner! Dolly is a Scottish sheep that you see in the
5 photo. But Dolly is not just a simple sheep. She is a clone of another sheep. A clone means: a copy. Cloning means copying 'from a single master copy'. Scientists succeeded in creating a sheep (Dolly) that
10 is identical to a sheep that functioned as a 'master copy'.
It was the Scottish scientist Ian Wilmut who designed the 'copying machine' for sheep. He took a very small piece from the
15 udder of an adult sheep (sheep 1).

From that small piece he removed the nucleus, then he transferred the nucleus into the egg-cell of another (female) sheep (sheep 2). But first he removed from that
20 egg-cell all the material that would have determined sheep 2 characteristics in a lamb produced from that egg-cell. Ian Wilmut implanted the manipulated egg-cell of sheep 2 into yet another (female)
25 sheep (sheep 3). Sheep 3 became pregnant and had a lamb: Dolly.
Some scientists think that within a few years it will be possible to clone people as well. But many governments have already
30 decided to forbid cloning of people by law.

Question 1: CLONING

S128Q01

Which sheep is Dolly identical to?

A Sheep 1
B Sheep 2
C Sheep 3
D Dolly's father

Question 2: CLONING

S128Q02

In line 14 the part of the udder that was used is described as "a very small piece".
From the article text you can work out what is meant by "a very small piece".

That "very small piece" is

A a cell.
B a gene.
C a cell nucleus.
D a chromosome.

FIGURE 5.1 Sample Test Question from PISA

The original English text and two questions for the item "Cloning," reproduced as they appeared in the student's questionnaire (OECD, 2009b, pp. 197–198).

PISA technical reports assert to readers that it uses a top-quality translation process:

> As in PISA 2003, one of the most important quality control procedures implemented to ensure high quality standards in the translated assessment materials consisted in having an independent team of expert verifiers, appointed and trained by the consortium, verify each national version against the English and French source versions.
>
> *(OECD, 2009a, p. 91)*

The procedure for the translation control is then described in detail. The "translation equivalence across PISA countries" is also thoroughly discussed in Grisay, de Jong, Gebhardt, Berezner, and Halleux-Monseur (2007). In light of this objective, it is rather surprising that big blunders can be discovered with just a cursory look at published items.

Even a hasty reading by nonexperts shows that the translated texts are put in a strange and awkward prose that one cannot find in any Scandinavian publications. Such texts cannot possibly be called "authentic." Arffman (2010) noted that bad translations also may cause readers to lose interest and motivation to become engaged with the text, and that this may have a severely negative effect on the test results. This effect, I assert, is likely to be greater in countries where students are critical, independent, and unwilling to obey the authority of schools and teachers. This point about students' motivation and willingness to engage in the whole exercise is elaborated elsewhere (Sjøberg, 2007).

Written Test as "Real Life" Situation?

The basic claims of the OECD as listed in its technical documents are that the PISA test results can provide reliable evidence about (a) how well young people are prepared for future challenges; (b) whether they can analyze, reason, and communicate effectively; (c) whether they have the capacity to continue learning throughout life; and (d) to what extent they have acquired some of the knowledge and skills essential for full participation in society. These ambitions are great, but they are contradicted by the very format of the testing: The PISA test is a traditional pen-and-paper test, where students sit for 2.5 hours to answer written questions, in solitude, and without access to sources of information. How "real life" is that test situation? How does it relate to the challenges that young people may face in their future life as citizens, as participants in tomorrow's democracy, and as members of a skilled workforce? The fact is that the PISA test situation does not resemble any real life, problem-based situations. The only place where you sit in solitude with a written test is in exams at schools and universities. The only places where students are not allowed to communicate, collaborate, or use modern information technologies are similar contrived test situations.

Real life, in private, at leisure, as well as at the workplace, is more or less the opposite of the PISA test situation. While one would expect that an organization like the OECD should emphasize the competencies needed by the big international actors in a competitive global market, the PISA test situation is different. Therefore, PISA does not even serve the political/economic goals of the OECD.

Test Scores and Economic Prosperity

It does sound like "common sense" that high scores on science and math tests at school are good predictors of future economic prosperity. The assumed strong connection between scores on tests like TIMSS and PISA and the economic competitiveness of the country is a core assumption behind these studies. As noted earlier in this chapter, bad rankings on PISA are thought to be bad signals for the future of a country. This assumption is probably the main reason for the extreme importance given to PISA results and rankings. PISA is, in fact, presented, marketed, and understood in this perspective, as also noted earlier.

But this commonsensical assumption may now be studied empirically. In January 2013, *New Scientist* published an article titled "West vs Asia education rankings are misleading," claiming:

> For developed nations, there is scant evidence that TIMSS rankings correlate with measures of prosperity or future success. The same holds for a similar test, the Programme for International Student Achievement (PISA). . . . Analysis of 23 countries found a significant negative relationship between 2009 PISA scores and ranking on the Global Entrepreneurship Monitor's measure of perceived entrepreneurial capabilities.
>
> *(Campbell, 2013)*

Among the references in this article is a study by Tienken (2008), who used a series of indicators for countries' economic competitiveness and prosperity, and looked at how these correlate with scores on international tests of TIMSS (using data since the early 1960s) and PISA (since 2000). Such studies are most interesting, because they undermine the fundamental premise behind PISA. Further studies of the connections between national test scores and economic prosperity are likely to shed more light on this important issue. Such statistical studies may be supplemented with studies undertaken by the actors on the market. Two examples follow.

Competencies for the Future: The Voice of Employers

Many sources provide qualified accounts of the skills and competencies that large employers in the high-tech sector require from their workforces. At the Official Bologna Seminar in 2008 on "Employability: The Employers' Perspective and Its Implications," Frank Stefan Becker (2008), head of Human Resources at Siemens, gave a presentation of his company's view regarding the competencies it needs from its employees. He presented the following list:

Professional Competence—Vital Skills for Today's Employees

- Thorough knowledge of one's subject;
- Ability to judge analytically, structure one's work, make "plausibility checks," carry out research, evaluate information, and identify problems;
- Ability to look beyond one's own area of competence and take other factors into account;

- Independence, initiative, independent learning, work techniques, discipline, frustration tolerance, ability to set priorities;
- Interpersonal skills: communication, feedback, a feeling for situations, capacity for teamwork, fluent English.

Siemens AG is the largest Europe-based electronics and electrical engineering company. Siemens and its subsidiaries employ approximately 360,000 people across nearly 190 countries. One may easily see that most of the competencies on the preceding list are not addressed on the PISA test.

The second example is an investigation done by Abelia, the Business Association of Norwegian knowledge- and technology-based enterprises. Based on a survey among 500 leaders in the most competitive sector of the Norwegian economy, the association ended up with the following ranking of competencies:

Competencies for Future Leaders and Key Personnel

- Good communication skills;
- Aptitude for strategic thinking;
- Ability to motivate;
- Concern for staff and coworkers;
- Self-confidence and self-efficacy;
- Solid educational background;
- Visionary;
- Understanding numbers and quantities.

(DAMVAD Group, 2013, Author's translation)

As one can readily see, the two examples emphasize similar competencies, but they are quite different from what PISA is testing. Interestingly, the perspectives expressed from high-tech industry in many ways coincide with the purposes and aims of schooling in many modern democracies, and they also are in line with many aspects of "progressive pedagogy." Advice based on PISA results may, in fact, be counterproductive even for companies that operate in the competitive global market.

Problematic Statistics and Lack of Transparency

The PISA project is a large undertaking that has many of the characteristics of "big science" and "techno-science." It is costly and involves the cooperation of approximately 70 countries. The logistics of the project are complicated, as specified in piles of documents with detailed instructions to the national groups who are responsible in the participating countries. Hundreds of experts from several fields of expertise are involved. Contracts with subcontractors are given by bids. Thousands of schools and teachers participate, with nearly half a million students spending 2.5 hours answering the test and the questionnaire. Data are carefully coded by thousands of specially trained markers. And the list goes on.

Some of the many problematic issues in the process from intentions to test items have been raised earlier, but there are more issues that are problematic. The final test consists of items that are selected according to a process previously described, but the actual test booklets and questions that are answered by the students are not identical. A system of "rotation" of items means that the students answer several different booklets. In this way, PISA can include a larger number of items in its test. After the time-consuming and tedious coding and data-entry process, the data undergo complicated statistical analysis. The statistical processes that lead from actual responses to these numbers is based on Item Response Theory (IRT) and Rasch modeling. Moreover, the final overall scores are normalized to provide an international mean score of 500 with a standard deviation of 100 for the OECD as a whole.

The road from the actual responses to the final numbers and rankings in the publicly available tables is long and not very transparent. The methods have been criticized by well-qualified statisticians, even among those who actually work on PISA data. Svend Kreiner, professor of biomedical statistics at Copenhagen University, argued that by simply changing some of the parameters in the complicated statistical analysis, Denmark's rank can fluctuate from as high as number 2 to as low as number 42. He also noted that the PISA methods of statistical calculations are published only in a general form, making detailed critique and replication difficult (Kreiner & Christensen, 2014).

Problematic and Intriguing Results

The political/economic aspects of PISA and the overall basic weaknesses of the project, as described, are primary concerns. But other serious concerns also should be addressed, especially by those who embrace PISA and believe that PISA provides valid data on educational quality and student achievement. The following is an overview of some of these concerns.

Resources and Finance Have No Influence?

From the beginning of the PISA project, the OECD has produced graphs and indicators that have shown small or negligible correlations between a country's PISA scores and its spending on education (OECD, 2001). This, of course, has led to the OECD advice that more spending on education will not improve its quality.

In the five Nordic countries, the relationship between public spending and PISA scores is actually strongly negative. Such findings are often used to the detriment of schools and teachers. Finland, a country that ranks high in all areas of PISA, has one of the lowest levels of spending. This example of an inverse correlation between public spending and PISA points is used by political actors in the ongoing debate about return on public investment. Finnish teachers have difficulties asking for higher salaries and more funding because the Finnish scores already rank so high and hence no changes need to be made. Norway, on the other hand, is lower in the PISA rankings, but with higher amounts of public spending on schools. Based on PISA, Norwegian politicians have argued that it has been demonstrated that more spending would not increase the quality of schools. As noted earlier, the OECD (2008) economic report to Norway actually warned Norway not to increase spending on schools, emphasizing that "this will not improve the quality."

High PISA Science Scores Bring Lower Interest and Negative Attitudes?

PISA scores are often presented as league rankings between countries, with the winners on top and the losers at the bottom. But PISA tests also include a questionnaire with many questions about attitudinal aspects of how young people relate to science and the other tested subjects. This was an important element of the PISA 2006 study, when science was the core subject. The definition of *science literacy* in PISA 2006 actually included "willingness to engage in science-related issues, and with the ideas of science, as a reflective citizen" (OECD, 2006a, p. 22). The indices and constructs that were developed for this broad category, however, were not included in the PISA scores that were used for rankings.

A special issue of the *International Journal of Science Education* (2011) presented several interesting results from analyses based on these data. The simplest and possibly most surprising finding was that many countries with the highest mean PISA science scores were at the bottom of the list rating students' interest in science (Bybee & McCrae, 2011). Finland and Japan were the prime examples. Both sat atop the PISA rankings for science scores, yet were at the very bottom on constructs like student "interest in science," "future-oriented motivation to learn science," as well as on "future science job," that is, inclination to see themselves as scientists in future studies and careers. In fact, the PISA science score correlated negatively with "future science orientation" ($r = -0.83$) and with "future science job" ($r = -0.53$), as Kjærnsli & Lie (2011) reported. These negative relationships are based on countries as the units of analysis. When individual students within each country are the units, some of the correlations are positive. Making unjust statistical inferences from groups to individuals is labeled "ecological fallacy."

Such findings are most disturbing for those interested in having more youth pursue careers in science. If the students in top-ranking PISA countries leave compulsory school with strong negative orientations toward science, one needs to step back and think about the reasons for this as well as the possible consequences. Of course, care should be taken not to interpret correlation as cause and effect, but one should at least think twice before using these countries as educational models and ideals to be copied if they are producing negative attitudes toward an important subject like science.

Interestingly, many of the winners in the PISA science test also have the largest gender differences in PISA scores. Finland is again a prime example, where girls outperform boys on all three PISA subjects. In reading literacy, the difference in means is about 50% of a standard deviation. Again, such findings should call for some caution against trying to copy the "PISA winners." What are these winners actually producing? It seems at least in science, the winners are producing inequity in science achievement with overall negative attitudes toward the subject. Is that something to be celebrated or copied?

Traditional Teaching Equates to Better Results?

The PISA student questionnaire includes a series of questions about family background, home environment, and cultural artifacts. It also contains a series of questions to students about the teaching methods and classroom practices that characterize their school experiences. When looking for possible relationships between these variables and the PISA scores, many of the results are surprising and should be given attention. The most intriguing aspect of the results is that they run contrary to current advice from science educators as well as "accepted wisdom" among policymakers and curriculum specialists on what constitutes good instruction. The following is a brief indication of some problematic results.

A trend in current science education is emphasis on active learning and inquiry. Such teaching methods are supported by panels of science education specialists (e.g., Osborne & Dillon, 2008) as well as OECD (2006b) experts and the influential European Union (European Commission, 2007). Policy statements made in these and other reports have channeled much of the research and development work supported by the European Union's current Framework Programme FP7 into inquiry-based science education (IBSE).

Reference is often made to the French program *La main à la pâte* organized by the Academy of Sciences. The key person in the project is Pierre Léna, a well-known astrophysicist as well as former Director General of Higher Education and Research at the Ministry of Education. This French program was inspired by a U.S. program with hands-on science initiated by the Nobel Laureate Leon Lederman. Such projects are seen as sources of inspiration by science educators as well as by national policymakers. PISA scores, however, seem to be negatively correlated with many active teaching methods like "formulating your own problems and finding answers" and doing experimental work (Kjærnsli, Lie, Olsen, & Roe, 2007).

Current science education trends and reforms are reviewed by Jenkins (2009). Key concepts and acronyms in current thinking in science education are well known: science in context, IBSE (inquiry-based science education), hands-on science, active learning, NOS (nature of science), SSI (socio-scientific issues), argumentation, STS (science, technology, and society). There seems to be no evidence from PISA to back up these recommended methods; PISA rather provides counterevidence. This possible contradiction should at least be seen as problematic when interpreting the value of high PISA scores in science.

Does the Use of ICT Lead to Lower Scores?

PISA includes several questions regarding the use of information and communication technologies (ICT) in schools and has made two constructs based on them. One construct or index is related to the use of the Internet in schools; the other is related to the use of software and educational programs. In a detailed study of the five Nordic countries, Kjærnsli et al. (2007) documented a clear negative relationship between the use of ICT and PISA scores. The PISA winner, Finland, has by far the lowest use of ICT of any Nordic country, and is actually below the OECD average. In contrast, Norway is top of the OECD in all indicators on the use of ICT in schools, but has only average PISA scores. Nevertheless, the policy advice in Norway is to increase the use of ICT in schools to improve achievement.

Intriguing PISA Results: Concluding Remarks

Some of the problematic results described here are not difficult to understand. A written test like PISA can hardly measure the skills and knowledge acquired in experimental work in a lab or on an excursion; neither can it capture the kind of interest, curiosity, and enthusiasm that may be the result of argumentation, inquiry, and the search for solutions to questions that students have formulated themselves. If the final test of quality is a written test, it is no surprise that teaching will be more cost-effective if students do not spend time on excursions, experimental work, or discussion of socio-scientific issues.

The use of PISA data for policy recommendations is, at best, very selective. If one believes in the free-market mission of the OECD and the meaningfulness of the PISA results, then one has to take all the results seriously, including those that are counterintuitive and at odds with other research findings and policies recommended by educational experts. PISA enthusiasts cannot selectively pick results that support their political positions while completely ignoring data that disprove their positions.

Critique from Academics

Parallel to the increasing global influence of PISA on educational debate and policy, there has been a growing critique of the PISA project in the academic world. Several anthologies have raised serious questions about the meaningfulness of the results (Hopmann, Brinek, & Retzl, 2007; Meyer & Benavot, 2013; Pereyra, Kotthoff, & Cowen, 2011). The authors raising important questions represent a cross-section of thinkers and researchers who come from many countries and academic fields, and include well-known philosophers, sociologists, economists, and educators.

In May 2014, a group of these and other academics sent an open letter to Andreas Schleicher, head of PISA and Director for Education and Skills at the OECD. In the letter (Meyer & Zahedi, 2014), they voiced a series of concerns about the growing influence of PISA. They argued that PISA is killing the joy of learning and is detrimental to basic values for which schools should strive. This initiative received public attention through coverage in *The Guardian* and other news media worldwide. The open letter has been signed by more than 2,000 academics from about 40 countries. Behind the initiative are leading educators such as Stephen Ball, David Berliner, and Robin Alexander. Noam Chomsky is also behind this initiative; likewise Diane Ravitch, who was previously U.S. Assistant Secretary of Education. Ravitch is now, as a distinguished professor of history and philosophy of education, the most influential critic of market-driven education policies. She is author of several influential books, including *The Death and Life of the Great American School System* (Ravitch, 2011) with the telling subtitle *How Testing and Choice Are Undermining Education.*

It seems fair to say that criticism of the uses and misuses of PISA is now common among most academics concerned about schooling and education. Because PISA has been extending its scope and influence during the past few years, this critique has been fueled. Further analysis of this development lies outside the scope of this chapter, but here are some aspects of the development.

PISA has recently established a close cooperation with Pearson, the owner of the *Financial Times, The Economist,* Allyn & Bacon, and Prentice Hall. Pearson has expanded its activities into the education sector and has become the world's largest company for testing and education programs, with 40,000 employees in more than 80 countries. Approximately 80% of Pearson's revenues now come from what Pearson terms the "education sector." Pearson won the bid for important parts of the PISA 2015 testing and has developed strong links with the OECD. Pearson has, of course, a vested interest in creating a market for its services and products. Through its close partnership with the OECD, it created a strong position to expand its market share as well as its global influence. Ravitch (2012) expressed her concern about this influence: "Are we prepared to hand over our children, our teachers, and our definition of knowledge to Pearson?"

Pearson has an even stronger grip over PISA 2018. The company won the bid for key elements of the entire undertaking. A joint press release (Pearson, 2014) from OECD and Pearson proudly announced:

> Pearson, the world's leading learning company, today announces that it has won a competitive tender by the Organisation for Economic Co-operation and Development (OECD) to develop the Frameworks for PISA 2018. . . . The frameworks define what will be measured in PISA 2018, how this will be reported and which approach will be chosen for the development of tests and questionnaires.

This key role in PISA does not, of course, mean that Pearson's staff will do the work. But they will organize and administer the process. Pearson will continue to forge personal links with countless academics in key positions and the countless representatives for national educational authorities. This contract is a most valuable investment for Pearson. The cooperation is already in place for several by-products, such as a video series about "Strong Performers and Successful Reformers in Education" (www.oecd.org/pisa/pisaproducts).

Andreas Schleicher is also on Pearson's Advisory Board. He is, among several roles, also heavily involved in the initiative called *The Learning Curve*, where the main "product" is a ranking of the quality of educational systems based on several data sources (e.g., PISA, TIMSS, PIRLS). This ranking list gets a lot of attention from the media as well as from politicians, who often panic when their country is lower than they expect or when they move down on the rankings.

PISA itself is also widening its repertoire. One new product, the PISA-based Test for Schools, is a complementary test used to assess local-level performance. The results of this local test are reported individually to the school or district, in contrast to the aggregate scores reported on the international PISA test. Individual schools or school districts may get "information and analyses . . . comparable to main PISA scales" (www.oecd.org/pisa/aboutpisa/pisa-basedtestforschools.htm). This, of course, may create an enormous market and also bring competition, testing, and rankings even closer to the daily activities in schools. The PISA influence on local education policy will also be stronger.

With its PISA for Development test product, the OECD is widening its influence over education in developing countries. Such a test will provide standardized definitions of worthwhile skills and knowledge that are measurable and common for developing countries, independent of their culture, economic contexts, traditions, natural resources, and local challenges. Such scores will be seen as "benchmarks" and objective measures of quality by both donors and national authorities. The OECD may thereby push aside the influence of

United Nations organizations like UNESCO and UNICEF, which may have different priorities than those of the OECD. PISA for Development has created close links with these organizations as well as with the World Bank.

While PISA has 15-year-olds as it target population, an emerging OECD project—Programme for the International Assessment of Adult Competencies (PIAAC)—has been labeled PISA for Adults. Results from the first full-scale data collection in 24 countries were published in 2013 (OECD, 2013b), and the program is likely to increase its importance for the higher education and training sector as well (www.oecd.org/site/piaac).

Conclusions

This chapter focused on the problematic sides of PISA, but the positive virtues of PISA should not be ignored. The PISA project has led to an increased interest in and concern for education and the competencies that young people need to develop to achieve the different "literacies" that are needed for their future lives as well as for the well-being of their societies. The data bank generated by successive rounds of PISA is tremendous, and is likely the largest and most professional data source in the history of social science and educational research. These data are also well documented and available for research purposes.

International comparisons in education are important: They can introduce new perspectives, and they can provide inspiration and ideas for educators, researchers, and policymakers. However, international comparisons have a kind of Janus face: They can be understood and used in two opposite ways. Such studies may acknowledge and give cause to celebrate the great variety among youth, nations, and cultures on aspects of education and, as such, serve as a source of inspiration. But they can also be used normatively, creating pressure to oblige and fit to allegedly universal and common standards set by the authority of external specialists.

What we are seeing is a prime example of New Public Management (Møller & Skedsmo, 2013) as well as a kind of global governance and standardization of education (Ball, 2012; Rinne, 2008). As indicated earlier, academics from several disciplines have raised concerns about various aspects of the PISA undertaking and about the OECD acting like a global ministry of education. The open letter to the OECD is also a sign of a growing concern about how PISA is used to overrule national and local priorities in education.

The official intentions of PISA, as cited earlier in this chapter, can easily be endorsed. No one can disagree with the need to ascertain whether young people are developing the knowledge, skills, and competencies needed to face the challenges as citizens of the future. But the underlying economic and political ambitions behind the OECD-driven PISA project are often ignored or undercommunicated. Even researchers in the PISA project seem not to realize (or accept) the overall political/economic aspects of the project.

The inherent difficulties in evaluating what PISA claims to measure are seldom fully understood or considered. The road from ambitious intentions to the actual test instruments and valid data to policy proposals is long and murky. This chapter has pointed to some of the problematic issues in the process. In this chapter and elsewhere, I stated that it is not just problematic to live up to the intentions laid down in the overall statements of PISA; it is, in fact, "mission impossible" (Sjøberg, 2007).

The public, media, and policymakers, however, often take the PISA numbers and rankings as given facts. They trust that the PISA experts know what they are doing and that the numbers are objective, reliable, valid, and neutral measures of education quality. They trust that PISA scores measure the stated intentions.

No test is better than the items of which it consists. The secrecy over most PISA items that appear on tests makes critique and scrutiny from the academic community, and even the public, difficult. Many of the publicly published PISA item samples have faced serious critique for issues related to content, language, and relevance. Translations into the many different languages have only begun to be examined, but it is easy to find flaws and even substantive changes and mistranslations. More research is needed there. The problematic use of statistics and the lack of transparency must also be examined.

Similarly, there seems to be little attention to the fact that many of the results of PISA are at odds with what educators recommend, and with what politicians propose as interventions to improve the quality of schools. Many politicians want to copy the PISA winners, but they don't fully understand the consequences; in order to copy the winners, policymakers often prescribe measures that are the opposite of what these winners actually do. There is a need to seriously address these paradoxical results. If one really believes in PISA, one also has to accept and address the contradictions.

PISA has a profound influence on educational policy in many countries, and this is indeed the intention behind the project. It is, however, obvious that PISA results are used selectively, misused, and even distorted for political purposes in many countries. The reference to PISA to justify and legitimize educational reforms is widespread. This influence ought to be better researched and scrutinized. PISA is, in essence, part of a free-market political project—a perspective that often falls outside the agenda of the educational research community. The recent expansion of PISA into schools and school districts, adult education, and education in developing countries needs to be followed with great concern; likewise the close connection between OECD and global, commercial actors like Pearson.

Extensive resources are used to run the PISA project and to produce reports and publications, but critical research is scarce and not well funded. A key aspect of the academic ethos is to provide a critical voice, and to question and challenge conventional wisdom. Given the great political and educational importance of PISA, there is a strong need for critical and independent research.

So What? Implications for School Policy and Leadership

For educators and school leaders, in particular, it is of paramount importance to understand the forces acting on the educational scene—globally, nationally, and locally. With PISA as an instrument, the OECD has become a key actor in education at all these levels. The OECD's perspective is mainly reflected by the E in its acronym: Economic. The preparation of human resources to be active participants in the global economy is the organization's prime concern, and this is also how it presents its results. Worldwide, governments look to PISA results and rankings as objective indicators and predictors of a country's future competitiveness on the global scene. In this chapter, I have cast doubt on the soundness of such "common sense" interpretations of PISA data. I also have pointed to serious concerns about other aspects of the PISA test. School leaders should be aware of these serious problems and the pitfalls of putting too much weight on PISA results.

The OECD boasts that PISA results have triggered educational policy reforms in nearly all participating countries (Breakspear, 2012). According to this analysis, the U.S. ranking on PISA has not yet triggered reforms. This is likely because of the decentralized structure of power in U.S. schools. However, as U.S. education policy becomes increasingly standardized and centralized, the influence of PISA will probably increase. Rutkowski (2014) considered this issue and asserted that the development of PISA may strongly increase the normative influence of PISA/OECD on U.S. schools. When local schools are able to compare themselves with international PISA winners such as Shanghai or Finland, one may expect a race to climb on this indicator.

Rutkowski, Rutkowski, and Plucker (2014/2015) addressed whether individual U.S. schools should participate in a PISA-like test. The authors provided detailed arguments against such participation, based on technical perspectives of the test as well as educational arguments. A key argument is that the PISA tests explicitly state that they do not address school curricula or school knowledge. As instruments to monitor how schools live up to the mandates from national or local authorities, PISA should by definition be ruled out. Schools are bound by state-mandated curricula in the United States. I do not claim to know every detail of the inner workings of the U.S. education system, but I endorse the conclusion that the PISA-based Test for Schools program will serve no good purposes in U.S. schools or schools in other countries. The economic argument for not administering this test might also be added, although the main arguments are educational.

Not only in the United States, but also worldwide, schools and the education arena in general have become open markets for corporations to snag large contracts and large profits. In recent years, the testing industry has expanded and become global. Large sums of public money float into the pockets of these companies. Competition, privatization, and market-orientation are threatening the values that used to be the cornerstone of public education in many countries. School leaders and principals should take a stance in this battle over priorities and should not become passive recipients of new ideas disguised as a means to increase quality and efficiency.

What about participating in the PISA test itself? This international version of the test is administered in only a sample of schools, to only some students in each school. Whole classes do not participate—only a certain number (about 30) from the whole school, all at the age of 15. This, of course, adds to the logistical complexity for the schools taking part. The participating schools and students do not get anything of educational value in return. The test is anonymous for the students as well as for the schools. The test booklets are meticulously collected and removed when completed. Test items are treated as secret. There is no possibility of discussing the items for the purpose of learning from them. No results are given back to schools.

In some countries, schools have refused to take part in PISA, a decision usually made by the principal. This may also be an option for U.S. principals and school leaders.

Note

This chapter is based in part on "PISA and global educational governance: A critique of the project, its uses and implications" by Svein Sjøberg. *Eurasia Journal of Mathematics, Science & Technology Education, 11*(1), 111–127. Copyright © 2015 by International Society of Educational Research. Used by permission of the publisher.

References

Alexander, R. (2012). Moral panic, miracle cures and educational policy: What can we really learn from international comparison? *Scottish Educational Review, 44*(1), 4–21.

Alliance for Excellent Education. (2007). Losing our edge: Are American students unprepared for the global economy? PISA 2006 Release Conference, Washington, DC. Retrieved from www.all4ed.org/events/losingedge

Arffman, I. (2007). *The problem of equivalence in translating texts in international reading literacy studies: A text analytic study of three English and Finnish texts used in the PISA 2000 reading test* (Research Reports 21). Jyväskylä, Finland: University of Jyväskylä, Finnish Institute for Educational Research.

Arffman, I. (2010). Equivalence of translations in international reading literacy studies. *Scandinavian Journal of Educational Research, 54*(1), 37–59.

Ball, S. J. (2012). *Global Education Inc.: New policy networks and the neo-liberal imaginary.* Abingdon, Oxon, UK: Routledge.

Becker, F. S. (2008, November). *What companies need and how they can cooperate with universities to get it.* Presentation at Official Bologna Seminar, Luxembourg.

Bergesen, H. O. (2006). *Kampen om kunnskapsskolen* [The fight for a knowledge-based school]. Oslo, Norway: Universitetsforlaget.

Breakspear, S. (2012). *The policy impact of PISA: An exploration of the normative effects of international benchmarking in school system performance* (OECD Education Working Papers, No. 71). Paris, France: OECD Publications. doi:10.1787/5k9fdfqffr28-en

Bybee, R., & McCrae, B. (2011). Scientific literacy and student attitudes: Perspectives from PISA 2006 science. *International Journal of Science Education, 33*(1), 7–26.

Campbell, M. (2013). West vs Asia education rankings are misleading. *New Scientist,* 22–23.

DAMVAD Group. (2013). *Integrating global talent in Norway: Survey report.* Oslo, Norway: Author.

European Commission. (2007). *Science education now: A renewed pedagogy for the future of Europe* (Rocard report). Brussels, Belgium: Author.

Grek, S. (2009). Governing by numbers: The PISA "effect" in Europe. *Journal of Education Policy, 24*(1), 23–37.

Grisay A., de Jong, J. H., Gebhardt, E., Berezner, A., & Halleux-Monseur, B. (2007). Translation equivalence across PISA countries. *Journal of Applied Measurement, 8*(3), 249–266.

Hopmann, S. T., Brinek, G., & Retzl, M. (Eds.). (2007). *PISA zufolge PISA [PISA according to PISA].* Berlin, Germany: LIT Verlag.

International Journal of Science Education. (2011). Special issue: Visual and spatial modes in science learning. Author: *33*(3).

Jenkins, E. W. (2009). Reforming school science education: A commentary on selected reports and policy documents. *Studies in Science Education, 45*(1), 65–92.

Kjærnsli, M., & Lie, S. (2011). Students' preference for science careers: International comparisons based on PISA 2006. *International Journal of Science Education, 33*(1), 121–144.

Kjærnsli, M., Lie, S., Olsen, R. V., & Roe, A. (2007). *Tid for tunge løft. Norske elevers kompetanse i naturfag, lesing og matematikk i PISA 2006* [Time for heavy lifting: Norwegian students' competence in science, reading, and mathematics in PISA 2006]. Oslo, Norway: Universitetsforlaget.

Kreiner, S., & Christensen, K. B. (2014). Analyses of model fit and robustness: A new look at the PISA scaling model underlying ranking of countries according to reading literacy. *Psychometrika, 79*(2), 210–231.

Lawn, M., & Grek, S. (2012). *Europeanizing education: Governing a new policy space.* Providence, RI: Symposium Books.

Loveless, T. (2009). *How well are American students learning?* [The 2008 Brown Center report on American education] (Vol. II, No. 3). Washington, DC: Brookings Institution.

Lundgren, U. P. (2011). PISA as a political instrument: One history behind the formulating of the PISA programme. In M. A. Pereyra, H.-G. Kotthoff, & R. Cowen (Eds.), *PISA under examination: Changing knowledge, changing tests, and changing schools* (pp. 17–30). Rotterdam, The Netherlands: Sense Publishers.

Maslen, G. (2013, November 29). Andreas Schleicher and the PISA phenomenon. *The Sydney Morning Herald.*

Meyer, H.-D., & Benavot, A. (Eds.). (2013). *PISA, power and policy: The emergence of global educational governance.* Oxford, England: Symposium Books.

Meyer, H.-D., Zahedi, K., et al. (2014). Open letter to Andreas Schleicher, OECD, Paris [Blog post]. Retrieved from https://oecdpisaletter.wordpress.com

Møller, J., & Skedsmo, G. (2013). Modernising education: New public management reform in the Norwegian education system. *Journal of Educational Administration and History, 45*(4), 336–353.

Organisation for Economic Co-operation and Development. (1999). *Measuring student knowledge and skills: A new framework for assessment.* Paris, France: OECD Publications.

Organisation for Economic Co-operation and Development. (2001). *Knowedge and skills for life: First results from PISA 2000.* Paris, France: OECD Publications.

Organisation for Economic Co-operation and Development. (2006a). *Assessing scientific, reading and mathematical literacy: A framework for PISA 2006.* Paris, France: OECD Publications.

Organisation for Economic Co-operation and Development. (2006b). *Evolution of student interest in science and technology studies* (Policy report from the Global Science Forum). Paris, France: OECD Publications.

Organisation for Economic Co-operation and Development. (2007). *PISA 2006: Science competencies for tomorrow's world* (Vol. 1: Analysis). Paris, France: OECD Publications.

Organisation for Economic Co-operation and Development. (2008). *OECD economic surveys: Norway 2008.* Paris, France: OECD Publications.

Organisation for Economic Co-operation and Development. (2009a). *PISA 2006 technical report.* Paris, France: OECD Publications. Retrieved from www.oecd.org/pisa/pisaproducts/42025182.pdf

Organisation for Economic Co-operation and Development. (2009b). Take the test: Sample questions from OECD's PISA assessments. Paris, France: OECD Publications. Retrieved from http://dx.doi.org/10.1787/9789264050815-en

Organisation for Economic Co-operation and Development. (2010a). *PISA 2009 results: What makes a school successful? Resources, policies and practices* (Vol. IV). Paris, France: OECD Publications.

Organisation for Economic Co-operation and Development. (2010b). *PISA computer-based assessment of student skills in science.* Paris, France: OECD Publications.

Organisation for Economic Co-operation and Development. (2013a). *PISA 2012 assessment and analytical framework: Mathematics, reading, science, problem solving and financial literacy.* Paris, France: OECD Publications.

Organisation for Economic Co-operation and Development. (2013b). *OECD skills outlook 2013: First results from the survey of adult skills.* Paris, France: OECD Publications.

Organisation for Economic Co-operation and Development. (2014). *PISA 2012 results in focus: What 15-year-olds know and what they can do with what they know.* Paris, France: OECD Publications.

Osborne, J., & Dillon, J. (Eds.). (2008). *Science education in Europe: Critical reflections* (A report to the Nuffield Foundation). London, England: King's College.

Pearson. (2014). Pearson to develop PISA 2018 student assessment 21st century frameworks for OECD [Press release]. Retrieved from www.prweb.com/releases/2014/12/prweb12386913.htm

Pereyra, M. A., Kotthoff, H.-G., & Cowen, R. (Eds.). (2011). *PISA under examination: Changing knowledge, changing tests, and changing schools.* Rotterdam, The Netherlands: Sense Publishers.

Popkewitz, T. (2011). PISA: Numbers, standardizing conduct, and the alchemy of school subjects. In M. A. Pereyra, H.-G. Kotthoff, & R. Cowen (Eds.), *PISA under examination: Changing knowledge, changing tests, and changing schools* (pp. 31–46). Rotterdam, The Netherlands: Sense Publishers

Ravitch, D. (2011). *The death and life of the great American school system: How testing and choice are undermining education.* New York, NY: Basic Books.

Ravitch, D. (2012, May 7). Pearson's expanding role in education. *The Washington Post.*

Rinne, R. (2008). The growing supranational impacts of the OECD and the EU on national educational policies, and the case of Finland. *Policy Futures in Education, 6*(6), 665–680.

Rutkowski, D. (2014). The OECD and the local: PISA-based test for schools in the USA [Online]. *Discourse: Studies in the Cultural Politics of Education.* doi:10.1080/01596306 .2014.943157

Rutkowski, D., Rutkowski, L., & Plucker, J. A. (2014/2015). Should individual U.S. schools participate in PISA? *Phi Delta Kappan, 96*(4), 68–73.

Sjøberg, S. (2007). PISA and "real life challenges": Mission impossible? In S. T. Hopmann, G. Brinek, & M. Retzl (Eds.), *PISA zufolge PISA [PISA according to PISA]* (pp. 203–224). Berlin, Germany: LIT Verlag.

Sjøberg, S. (2015). PISA and global educational governance: A critique of the project, its uses and implications. *Eurasia Journal of Mathematics, Science & Technology Education, 11*(1), 111–127. doi:10.12973/eurasia.2015.1310a

Steffen B., & Hößle, C. (2014). Decision-making competence in biology education: Implementation into German curricula in relation to international approaches. *Eurasia Journal of Mathematics, Science & Technology Education, 10*(4), 343–355.

Tienken, C. H. (2008). Rankings of international achievement test performance and economic strength: Correlation or conjecture? *International Journal of Education Policy and Leadership, 3*(4), 1–15.

6

HIGH SCHOOL MATHEMATICS IN TEXAS: FREEDOM AND SHACKLES

Michael Marder

UNIVERSITY OF TEXAS AT AUSTIN

In the spring of 2013, the Texas legislature passed House Bill 5 (HB5), and former Governor Rick Perry had signed it into law by that summer. The bill eliminated 10 of the 15 high-stakes, end-of-course standardized tests that previously had been required for high school graduation. It also introduced major changes into high school curriculum sequences required for graduation. The previous *Recommended* High School Graduation Plan was called the "4 by 4": four years each of science, mathematics, language arts, and social studies. In the new plans, the number of required courses in each subject area was reduced, particularly for mathematics and science. Chemistry and Physics were no longer mandatory parts of the science requirement, and Algebra II was no longer a mandatory part of the mathematics requirement.

The spirit of HB5 was to allow students more freedom to define their own path through high school. The minimum levels of mathematics required in the bill were Algebra I, Geometry, and an additional advanced mathematics course that could be selected by the student. The required science was Biology and two other science courses that had to include the option of Integrated Physics and Chemistry. Although students could graduate high school with what was termed the *Foundation* Plan, high school students were expected by default to construct personalized graduation plans called *endorsements*, which included sequences of courses corresponding to their interests.

The *STEM* endorsement would allow students to select a variety of courses that could include Algebra II, Chemistry, and Physics, but also could let them specialize instead in Computer Science. The only endorsement school districts were required to offer was the *Multidisciplinary Studies* endorsement, and the requirements could be satisfied with a grab bag of courses the district was able to offer. Students also could choose the *Distinguished Level of Achievement*

Graduation Plan, the only plan that continued to make students eligible for automatic admission to Texas colleges if they were in the top 10% of their graduating class. The *Distinguished* Plan required Algebra II, Chemistry, and Physics, whereas the other plans did not.

The State Board of Education had to oversee implementation of the bill in cooperation with the Texas Education Agency. Whether to require Algebra II of most students was one of the chief points of contention considered by the Board. The question was debated at length, and eventually a compromise plan was devised where students had to choose math courses from state-approved lists in such a way that almost all of them would take Algebra II or a more difficult mathematics course.

Critical Issue

Although the debates in Texas over Algebra II, Physics, and Chemistry directly affect only Texas students, the national curricular issues they are raising are more general:

- What should be the minimal curricular requirements of a state education system to ensure that students are college- and career-ready?
- What should be the requirements for students interested in a career, but not in college?
- How much mathematics should students have to take to graduate high school?

Most public school education personnel find themselves knee-deep in implementing Common Core State Standards (CCSS) and Next Generation Science Standards (NGSS). Although Texas is not a Common Core state, the arguments that arose around curricular issues in that state need to be explored because similar debates are taking place all over the country. The issue of what math and science courses should be required to prepare students for the future is of national importance.

Cases Against Algebra II

Algebra II was a contentious topic in the changing standards for high school graduation in Texas. That course was singled out in HB5, which clearly indicated that it could not be required of all students. The nuts and bolts of actually implementing the bill with its various pathways and requirements were the subject of intense debate that lasted for months and involved several public hearings.

Other STEM subjects also were affected by the law. Chemistry and Physics were removed from the list of generally required courses, but not much of a debate surrounded that decision. Only enough energy seemed available to argue about one thing in the STEM area, and Algebra II was it. I believe that is because Algebra II is more important than Chemistry and Physics.

The special role of Algebra in school curricula has been clear for a long time. Robert Moses (Moses & Cobb, 2002) wrote,

> I know how strange it can sound to say that math literacy—and algebra in particular—is the key to the future of disenfranchised communities, but that's what I think, and believe with all of my heart.... [A]lgebra, once solely in place as the gatekeeper for higher math and the priesthood who gained access to it, now is the gatekeeper for citizenship.
>
> *(pp. 5, 14)*

Nevertheless, in 2013, the decade-long requirement that all high school graduates in Texas have Algebra II by default was rolled back. Three basic arguments were commonly given for why it should not be required: The first was that it is a traumatic learning experience for many students; the second was that it held students back and prevented them from graduating high school; and the third was that it is not really necessary for careers at all. I examine each of these arguments in turn.

Algebra II as a Traumatic Learning Experience

The argument about the traumatic effects of Algebra II on students was beautifully explained by Baker (2013) just as the debate in Texas was playing out. I also heard stories from friends and colleagues that captured the personal essence of Baker's argument. One colleague who grew up in Texas described her own experiences with Algebra and allowed me to share them:

> My high school was tiny.... For the sake of full disclosure, there were some students who thought the Algebra teacher was simply wonderful. These were the students who went to college and often majored in mathematics or engineering. She worked well with them and had animated conversations with them, and they were all in the math club with her as the faculty sponsor.
>
> Then there were the rest of us. My entire experience in Algebra II was complete bewilderment. The teacher read the instructions in the book and put problems on the board. She liked very much to send students to the board who did not know how to do the problems. She knew it and all the students knew it. The students she sent most frequently were the ones who excelled in other subjects, particularly English and foreign languages. The student would stand there, not writing anything, until the teacher would sigh loudly and send one of the younger students

who could do the problem without help (the mathematically apt eighth graders were allowed to take Algebra I with the ninth graders). Ask a question and frequently the teacher would have the younger students help the older ones. That was class, maybe some worksheets. I have no memory of actual instruction.

Every time I looked at a problem, I genuinely had no idea what I was supposed to do to get somewhere with it, to even attempt a solution. I didn't know what the solution itself might even look like. The vocabulary made no sense. None of the ideas related to each other; none of the skills built on anything I'd ever seen before. I felt like I was slipping and sliding the whole time, no traction, no purchase on ideas or understanding that might help me figure out where I was supposed to go. There were no principles or large, organizing ideas that I could use to figure out a solution. I never knew what I was doing or why. Solutions, once presented, seemed random and disconnected or overly complicated for no discernible reason. I had no recourse. There was only the one teacher. The school didn't have the resources to offer extra help. My family didn't have the money to hire a tutor even if one had been available. I felt trapped and frequently desperate. I had to have this course, this one course to graduate from high school.

I managed to get out and earn several degrees, get nice jobs, earn a decent living working with students. I write and publish. All without Algebra II.

Just as some students in my colleague's classes found the course traumatic to take, some teachers found it traumatic to teach. One teacher explained to the State Board of Education why Algebra II should not be required:

As a certified math teacher, naval nuclear veteran, former commercial senior nuclear reactor operator, Republican for 35 years, and concerned native Texan, I urge you to use your influence to prevent making Algebra II mandatory for graduation. I teach Algebra II and Algebra I in high school this year (I taught Algebra I and eighth grade regular math the last two years), and I want you to know that Algebra II is a tough course that is not meant for students who do not have the strong desire to learn the multistep complex math processes required to succeed. Many groups try to make this an ethnic issue claiming that the course will somehow magically prepare anyone who passes for college and certain careers—not so! Teachers can't apply the necessary rigor needed by the potential engineers, computer programmers, actuaries, physicists, and chemists because of the students who do not have the drive to succeed. Forcing the course on those who do not want it creates difficulty for us who labor on the educational front line because those students typically fail or marginally pass causing them to chronically express their disdain for math verbally and through their overt behavior. I don't want electricians, military electronics technicians, nuclear operators, etc., who are so-so in math.... I teach many marginal math students in Algebra II, and they declare openly their intent to shut down mentally when they must calculate an inverse matrix or factor a quadratic equation because they *don't want* to master that many steps. Please bring common sense to this issue.

These examples of teachers' arguments against mandating Algebra II for all students are powerful and representative of those that swayed the legislature. It is difficult not to feel sympathy for students who hated Algebra II as much as my colleague. Everyone deserves a course taught well enough not to produce such a negative experience. However Algebra II is too important simply to drop because of cases in which it is not well taught.

Graduation Rates as an Algebra II Problem

In my opinion, the most worrisome charge against Algebra II as a mandated requirement for high school graduation was that it stopped many students in their math tracks, so to speak, and kept them from graduating high school. Here is an expression of this view from a school official who represented concerns shared by administrators in many small schools and districts:

I am a superintendent of a 3-A school with 2,000 [students], and we have over 70% living below the poverty rate.... Our school is the center of our community, and our students' high school education is vital to our city and county's progress. We sit on the edge of the Eagleford Shale; thus, there are countless high-paying jobs just 30 minutes south of us if our students have adequate career-technology skills. It is our school's responsibility to help our students plan for a graduation endorsement that will give them a good future and a career.

During the 2013 legislative session, parents and taxpayers made their wishes known regarding EOCs [end-of-course exams] and flexibility in graduation plans. Thus, I believe that the true intent of HB5 and the desire of parents of the great state of Texas is not being served by "adding back" Algebra II as a requirement for *all* five of the endorsements for graduation. I agree with the Texas PTA that has developed a petition to "Keep House Bill 5 Alive" by showing their support for Algebra I only as an end-of-course exam, a required math course for *all* five graduation endorsements.... I urge you to refrain from adding Algebra II as a required math for all five graduation endorsements as this will limit the flexibility intended in HB5.

Was there evidence that Algebra II was in fact stopping students from graduating? If so, graduation rates might have been expected to drop after Algebra II became required across the state. The requirement of Algebra II was relatively recent. For students who entered ninth grade in 2004–2005 (the class of 2008), Algebra II became required to graduate by default; and for students who entered in 2007–2008 (the class of 2011), the total number of mathematics and science courses in the default graduation plan increased as well (Texas Education Agency, 2014e).

As shown in Figure 6.1, the four-year graduation rate in Texas did in fact fall between 2005 and 2007, but this was just before Algebra II became required by default; after that, graduation rates rose every year. Official high school graduation rates in Texas are, in fact, remarkably strong compared to those of other states. For the class of 2012, the U.S. Department of Education (2014), employing reporting standards promoted by the National Governors Association Center for Best Practices (NGA, 2008), listed Texas graduation rates as:

- No. 2 overall at 88%, tied with Nebraska, Vermont, and Wisconsin and 1 point behind Iowa;
- No. 2 for Asians at 94%;
- No. 1 among low-income students at 85%, tied with Indiana;
- No. 1 among White students at 93%, tied with New Jersey;

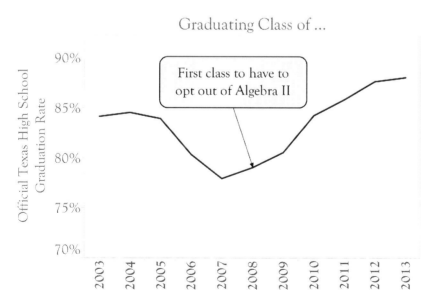

FIGURE 6.1 Texas Four-Year Graduation Rate, as Officially Reported by the Texas Education Agency (2014d)

- No. 1 among Hispanics at 84%, 4 points above the next state; and
- No. 1 among African Americans at 84%, 5 points above the next state.

For those surprised by these numbers, I must acknowledge that Texas graduation rates have been the subject of controversy in policymaking arenas and in the court of public opinion (see Figure 6.2). For example, the president of the Texas Association of Business responded to an official four-year graduation rate of 88% reported for 2013 by writing,

> This is so far removed from reality it is Orwellian in nature. If you look at the raw data—ninth graders and then those who walk across the stage four years later—the graduation rate is closer to 72, 73 percent.
>
> (B. Hammond as quoted in Smith, 2014)

It is true that the ratio of ninth to 12th graders is much smaller than the four year graduation rate, but there is an explanation. The data in Figure 6.2 show the ratio of students in each grade to graduates for Grades 6–12 over the period 2005–2012. The ratio is nearly constant through middle school. Then it drops precipitously in ninth grade, before jumping back up by the same amount in

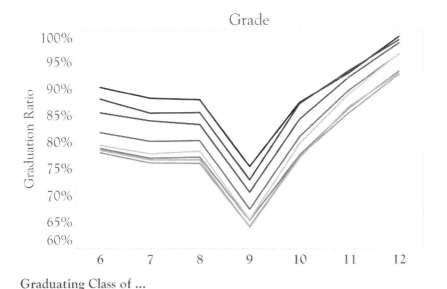

FIGURE 6.2 Ratio of Students in Each Grade to the Number of Students Eventually Graduating With Their Cohort

The ratio of eighth graders to graduates is close to the official graduation rates.

10th grade. The reason is that about 10% of Texas high school students are made to repeat ninth grade in order to pass required exams. Without defending the practice of retention, the figure makes clear that using the number of students in ninth grade in a simple formula for graduation rates is misleading. If one wants to use a simple ratio as a check on the more complicated procedures employed by the Texas Education Agency (2014a), enrollment in middle school is a better indicator.

Heilig and Darling-Hammond (2008) also criticized Texas graduation rate figures, based on a different argument. They presented a detailed case study describing how a large Texas district gamed the graduation rate system during the period 1997–2002. A feature of the gaming was that few students moved from grade to grade in successive years. Students might stay in ninth grade for several years and then jump to 12th. So an additional question about the rising Texas graduation rates is whether they might be due to this sort of manipulation of student enrollment.

I examined the possibility of grade advancement gaming strategies as a cause for increased graduation rates by making use of a longitudinal data set that contained records of all student mathematics exams for Texas over the period 2003–2012. If students repeated a grade or skipped a grade, their scores showed up in the grade level assigned to them when they took the exam. State officials I questioned could not think of any reason that registration for high-stakes exams would not be an accurate measure, in all but a handful of rare cases, of attendance and grade level.

As shown in Figure 6.3, for students who entered high school over the period 2003–2009, anomalies in the pattern of grade advancement decreased. In particular, the number of low-income students who were enrolled in Grades 9, 10, and 11 in sequence increased by nearly 50% over this time period, from 80,000 to 120,000 students; and this was by far the most common enrollment pattern. The next two most common enrollment patterns were "enroll in ninth grade and disappear" and "enroll in ninth and 10th and disappear." The numbers of students in these two patterns were much smaller than the numbers progressing normally, and they dropped as time went on.

Thus, so far as I can tell, the graduation rates reported by the Texas Education Agency (2014b, 2014c, 2014d) have been consistent with simple estimates produced by the ratio of eighth graders to graduates since 2008; and if the graduation results have been produced to some extent by gaming the system, the problem has been diminishing rather than getting worse. In turn, the argument that requiring Algebra II by default from 2004–2005 onward damaged graduation rates is weak. Graduation rates might have been even higher if Algebra II had not been required, but the increase in graduation rates has been so large, and the comparison with the rest of the nation is so favorable, that it is difficult to believe that Algebra II constituted a major barrier to high school graduation in Texas.

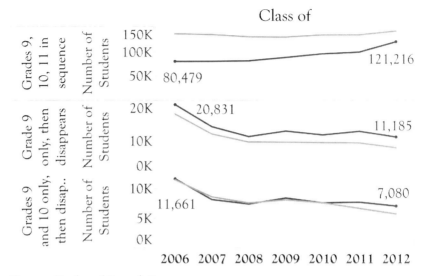

Class of

Free or Reduced Lunch Status
▩ Not Eligible   ■ Eligible

FIGURE 6.3 Numbers of Students Proceeding Through High School in a Normal Fashion, Deduced From Registration for Mathematics Exams

Numbers next to the curves indicate numbers of students eligible for free/reduced lunch. The number of low-income students advancing normally increased by 50% between 2006 and 2012. While these are the most common enrollment patterns beginning with ninth grade, there is a total of 3,211 distinct patterns students turn out to follow, although only 47 patterns with more than 1,000 students. Data from Texas Education Agency, Public Education Information Management System.

The Case That Algebra II Is Not Necessary

The argument that students do not need Algebra II relies on two primary claims. The first claim is that students will not use algebra as part of their adult work life, either frequently or occasionally. The second claim is based on questioning whether mastery of Algebra II is necessary to have a career. Few students will need Algebra II as part of their daily working life. Certainly they will need it if they work as research professors in science or engineering. They will need it in many engineering jobs. They will need portions of it for many accounting jobs. However, in truth, the fraction of jobs for which Algebra II is part of daily life is small. If one were to base the requirement of Algebra II on the realistic possibility of its direct lifelong use, one should leave it optional.

The case for Algebra II as a requirement for credentials, however, is much more significant. Here are some consequences for students who do not take and pass it:

- They are not eligible for automatic admission to Texas universities under the top 10% rule.
- It will be difficult for them to be accepted into four-year colleges and universities, all of which require mathematics at or above the level of Algebra II.
- It will be difficult for them to obtain an associate degree or even a long-term certificate at a community college.

One can hold that college is not for everyone, and that we should not try to extract engineers from populations of students who have panic attacks during mathematics exams. However, in my opinion, putting students at risk of not being able to obtain a community college certificate is more troubling, and I turn to this point next.

Community College Requirements

Texas community colleges provide three basic types of services: (a) They provide students the opportunity to earn certificates, which are collections of linked courses mainly requiring less than 42 hours leading to the acquisition of specific technical skills; (b) they let students earn associate degrees, which are two-year degrees that involve some general education requirements in addition to building specific skills; and (c) finally, Texas community colleges provide a stepping stone to four-year colleges and universities.

The significance of 42-hour degrees is that above this point students must take the Texas Success Initiative (TSI) examination; unless they obtain a satisfactory score on the mathematics portion (as well as other parts of the exam), they must then begin to take "developmental" mathematics. The descent into remedial mathematics is a substantial barrier to a large fraction of students who enter community college. Graduation rates from community college in turn are low—in the range of 3–15% (three years after beginning a two-year degree for full-time fall entrants) except at some of the smaller regional community colleges.

Austin Community College, for example, offers more than 100 certificates ranging from American Sign Language Studies to Biotechnology, Firefighter, and Ultrahigh Purity Piping. Only a few of the certificates have a mathematics requirement. Most of the certificates require fewer than 42 hours, so these students need not take the TSI examination.

The associate degrees by contrast all have a mathematics requirement. For most of them, the lowest level mathematics course allowed is College Algebra, which both covers material at a somewhat higher level than Algebra II and proceeds much faster at the community college than it does in high school. Students whose TSI scores are too low or who are not otherwise exempt end up in the developmental sequence—Basic Math Skills, Elementary Algebra,

Intermediate Algebra—before they can take the first credit-bearing courses, including College Algebra.

Algebra in the Paycheck

Because a sharp line divides certificates and degrees that do and do not require students to master algebra, it is interesting to check whether any economic consequences correlate with getting certificates of one type or the other. Texas is not unusual in its organization of community colleges, and the best evidence comes from elsewhere in the country. Jepsen, Troske, and Coomes (2014) studied certificates in Kentucky and distinguished among associate degrees, which require 60 or more credits; diplomas, which require between 36 and 68 credits; and certificates, which require less than 40 credits. A study in Washington State distinguishes similarly among long-term certificates, which take more than a year; and short-term certificates, which take less than a year (Dadgar and Trimble, 2014). The findings of the two studies are consistent.

Short-term certificates offer little to no financial benefit to their recipients after a period of five to seven years. The Washington State study found a net loss of income for the shorter certificates, while the Kentucky study found an earnings gain of about $1,000 per year. By contrast, the diplomas, long-term certificates, and associate degrees lead to much larger improvements in income. In Kentucky, women increased their annual income by around $8,000 and men by $6,000. The Washington State study similarly found that long-term certificates and associate degrees provided a benefit (seven years after beginning the community college program) of $6,000 to $8,000 per year in comparison to those who obtained a short-term certificate or no certifications. The Washington State study also concluded that long-term certificates and degrees increased their recipients' employability rather than their wages. It is not their hourly rates that went up as much as the ease with which they obtained a job at the outset.

Career Readiness and Algebra II

Thus, it is reasonable to connect the term *career readiness,* so often invoked, so rarely defined, with readiness to complete a long-term certificate or associate degree at community college. I define career readiness in mathematics at the end of high school to mean exemption from any diagnostic tests at university or community college that could lead to placement in developmental mathematics. That is because for any Texas degree requiring more than 42 hours, mastering mathematics at the level of Algebra II is nearly unavoidable. Even a 55-hour Automotive Technician Certificate requires passing TSI or completion of developmental mathematics. A comparison of Algebra II topics with the developmental mathematics topics reveals correspondence with Intermediate Algebra, the highest developmental course prior to the credit-bearing College Algebra. Thus Algebra II is the minimal level of mathematics that high school leaders owe to students if they are to be called "career ready."

After Texas required Algebra II for the class of 2008, graduation rates went up. But did a greater fraction of students leave high school career ready? Yes. Since 2005, Texas has reported the percentage of students whose high school mathematics exam scores exempted them from taking the TSI mathematics exam when they went to college. The percentage of students who met this state standard in mathematics went up greatly, particularly in schools with high concentrations of poverty. In 2005, 32% of economically disadvantaged students left high school career-ready in mathematics. In 2013, the number had reached 57% (77,741/136,989), an increase of almost 100%. From 2005 to 2013, 90% of Texas high schools improved their average score on TSI mathematics, as shown school by school in Figure 6.4.

Students who do not leave high school career-ready are not excluded from community college. For long-term certificates or degrees, they must take the TSI examination; if they do not pass it, they take developmental coursework. But the odds of passing the TSI without having passed high school Algebra II are stacked against them. Only one quarter of those students who do not leave high school having passed Algebra II go on to pass TSI mathematics. Only 18% eventually pass a first college-level mathematics class. Thus mathematics emerges as a major barrier to completion of community college degrees and certificates (Texas Higher Education Coordinating Board, 2014).

The proliferation of high-stakes exams led to a popular revolt in 2013 by some educators and parents, but one feature of those exams does not seem to have penetrated the public debate. Some of those exams gave students a ticket to start community college degrees, and the number of students getting the ticket that way had soared over time. The exam most recently designated to demonstrate that students were career-ready in mathematics was the Algebra II end-of-course exam (University of Texas at Austin, 2015). In 2013, that exam became optional because of HB5, allowing school district administrators and boards of education to decide whether or not to administer it. If they choose not to, then the ticket is no longer available for the students in that district.

Students can still show they meet state standards by scoring above 1,070 (in Reading plus Math) on the SAT or 23 on the ACT. But the percentage of low-income students who do this is small. The state reports a slightly different number: the fraction of students scoring above 1,110 (Reading plus Math) on the SAT or 24 on the ACT. No Texas high school where more than 80% of the students are eligible for free or reduced lunch has ever had more than 30% of its students reach the 1,110 threshold.

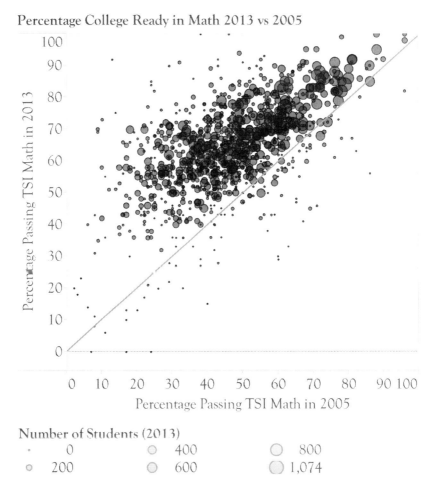

Percentage College Ready in Math 2013 vs 2005

Number of Students (2013)

| · | 0 | ○ | 400 | ○ | 800 |
| ○ | 200 | ○ | 600 | ○ | 1,074 |

FIGURE 6.4 Percentage of Students at Each High School in Texas Who Scored High Enough on a Mathematics Exam While in High School That They Were Exempt From Further Examination

The plot compares the percentage in 2013 with the percentage in 2005; if a circle lies above the straight line, the percentage went up. Data from Texas Academic Excellence Indicator System.

Another provision in HB5 attempts to compensate for the threats to readiness. Each district must offer a course in English and a course in mathematics in partnership with an institution of higher education. If 12th graders are thought to be unready for college, they are to be advised to take the classes. Passing the courses gives them corresponding credit at the partner college. But this mechanism for reaching career readiness is, for the moment, optional and the way it will work out in practice is still unknown.

This story may seem complicated, but it is not. For many years, Texas required students by default to take Algebra II and an exam that evaluated their proficiency. A passing score on the exam meant that students could move straight into credit-bearing coursework at community colleges when they chose, without remedial mathematics. The numbers of students becoming career- or college-ready in this way soared over time. Then in 2013, the course and the exam became optional. Alternative means to establish career readiness in mathematics during high school were either unlikely to succeed or untried. The attraction of the changes was that they offered increased curricular freedom. But in the name of freedom, a decade of work that tried to guarantee low-income students access to community college was undone.

Arguing for Algebra II

The questions concerning Algebra II may come down to these: (a) Is there a difference between a job and a career? and (b) should education policy regarding graduation requirements increase the probability that public high schools prepare every graduate for a career, not just a job? Some defining characteristics of a career include the possibility of advancement, of acquiring some management responsibility, or starting one's own business. The default minimal education for managers across the United States is an associate degree or above. And only long-term credentials and degrees provide substantial income increases five to seven years after graduation. Employers appear willing to pay a premium for credentials that include mathematics at a level just above Algebra II.

The U.S. higher education system has gone to great lengths to prevent students from obtaining advanced credentials without reaching this level of mathematics. Jobs that pay larger than average salaries and include leadership or management responsibilities almost always demand advanced degrees. Algebra II is in practice a requirement to have a career and not just a job. This is a judgment of the labor market, enforced by policies in higher education; and it is unlikely to change quickly or at all no matter what anyone likes or dislikes during high school. If high schools stop teaching and assessing Algebra II, the requirement does not go away; it moves to community colleges and universities, to the great disadvantage of low-income students.

One can only speculate why employers are more likely to hire people who have mastered Algebra II, given that so few jobs make use of it on a daily basis. Probably the degrees, and therefore algebra mastery, signify persistence, logical thinking, ability to solve complicated multistep problems, and willingness to perform tasks whose importance is not immediately evident. These are desirable qualities in an employee, and particularly in a manager. The British Empire selected its elite by demanding the mastery of the Classics (Orwell, 1953). Such were the joys of British high school. The United States chose mathematics.

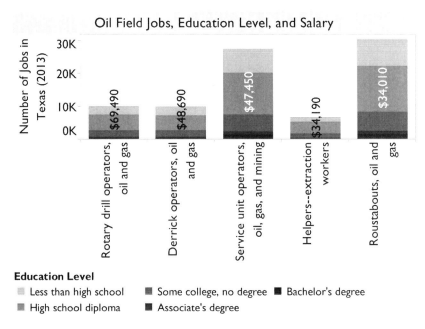

Oil Field Jobs, Education Level, and Salary

FIGURE 6.5 Oil Field and Mining Jobs in Texas

The figure show the educational level of workers holding various types of positions, and their mean annual salary. Bureau of Labor Statistics, 2013.

A few spot checks may help reinforce the importance of Algebra II in the U.S. job market. In talking about good jobs and careers that do not need mathematics, Texans sometimes mention opportunities in the oil fields. Figure 6.5 shows oil field jobs in Texas, indicating educational level and salary. The jobs pay well, but not exceptionally well, and are not very numerous; many of the employees holding these jobs have not even completed high school. These jobs should not be confused with the positions available to geoscientists and petroleum engineers, who require mathematics through calculus and command average salaries well in excess of $100,000.

Alternatively, one can check the percentage of workers in each level of educational attainment who are in management or executive positions. These data for the U.S. are shown in Figure 6.6. The odds of being in management roughly double each time students move from below high school to high school diploma, from high school diploma to associate degree, and from associate degree to master's. There is a drop in management positions for holders of doctoral and professional degrees, but that is because most of them are doctors, lawyers, and professors, and therefore have autonomy and relatively high salaries without management titles.

Finally, an overview of the entire U.S. labor market, showing numbers of jobs in every salary band for each level of education appears in Figure 6.7. In nearly

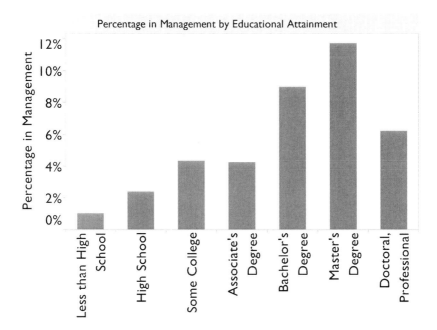

Percentage in Management by Educational Attainment

FIGURE 6.6 Percentage of Employees in Management Positions, for Various Levels of Education

Bureau of Labor Statistics, 2013.

every case, a rising level of education leads to a rising probability of higher salary. The one exception comes with master's degrees, which have a peak between $20K per year and $40K per year. This group is dominated by social workers, librarians, and school counselors.

So What?

Texas is the second-largest state, and its influence on education policy for the rest of the country recently has been even larger than its size would warrant. The Texas Miracle in education played a role in the election of George W. Bush in 2000, and this led in turn to the passage of No Child Left Behind, which imposed test-based school accountability on the entire country. The allure of improving education nationwide through computerized standardized tests with unified rules was strong enough to survive the transition from the Bush presidency to the Obama administration.

Apart from contributions of isolated scholars and research centers, Texas has played no role in the development and promotion of the Common Core State Standards (CCSS) and Next Generation Science Standards (NGSS). Indeed HB 462 of 2013 prohibits Texas school districts from adopting those standards.

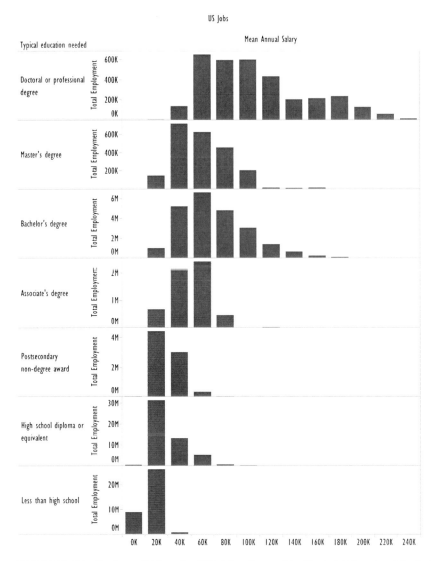

FIGURE 6.7 Distribution of Salary for U.S. Jobs Grouped by Typical Education Needed for Entry

However, the path Texas chose with HB5 could turn out to have great influence in many other states on the question of whether or not to keep the new standards and the accompanying tests. The two key ideas were that "one size does not fit all" and we must "prepare students for the workforce." The promise was that the changes in high school requirements would "improve workforce quality so that more young Texans are ready and able to step into demanding, productive and prosperous careers" (Rivero, 2013).

An interesting feature of the Texas rebellion against high-stakes testing and college-ready standards is the coalition that formed around it. The visible face of the coalition was Texans Advocating for Meaningful Student Assessment (TAMSA) which Robert Scott, just before stepping down as Commissioner of Education, nicknamed Mothers Against Drunk Testing (Michels, 2013; Weiss, 2014a, 2014b, 2014c). This group of angry mothers was bipartisan, geographically distributed, and middle-class. Supporting the same bill as the mothers was a group known as Jobs for Texas (2014), "a coalition consisting of 22 trade associations representing 300,000 businesses and 6 million jobs". The two lead organizations were the Texas Association of Manufacturers, representing 450 companies in the manufacturing sector and the Texas Chemical Council. They celebrated HB5 for providing "flexibility to ensure that students can graduate from high school well prepared to take on the challenges of a two-year or four-year college, or to seek out a professional certificate" (Bennett, 2013).

A bit further down the list are Associated Builders and Contractors of Texas, who declared,

> We finally [may] make real headway in trying to address dropout rates caused by students questioning the relevance of their high school education. We need an education system that serves 100% of the students and prepares all who are able for post-secondary education whether it be college or a career path that involves technical training. We have to develop more flexibility in the curriculum while continuing to provide accountability and rigor. ABC of Texas is a member of the Jobs for Texas coalition which is promoting these principles.
>
> *(Fisher, 2013, p. 6)*

Although the attention of the state and nation was captured by mothers protesting against testing, it is imaginable that legislators also were being swayed by businesses pursuing business interests. Changes in high-stakes testing requirements and changes in high school graduation requirements did not have to be combined into one bill; but, in fact, they were. In the case of Algebra II, both the course and the exam became optional. The potential effect on low-income students would have been less had either one remained mandatory.

A coalition of liberals and conservatives, representatives of the cities of Dallas, Austin, and Houston, manufacturers, and mothers united swept away most of the high school testing and course requirements. Yet one of the central problems the coalition claimed to address—dropout rates—did not exist. There was no crisis of dropout rates. As the bill was being debated, Texas had the highest graduation rates for low-income students in the United States. If anyone in the media or legislature acknowledged this, I found no sign of it.

HB5 removed the high school coursework and exams that made it possible for students to complete certificates and degrees at community colleges, and thus made their career paths more difficult to tread. This possibility also was never highlighted in the public debate. The narrative claiming that public schools are broken and ineffective has so completely dominated public discourse for the last several decades that it has become nearly impossible to advertise their successes. Thus it becomes increasingly easy to remove resources from the public schools and change the policies that govern them. Those who genuinely wish to improve the prospects of public school students can become unwitting allies of those who do not.

And Now What?

The debate on whether to require students to take and pass an Algebra II course could well come to your state, if only because of the Common Core State Standards (NGA & Council of Chief State School Officers, 2010). Standardized curricular tracks and accountability enforcing them have earned fierce opposition (e.g., Ravitch, 2013) and produced distasteful outcomes, such as having students take Algebra II multiple times and lose the opportunity for electives (Fensterwald, 2012). Yet removing a mandatory Algebra II course and its test results in serious consequences for the vulnerable. So, what should you do?

- Learn about the education statistics for your state and community, both good and bad. Make sure you pay attention to results disaggregated by income and race. Note whether the results describe elementary, middle, and high school, and whether they correspond to problems of struggling learners or advanced students. As proposals arise for educational reform, constantly ask whether the proposals address the points at which the educational system in your community is weak, rather than areas where it is strong. If your community is hampered by a lack of Advanced Placement (AP) calculus teachers, question the need for a response that involves firing third-grade reading teachers.
- Pay particular attention to the transition between high school and community college. Learn precisely the requirements in your state for a student or an adult to be able to obtain a long-term certificate from a community college. If you are working in a high school, learn what students must be able to do in order to gain admission to both two-year programs and four-year colleges and universities. If you are working in a college or university, learn which high school courses prepare students for the entrance examinations of your institution.
- Make sure that someone in your organization or professional association is monitoring education bills emerging in your state. Take nothing for

granted as you listen to descriptions of what the bills will do and who backs them. Make sure someone connected to you has read the bill and thought through the consequences—for you, for low-income communities, and for communities of color. Imagine that a bill advertised for the freedom it gives your child to pursue her dreams, and the freedom it gives your teachers to throw off the constraints of testing and teaching, may also shackle low-income students to a lifetime of minimum-wage work.

Policymakers

The consequences of laws passed today may not fully appear for 10 to 15 years. When examining current education statistics, policymakers and practitioners should keep in mind that current circumstances can be due to laws passed 15 years ago, implemented 12 years ago, and producing the first high school graduates now. Students will pass sequentially through elementary, middle, high school, and post-secondary education whether or not the legal framework and policy landscape provides them a coordinated path toward college and careers. If the curricular path is uncoordinated, confusing, or changes rapidly, middle-class professionals are much more likely to find the way through for their children than parents with fewer monetary resources and personal experiences with the educational system.

Canceling the high school requirement for Algebra II and the associated exam in high school, while leaving it for exams students must pass to begin credit-bearing work in community college, is an example of an uncoordinated path. School officials and teachers are in a weak position to make sure that different parts of the educational system mesh well with one another; this task is yours.

Public School Leaders

Although the connections between different levels of the educational system are not under your control, you can try to understand them and make sure that students, parents, and counselors get accurate information. Student choices about programs of study and specific courses become particularly consequential in high school. Algebra II is just one example of a course with potential long-term consequences for students who take it and for those who do not. Please consider helping the students who attend your schools and their parents to understand clearly the implications and consequences of not taking Algebra II or other courses in high school.

Journalists

When you obtain statistics, please go to primary sources maintained by your state education agency and examine unfiltered results. Learn how to interpret them, to the extent practical, by yourself. Examine reports in which data have been heavily processed by complicated models with some skepticism. Worry about whether the loudest voices and pithiest quotations on a topic best serve the public interest. Above all, be informed consumers of data and dig below the headlines of your editors.

Academic Researchers

Look up lists of hearings in advance of legislative sessions so that you can make time to attend ones that seem important. Keep abreast of bills that could change the educational system and be prepared to offer written comments or testimony in person. Put national, state, and local data into forms that the public can understand. Ask how your research area impacts public debates about education. Write about what you find. Speak at hearings as often as you speak to other academics within your silos. Get out of your office more often to see the effects of various policies on children and take action to ensure those policies serve them well now and into the future.

Freedom or Shackles

By opening the option of avoiding Algebra II, Texas policymakers raised the possibility of a devastating freedom. Students in ninth or tenth grade have the chance to evade a course that many of them may hate, that some of their teachers would just as well not teach, and whose content quite realistically most of them will never use. Yet by never training their minds to this level of mathematics, students risk closing off the possibility of advancement for themselves forever. When someday they tire of minimum-wage jobs in retail and try to obtain a certificate as an automotive technician, an algebra exam will stand in their way. College doors will be closed.

It would be difficult to devise a more effective and objective way to secure privilege for children of the middle class, who mainly jump over the mathematics barriers as a matter of course while they are young. And what a temptation this new high school education must present to certain businesses, which by working with their local school districts may be able to secure pools of low-wage labor unable to move upward, even if during or after high school they acquire the resolve to do so.

How the curricular freedom in Texas will work out remains to be seen. Some districts are requiring all students to enroll by default in a college preparatory track. There is no sign yet that many districts are racing to offer the minimum allowable under law to their students. It is possible that the experiment will work out well. Yet given severe shortages of secondary science and mathematics teachers (U.S. Department of Education, 2011), I fear schools will give in to the temptation to offer what is easy, and low-income and rural students will face receding economic opportunity.

The forces that led Texas to its current situation press on other parts of the country. Rebellion against the Common Core State Standards and Next Generation Science Standards is growing. A coalition to reduce testing and increase workforce quality can form in any state. In the name of freedom and opportunity, a strange new set of shackles made of mathematics can form to bind to low incomes those students who already have the least.

Acknowledgments

I thank Chris King for information about the labor market for community college graduates. I also thank the authors of statements opposing Algebra II for granting permission to quote them. And finally I thank Christopher Tienken for soliciting this piece, pressing me to keep writing, and spending more time editing than I would ever have expected.

References

Baker, N. (2013, September). Wrong answer: The case against Algebra II. *Harper's*, 31–38.

Bennett, T. (2013, June). Manufacturers applaud Governor Perry, Texas lawmakers for broadening educational opportunities for Texas students. Austin, TX: Texas Association of Manufacturers. Retrieved from www.manufacturetexas.org/content/manufacturers-applaud-governor-perry-texas-lawmakers-broadening-educational-opportunities-te

Bureau of Labor Statistics. (2013). *Occupational employment statistics by state.* Washington, DC: Author. Retrieved from http://1.usa.gov/1wOAMbx

Dadgar, M., & Trimble, M. J. (2014, November 6). Labor market returns to sub-baccalaureate credentials: How much does a community college degree or certificate pay? *Education Evaluation and Policy Analysis.* Retrieved from http://bit.ly/1Ep1N5d

Fensterwald, J. (2012, December 6). Many math students are flailing, repeating courses without success. *Edsource.* Retrieved from http://edsource.org/2012/many-math-students-are-flailing-repeating-courses-without-success-2/63653#.VHZAo4dSaIQ

Fisher, J. (2013, January). ABC of Texas priority issues. *Texas Merit Shop Journal,* 6–7. Retrieved from www.abctexas.org/pdf/journal_jan13.pdf

Heilig, J. V., & Darling-Hammond, L. (2008). Accountability Texas-style: The progress and learning of urban minority students in a high-stakes testing context. *Educational Evaluation & Policy Analysis, 30*(2), 75–110.

Jepsen, C., Troske, K., & Coomes, P. (2014). The labor-market returns to community college degrees, diplomas, and certificates. *Journal of Labor Economics, 32*(1), 95–121. Retrieved from www.jstor.org/stable/10.1086/673389

Jobs for Texas. (2014). Texas association of builders. Retrieved from http://jobsfortexascoalition.org

Michels, P. (2013, February 21). Testing the limits: A Texas mother's radical revolt against standardized tests. *The Texas Observer.* Retrieved from www.texasobserver.org/mother-against-standardized-testing

Moses, R. P., & Cobb, C. E., Jr. (2002). *Radical equations: Civil rights from Mississippi to the Algebra Project*. Boston, MA: Beacon Press.

National Governors Association Center for Best Practices. (2008). *Implementing graduation counts: State progress to date, 2008*. Washington, DC: Author. Retrieved from www.nga.org/cms/home/nga-center-for-best-practices/center-publications/page-edu-publications/col2-content/main-content-list/implementing-graduation-2008.html

National Governors Association Center for Best Practices & Council of Chief State School Officers. (2010). *Common Core State Standards for mathematics: Appendix A*. Washington, DC: Author. Retrieved from http://bit.ly/1Dqlr36

Orwell, G. (1953). *Such, such were the joys*. New York, NY: Harcourt Brace Jovanovich. Retrieved from http://orwell.ru/library/essays/joys/english/e_joys

Ravitch, D. (2013). *Reign of error: The hoax of the privatization movement and the danger to America's public schools*. New York, NY: Vintage Books.

Rivero, H. (2013, April 7). Not lowering academic bar but better preparing students for workforce. *Abilene Reporter-News*. Retrieved from http://bit.ly/RiveroHB5

Smith, M. (2014, August 5). Texas posts top high school graduation rates, again. *The Texas Tribune*. Retrieved from www.texastribune.org/2014/08/05/texas-posts-top-high-school-graduation-rates-again

Texas Education Agency. (2014a). *Secondary school completion and dropouts in Texas public schools 2011–12*. Austin, TX: Author. Retrieved from www.tea.state.tx.us/acctres/DropComp_2011-12.pdf

Texas Education Agency. (2014b). 2012–13 *Texas academic performance report (TAPR) data download*. Austin, TX: Author. Retrieved from http://ritter.tea.state.tx.us/perfreport/tapr/2013/download.html

Texas Education Agency. (2014c). Glossary for the Texas academic performance report for 2012–13. Austin, TX: Author. Retrieved from http://ritter.tea.state.tx.us/perfreport/tapr/2013/glossary.pdf

Texas Education Agency. (2014d). High school completion, four-year rates. Austin, TX: Author. Retrieved from www.tea.state.tx.us/acctres/dropcomp/years.html

Texas Education Agency. (2014e). State graduation requirements. Austin, TX: Author. www.tea.state.tx.us/graduation.aspx

Texas Higher Education Coordinating Board. (2014). 2014 Texas public higher education almanac: A profile of state and institutional performance and characteristics. Austin, TX: Author. Retrieved from http://bit.ly/THECB2014Almanac

U.S. Department of Education. (2011). Number and percentage of public high school-level classes of specific subjects taught by a teacher with a major and certification in that subject area, by selected subject areas: 2007–08. Retrieved from http://1.usa.gov/tXiCy0

U.S. Department of Education. (2014). Ed data express. Washington, DC: Author. Retrieved from http://eddataexpress.ed.gov/state-tables-report.cfm

University of Texas at Austin. (2015). Texas success initiative exemptions. Retrieved from http://bit.ly/1xqTgJS

Weiss, J. (2014a, March). One mom's ire becomes a cause. *The Dallas Morning News*. Retrieved from http://res.dallasnews.com/interactives/2014_March/standardized_tests/part1

Weiss, J. (2014b, March). 'The heart of the vampire.' *The Dallas Morning News*. Retrieved from http://res.dallasnews.com/interactives/2014_March/standardized_tests/part2

Weiss, J. (2014c, March). Testing system shaken to its core. *The Dallas Morning News*. Retrieved from http://res.dallasnews.com/interactives/2014_March/standardized_tests/part3

7

STANDARDIZED TEST RESULTS CAN BE PREDICTED, SO STOP USING THEM TO DRIVE EDUCATION POLICYMAKING

Christopher H. Tienken

SETON HALL UNIVERSITY

Education bureaucrats and governors from most of the 50 U.S. states volunteered students, parents, teachers, and school administrators from public schools to participate in one of two national standardized testing programs aligned to the Common Core State Standards (CCSS) (National Governors Association Center for Best Practices [NGA] & Council of Chief State School Officers [CCSSO], 2010) in mathematics and English language arts: (a) the Partnership for Assessment of Readiness for College and Careers (PARCC), or (b) the Smarter Balanced Assessment Consortium (SBAC). As of November 2014 there were 12 states plus the District of Columbia participating in the PARCC (2014) consortium and representing approximately 12 million public school and charter school students, and the SBAC (2014a) consortium included 19 member states representing approximately 19 million public school and charter school students. Education bureaucrats in non-PARCC and non-SBA states use their existing state-mandated tests of academic skills and knowledge first developed as part of the No Child Left Behind Act of 2001 (NCLB, 2003) requirements or updated versions as the main part of their states' overall education accountability data collection systems.

Clearly, data generated from these new national assessments and existing state assessments will be used in a high-stakes manner to judge student, teacher, and school administrator performance in the states granted NCLB waivers (U.S. Department of Education [USDOE], 2012). According to the USDOE (2012) website, the NCLB waiver program gives the U.S. Secretary of Education the ability to "waive statutory or regulatory requirements of the ESEA that are applicable to State Educational Agencies, local educational agencies, Indian tribes, or schools," which means that individual or small groups of state bureaucrats are allowed to redefine the accountability systems in their states to align with the test-based requirements of the NCLB waiver program. The alignment aspect of the waiver program resulted in revised education accountability policies in the states that received waivers. The new or revised policies rely on the student results from PARCC, SBAC, or existing state tests as the centerpiece of the accountability structure for students and educators.

As of August 2014, the U.S. Secretary of Education granted 42 states, territories, and the District of Columbia NCLB waivers, and two more states were under review (USDOE, 2014). State education bureaucrats must make specific policy and program promises in order to receive waivers. One such promise is to participate in a standardized testing program that provides data on teacher and school administrator effectiveness, and student achievement of the CCSS via results from state-mandated tests of language arts and mathematics in Grades 3 through 8 and one year in high school. State education bureaucrats use the results from the tests as part of the educator and student accountability portions of NCLB waiver programs to make inferences of significance about teacher effectiveness, student readiness for college and careers, and school administrator effectiveness. Some other examples of the important, or high-stakes, decisions made in some states based on the test results include, but are not limited to, student promotion to the next grade level, eligibility to graduate high school in more than 20 states, gaining and retaining teacher tenure, teacher and school administrator merit or bonus pay, and school administrator employment and career advancement.

Results from previous studies (Maylone, 2002; Tienken, Tramaglini, & Lynch, 2013; Turnamian & Tienken, 2013) demonstrated that it is possible to accurately predict the percentage of students who will score proficient or above on state standardized tests in language arts and mathematics at the district level by using community and family-level demographic variables found in the U.S. census data. If the percentages of students who score proficient or above on high-stakes state tests can be predicted statistically using only community and family-level demographic variables, then how appropriate are those results for making significant decisions about student achievement, educator effectiveness, or the overall quality of public schooling?

Previous studies such as Maylone (2002), Jones (2008), and Turnamian and Tienken (2013) that used algorithms to predict the percentages of students rated proficient or above on state tests, however, were cross-sectional, looking at only one year in time. Those previous studies do not provide insights into how predictable state test results are over time with different cohorts of students when one uses community and family U.S. census data as the independent variables. Little is known about the accuracy of family and community demographic variables to predict the percentage of students who score proficient or above on state tests over the course of multiple years in a single grade level.

I organized my research report around (a) a central purpose and argument, (b) a brief overview of the existing arguments found in the literature for and against the use of standardized test results as accountability levers in policy, (c) two main competing theories for the use or lack of use of results from standardized tests, (d) the theoretical construct for my analysis strategy, (e) methods, (f) results, and (g) implications for policy and practice.

Purpose and Argument

My purpose for this chapter was to explain how well family and community wealth and education variables predicted the percentage of students who scored proficient or above, at the school district level, on state-mandated tests of mathematics and language arts in Grade 5 over a three-year period. I present results from a longitudinal study in which I used community and family demographic variables found in the U.S. census data to predict the percentage of Grade 5 students who would score proficient or above, at the district level, on the New Jersey state assessments in mathematics and language arts during the 2010, 2011, and 2012 testing cycles.

My thinking was that if it was possible to predict the actual percentages of students who scored proficient or above on the state tests over multiple years, then the use of such testing schemes as part of public school accountability policies might not be necessary. Perhaps policymakers, education bureaucrats, school administrators, and other public school stakeholders would question the seemingly unchallenged assumption that the results provide detailed insights about educator quality and student achievement. At the very least, I think that the results from standardized tests would not be the centerpiece of policy proposals to make important decisions about children and educators.

In this chapter I argue, based on the results from my study and those of others, that the results from high-stakes state standardized tests are inappropriate for use in education accountability policies aimed at making judgments about educators' and children's productivity. The proclivity of the results to be influenced strongly by out-of-school demographic factors renders them dangerous for policymaking by bureaucrats and education leaders if the resulting policies and practices rely on the results from standardized tests as a deciding factor from which to make life-influencing decisions.

I guided the empirical exploration of this topic with an overarching question: How well do family and community-level demographic variables, found in the U.S. census data estimates from 2009, predict the percentage of students scoring proficient or above on state tests of mathematics and language arts? More specifically, I sought to determine how well such variables predicted Grade 5 results in mathematics and language arts over a three-year time span, from 2010 through 2012.

Overview of Existing Literature

Advocates' arguments for the use of standardized test results for education accountability policymaking—found in the non-peer reviewed sources such as magazines, newspapers, reports by think-tanks, publications by interest groups, and other similar literature—separate into six categories. Advocates argue that results from standardized tests (a) provide a measure of quality control for the public school education being paid for by taxpayers, (b) motivate students and teachers to do their best, (c) represent universal content, (d) foster equal education opportunities for all students (e) provide accountability for students and teachers, and (f) provide a reliable measure of individual achievement (Achieve, Inc., 2004; Amrein & Berliner, 2002; Freedman, 2004; Greene & Winters, 2004; Hanushek & Welch, 2006; Hoover Institution, 2004; Rose, 2012).

For example, the producers of advocacy literature at Achieve, Inc. proclaimed when discussing the appropriateness of high school exit exams, "*First,* it is perfectly reasonable to expect high school graduates to pass these tests" (Achieve, Inc., 2004, p. 1). Likewise, leaders of groups leaning toward neoliberalism who supported the design and now support the vending of the CCSS stated that the standardized tests that would be developed to monitor implementation of the CCSS were necessary and would provide detailed information about student college and career readiness in Grades 3 through 8 and high school (NGA & CCSSO, 2010):

> Two state-led consortia, PARCC and SBAC, are currently working to develop assessments that aim to provide meaningful feedback to ensure that students are progressing toward attaining the necessary skills to succeed in college, career, and life.

PARCC and SBAC developers published glowing endorsements as to how the results from each test will provide meaningful information about student achievement and readiness for college and careers. For example, the developers of SBAC claimed, "Scores from the new assessments represent a realistic baseline that provides a more accurate indicator for teachers, students, and parents as they work to meet the rigorous demands of college and career readiness" (SBAC, 2014b).

Similarly, the PARCC (2013) creators claimed that the results from its test will provide stakeholders with information about how well students are prepared to attend the approximately 4,400 colleges, ready to embark on one of tens of thousands of possible careers, or even ready for life: "The PARCC assessments in English Language Arts (ELA/Literacy) and Mathematics are carefully crafted to give teachers, schools, students and parents better and more useful information on how we're preparing our kids for careers and college—and life" (p. 1).

The preceding examples represent just a couple of the stunning claims made about the usefulness and fine-grained insights that the results from PARCC and SBAC will provide. The claims are even more interesting given that the tests were not completed or finished with field testing at the time the claims were made. In essence, there is no empirical evidence to support the claims being made about the efficacy of the test results to determine overall student achievement or teacher and school administrator effectiveness.

The results from the empirical literature distill into three common claims about the use of results from high-stakes tests as tools for education accountability policy:

1. improve overall student achievement and increase high school graduation rates (Stringfield & Yakimowski-Srebnick, 2005);
2. suppress overall achievement and high school graduation rates, and have negative unintended consequences, especially for minorities (Heilig & Darling-Hammond, 2008; Hursh, 2008; Lee & Wong, 2004); and
3. provide mixed, uneven, or inconsistent results about the efficacy of use to attain stated policy goals (Allensworth, 2005; Dee & Jacob, 2009; Fuller, 2014; Russell, Ramos, & Miao, 2003).

Those who provide empirical arguments against the use of standardized test results as part of national, state, or local education accountability policies claim that the exams (a) lack construct validity, (b) are not suitable to make high-stakes decisions about individual student achievement or teacher effectiveness, (c) penalize minorities, special education students, and English language learners, (d) increase dropout rates, and (e) worsen test-gaming strategies, such as test preparation and narrowing the curriculum (Amrein-Beardsley & Berliner, 2003; Au, 2011; Koretz, 2008; Messick, 1994; Nichols, Glass, & Berliner, 2012; Papay, Murnane, & Willett, 2010; Penfield, 2010).

In general, the use of any single result from a standardized test to make life-influencing decisions about a child has been viewed as unprofessional by many educators. For example, this point has been made by the authors of the *Standards for Educational and Psychological Testing* (2014): American Educational Research Association (AERA), American Psychological Association (APA), and National Council on Measurement in Education (NCME). Other professional associations that oppose the reliance on the results from one high-stakes test include American Evaluation Association, National Council for Teachers of English, National Council for Teachers of Mathematics, International Literacy Association, College and University Faculty Assembly for the National Council of Social Studies, Association for Supervision and Curriculum Development, and Alliance for Childhood.

Not all the literature on the subject of the advantages and disadvantages of using results from high-stakes standardized tests as policy tools to improve student achievement or to increase educator accountability rises to the level of empirical research (as defined by Haller & Kleine, 2001). Nonetheless, the aggregate literature has influenced education policy at the federal and state levels through legislation and programs such as Goals 2000, Education America Act, NCLB Act, Race to the Top competitive grant program, and PARCC and SBAC testing programs. Claims from standardized testing advocates at nonempirically based sources such as the Hoover Institution, American Enterprise Institute, Thomas B. Fordham Institute, and similar organizations are sometimes quoted by employees of school board associations, professional education organizations and associations, state education agencies, and members of federal education commissions.

The use of nonempirical, nonpeer-reviewed information by policymakers and members of education associations and organizations presents the potential for untested and ideological policy proposals to enter the public education arena. The CCSS represent such an example. The claims about the CCSS being internationally benchmarked, more effective than existing state curriculum standards, and more comprehensive than existing standards have received short shrift in the empirical literature. Similarly, the claims made by standardized testing proponents about the ability of the PARCC and SBAC results to meet their objectives have not been demonstrated empirically. So now a situation exists in which students and educators forced to use an untested set of curriculum standards are judged by outputs from a nonempirically vetted assessment mechanism.

Competing Theories About the Use of Test Results

Education policies and practices do not simply appear from thin air. Policymakers and practitioners consciously or subconsciously cultivate policies and practices from theories or philosophies. Generally speaking, a policy that is intended to influence the behavior of educators and students comes from a theory. For example, a common theoretical framework used for test-based accountability policies is that if a policy mandates a specific level of student achievement on a state-mandated standardized test, then teachers and students will work harder to achieve that level. There exist two basic families of theories that drive test-based policymaking: (a) Instrumental use, and (b) Self-determination. In this section, I provide an overview of each theory so the reader can better understand the underlying foundation of the current education accountability landscape as it relates to testing.

Instrumental Use "Carrots and Sticks" Policymaking

Advocates for using the results from standardized assessments as part of policy schemes to impose accountability upon public school educators and students generally extort their policy frameworks from rationalist and behaviorist theories of education. The rationalist and behaviorist theories are operationalized via policies and practices that use positive reinforcement and negative reinforcement, known idiomatically as the carrot and stick approach (Andreoni, Harbaugh, & Versterlund, 2003). Bryk and Hermanson (1993) first described the carrot and stick approach as an "instrumental use model" of policymaking (p. 453).

The linear sequence inherent with instrumental use models is that a policy body develops a set of desired education outcome measures, monitors the relationship between the measures and school processes (e.g., teacher evaluation schemes linked to test results), and then implements a series of punishments or rewards in an attempt to change behavior through distal force to maximize performance of the intended outcome measure (Baker, Oluwole, & Green, 2013). Advocates of test-based educator and student accountability policies postulate that the test results are meaningful indicators of output (Smarick, 2014). Furthermore, advocates proclaim, without empirical evidence, that the use of results from state standardized tests in overtly public ways causes students and teachers to work harder and achieve higher levels of the intended outcome because the tests create teaching and learning targets that have perceived meanings for both groups (Reed, Scull, Slicker, & Northern, 2012).

In the example of teacher evaluation policies that use high-stakes test results as part of a teacher rating system, the assumption is that teachers will teach harder and be more aligned to the expected testing outcomes because they are being judged on how well students perform on those outcomes as measured by the results of the standardized test. An underlying assumption that rests upon McGregor's (1960) Theory X is that teachers choose not to teach harder or better because they are lazy and they need authoritarian leadership to motivate them to higher levels of performance.

Another example of instrumental use policies that rely on the results from state tests as an important decision-making tool is student grade promotion programs. More than a dozen states and multiple cities, including the District of Columbia, now use the results from state standardized tests as the deciding factor regarding whether to retain a student in grade (Rose, 2012). In many cases, the decision to retain a student in a grade based on the test results is made regardless of the report card grades or other information about student academic achievement. Similar to some teacher evaluation programs in effect around the country, a Theory X (McGregor, 1960) mindset about students being lazy prevails and undergirds promotion policies, suggesting that grade retention in those cases is based on an ideological romance with a curriculum monitoring tool whose marketing prowess outweighs its limited psychometric properties.

Yet another example of an instrumental use policy includes the threats from state education bureaucrats to withhold funding as a result of poor academic performance on state-mandated standardized tests. School personnel are then compelled to work harder to avoid losing funding. A variation on this is the use of public castigation via the press and horse-race style ratings or rankings of schools, school districts, and even teachers by state education personnel to spur educators to work harder to achieve outcomes (Santos, 2012). The underlying assumption, yet again, is that school personnel do not work hard and that the threat of a negative consequence will change their behavior to align with the externally imposed teaching and learning expectations in order to preserve their jobs and protect their families from financial ruin.

Instrumental use policies implemented as part of the current education accountability reform landscape share a general presumption: High-stakes test results are important indicators of the quality of educator and student output. The commercially prepared standardized test is the centerpiece and chief monitoring tool in all accountability schemes based on instrumental use theories and the tool de jure for all states with NCLB waivers. The faith placed in the validity and reliability of the results by policymakers, bureaucrats, and some educators and members of the public underscores the significant position that test results occupy in the policymaking arena and the trust placed in their meaningfulness.

Self-Determination Policymaking

Conversely, opponents of the use of standardized test results as the core of education accountability policy derive theoretical guidance from an enlightenment model based on self-determination theory (Deci & Ryan, 2012). Creators of education accountability policies derived from an enlightenment model or self-determination theory seek to foster greater discussion, study, and reflection of education practices and student learning from the indicators of an assessment system structured from multiple measures and multiple data points (Laitsch, 2006). Results from standardized tests might be part of overall assessment or accountability policy, but their uses and interpretations are different compared to those within an instrumental use model. Informing teaching and learning in real time with meaningful and varied indicators of cognitive, social, and emotional learning is at the center of education policy derived from self-determination theory.

One example of such a system based in part on an enlightenment model used in the current standardized era of education was the Nebraska School-based, Teacher-led Assessment and Reporting System (STARS) program. Nebraska STARS represents a recent attempt to deploy, on a statewide scale, school accountability policy based at least in part on self-determination theory. The purpose of assessment within STARS was to inform learning and instruction from a student-centered perspective, but also to give required accountability feedback to state bureaucrats to fulfill requirements of the NCLB Act (2003). The system began prior to the inception of the NCLB Act and ended in 2009 after a change in state education commissioner from one more aligned to self-determination theory to one sympathetic to NCLB testing. Of course, intense pressure and the threat of sanctions by U.S. Secretary of Education Margaret Spellings also propelled the transition to a more regressive carrot and stick model.

The STARS system was compiled from locally developed, school-based criterion-referenced assessments and state-mandated norm-referenced assessments. District personnel had the choice of purchasing criterion-based assessments as part of their local system (Dappen & Isernhagen, 2005). The criterion- and norm-referenced assessments were mandated only for students in Grades 4, 8, and 11 in mathematics, English language arts, science, and social studies. Other grade-level assessment systems could be wholly district-designed.

School district officials had some flexibility in the type of norm-referenced tests administered to students. They had to choose a test from a state-provided list, but were able to make a choice based on what they thought would be best for the students in their district. Criterion-based assessments, including writing prompts, were scored locally. State education bureaucrats acted in a support role and provided assessment development and scoring training for the school district personnel. They also audited small percentages of district criterion assessments to provide quality control and feedback to educators regarding progress being made in assessment development and scoring.

Prior to the inception of high-stakes accountability brought on by the NCLB Act, the results were reported to the state; but negative policy sticks were not used against districts. Instead, results were used to drive school planning and teaching along with results from district and school-level measures. The state test results were not the deciding factor in decision-making about educator quality and student achievement. They were interpreted in concert with other indicators to help educators better triangulate data to make more informed interpretation of assessment results.

The New York Performance Assessment Consortium, a group of 50 schools, is an example of a current assessment system based on self-determination theory. The Consortium has been operating since 1997. Consortium "schools have devised a system of assessment which consists of eight components including alignment with state standards, professional development, external review, and formative and summative data" (New York Performance Assessment Consortium, 2015). Consortium educators develop assessment tasks that facilitate student demonstration of learning 21st century skills, and the results are used along with other indicators from the classroom to inform instruction, not to punish.

All the traditional 20th century skills are accounted for in the assessment system, but the Consortium also uses tasks that provide feedback about student learning in analytic thinking, problem-solving skills, and scientific methodology, especially the use of the scientific method to solve ill-structured problems, "appreciation of and performance skills in the arts, service learning and school to career skills" (New York Performance Assessment Consortium, 2015). The Consortium uses outside experts to provide a more authentic review of student learning to inform teaching. Teachers and school administrators use the results from the assessments in conjunction with other indicators, and the results are not used to punish school personnel or teachers. Instead, school personnel use the results from the varied assessment tools to inform students and teachers, and to plan future instruction and learning goals.

The landmark Eight-Year Study (Aikin, 1942) provides educators and policymakers with a classical, empirically vetted example and perhaps the most comprehensive description of an assessment system built on multiple data points and self-determination theory. Although the study began more than 80 years ago in 1933, in 30 high schools in 30 school districts across the country, the study has currency because it provides educators and policymakers with a treasure trove of examples from which to design comprehensive, mixed-methods assessment systems for informing curriculum, teaching, school program planning, assessment, and student advisement.

Developed, in part, to supplement the narrow set of college entrance requirements accepted at the time, teams of teachers, university professors, and school administrators developed more than 250 qualitative and quantitative assessments during the course of the Eight-Year Study. One of their goals was to demonstrate that local assessment systems could provide more fine-grained and descriptive information about students' readiness for college and careers than a standardized test. Education leaders in the 30 districts entered into agreements with more than 300 colleges to waive the traditional college entrance exam in favor of a student portfolio. Although there was not a one-size-fits-all curriculum across all 30 school districts, the educators from those districts were united around a curriculum and assessment paradigm. Within it, the student was construed as an active constructor of meaning and as the centerpiece of the curriculum and assessment system (Kridel & Bullough, 2007).

The assessment system developed by those courageous educators involved in the Eight-Year Study helped paint a vibrant picture of each student's cognitive, social, and emotional growth through the use of quantitative and qualitative methods using instruments customized to the individual high schools in which they were used. Each student had a personal portfolio with detailed examples of his and her social, emotional, and cognitive growth based on multiple indicators and data points. Teachers also wrote narrative descriptions of students to augment the various interviews, observations, surveys, and traditional assessments that went into each portfolio. The depth of information for each student was more than ample to allow the admissions officers from some of the 300 colleges and universities to make informed judgments about the students (Aikin, 1942).

The assessments used during the study were embedded into instruction, formatively. In many cases, the assessments were made on site by teams of teachers, aligned to the curriculum and long-term learning goals. Assessment was viewed as a tool to inform and created first and foremost to provide the teacher, student, and parent with timely and reliable feedback about student cognitive, social, and emotional growth. The students in the 30 experimental school districts outperformed their peers in traditional schools on academic, social, and emotional measures, including scores on traditional standardized tests (Aikin, 1942).

Regardless of the examples one chooses to use, assessment policy based on self-determination theory focuses on assessment as a tool to inform, not to punish. Assessment in an accountability model based on self-determination theory would itself be accountable to the users of the results, not drive the behavior of the users. Importantly, assessment based on self-determination theory does not supplant the judgment and evaluation of the teacher; it merely provides yet one more data point to inform that judgment.

Theoretical Construct for the Study

One construct usually omitted from consideration by proponents of using high-stakes standardized tests for accountability and monitoring is the influence of community and family demographic characteristics on the results from state standardized tests. The conditions of the community in which a child lives and matures and the economic security of the family in which he or she is nurtured have an influence on the child's achievement as represented in standardized test results (Sirin, 2005).

Wilkins (1999) identified four categories of out-of-school factors that can predict the percentage of students who would be proficient on the Virginia state tests of mathematics and language arts: (a) financial capital of a community, (b) social capital of a community, (c) human capital of a community, and (d) the geographic capital of a community. Similarly, Maylone (2002) identified (a) median household income of a community, (b) education level of a community, and (c) the percentage of lone parent households in a community as broad factors that predict the percentage of students proficient or above on Michigan's state-mandated high school tests of mathematics and language arts.

Turnamian and Tienken (2013) demonstrated that factors found in the U.S. census data related to household income, percentages of lone parent families, and the education levels of residents in a community can be used to predict the percentage of students scoring proficient or above on New Jersey's state-mandated tests of math and language arts in Grade 3. Jones (2008) used a combination of community demographic and school characteristics to predict the percentages of students scoring proficient or above on the New Jersey high school exit exam in math and language arts.

Family characteristics and the characteristics of the community in which a student lives are important factors that can predict academic achievement on standardized tests. As children grow up, positive influences on student achievement on standardized tests at all levels of education include households with two parents, family income levels above the poverty line, one parent employed in a secure job and the other parent at home during the early formative years or working only part time, and parents with at least a high school education (College Board, 2012; Davis-Kean, 2005; Dawson, 1991; Weinberg, 2001). Although the environment does not destine a student to a certain level of achievement, it does influence ultimate achievement on standardized tests.

A common line of research about the influence of family characteristics on student academic achievement includes using student eligibility for free or reduced-price lunch as a proxy for student socio-economic status (SES) at the individual level or a proxy for school- or district-level SES. Approximately 20% of the studies reviewed by Sirin (2005) for the meta-analysis of SES influence on achievement conducted between 1990 and 2000, and those reviewed by Harwell, Maeda, and Lee, (2004) conducted between 1996 and 2000 used free/reduced lunch status as the SES variable.

Harwell and LeBeau (2010) raised important issues regarding the weaknesses of using free/reduced lunch status as an indicator of student, school, or school district SES. Overall, student eligibility for free/reduced lunch is not as fine-grained an indicator of poverty as researchers might believe or desire. That is one reason I used more focused U.S. census data to capture the influences of family characteristics on student achievement.

The community in which a student lives is also an important influence on academic achievement. In this work, I connect the community demographics to the social capital as described by Coleman (1988):

> Social capital is defined by its functions. It is not a single entity but a variety of different entities, with two elements in common: they all consist of some aspect of social structures, and they facilitate certain actions of actors—whether persons or corporate actors—within the structure. Like other forms of capital, social capital is productive, making possible the achievement of certain ends that in its absence would not be possible. . . . A given form of social capital that is valuable in facilitating certain actions may be useless or even harmful for others.
>
> *(p. 98)*

Whereas physical capital refers to equipment and concrete resources necessary to progress economically, and human capital refers to changes to people's skills and abilities that allow them to act differently and become more economically productive, social capital is formed through formal and informal relationships and interactions (Coleman, 1988; World Bank, 2011).

Community groups for adults, recreation programs for children, a local League of Women Voters, formal and informal parent groups, church groups, a local arts council, and other similar resources all contribute to the social capital of a town (Putnam, 2000).

When children grow up in towns with access to high levels of social capital, one can conclude that it increases the chances that children and their families will interact with and develop formal and informal relationships with people who have higher levels of human capital. Thus, children have the potential to be exposed to more academic ideas and situations that influence their learning in school directly and indirectly. Children living in communities with higher levels of human and social capital are then more likely to have access to varied life experiences that build academic background knowledge—the knowledge they bring to school to connect their experiences to new content and better transfer ideas from school to other situations (Tanner & Tanner, 2007). In these ways, access to varied types and quality of social and human capital influences student learning in more authentic classroom situations where children need to connect the content to their life experiences, but also social and human capital play a role in ultimate achievement on standardized tests.

Based on my reading of the literature, I understand social capital and human capital as having reciprocal relationships, each needing and each nurturing the other. I view the family in which a child is raised as the initial provider of human and social capital, and the community in which that family lives as a complementary provider of social capital and indirect facilitator of individual human capital. Based on results from earlier studies (e.g., Maylone, 2002; Wilkins, 1999), I theorize that the influence of the social and human capital present in the family and community demographic factors on standardized state test results is sizable.

I propose that variables found in the U.S. census data that represent various aspects of human and social capital at the family and community levels that a child experiences and has access to can be used to predict within a margin of error the percentage of students in a school district that will score proficient or above on state assessments. I see the equation as $C_i (A_i) + C_{ii} (A_{ii}) + C_{iii} (A_{iii})$ ... = Influence on Academic Achievement, where C is the specific type of capital, such as lone parent households or families in poverty, and A is the percentage of those factors in a community.

Methods

I used a correlational, explanatory, longitudinal design with quantitative methods. I included 12 independent community demographic variables associated with family and community human and social capital found in the extant literature and represented in the 2009 U.S. census data related to community income, community education levels, and lone parent households.

The dependent variables were the 2010, 2011, and 2012 Grade 5 New Jersey Assessment of Skills and Knowledge (NJASK) percentages of students scoring proficient or above, at the school district level, in mathematics and language arts.

Sample

The total available population for this study was 100% of New Jersey school districts that had (a) more than 25 Grade 5 students, (b) valid 2010, 2011, and 2012 results from NJASK mathematics and language arts sections, and (c) complete census data for the communities served. New Jersey is generally considered a home-rule state, so most school districts serve only the students who live in the community in which the district is located. Because of this correlation, I was able to use the community census data as a proxy for demographics of the community the school district served.

Some of the 572 school districts in New Jersey included regional schools that drew students from various communities, or school districts that did not house fifth-grade classes, and thus were excluded from the sample. Only schools that served Grade 5 students from their hometown were included in order to decrease the chances of compromised data that can occur from including students from multiple communities in a sample from one school district. It is impossible to parse out the multiple community and familial demographic factors for a school district that serves students from multiple communities when one uses only publically available data. Researchers need to have student-level data to do that type of analysis or to perform a study like this one at the individual school level. Those data do not exist in the U.S. census database and would have to be collected from each of the more than 500 individual schools in New Jersey.

Therefore, the study was conducted at the district level of analysis. The population available for this study was 399 school districts for the 2010 sample and 398 school districts for the 2011 and 2012 samples. The difference between the number of eligible districts in the 2010 sample versus those in the 2011 and 2012 samples was that one school district had less than 25 students in Grade 5 during the 2011 and 2012 school years. All the schools in the samples that met the criteria were used in the analyses. The sample sizes for the study represented all the districts that met the sampling criteria. I conducted an a priori calculation to ensure appropriate sample size power. The work of Field (2009), who referenced Green (1991), guided the establishment of a minimum acceptable sample size. Field (2009) stated,

> If you want to test the model overall, then he [Green] recommends a minimum sample size of 50 + 8k, where k is the number of predictors. So, with five predictors, you'd need a sample size of 50 + 40 = 90. If you want to test the individual predictors then he suggests a minimum

sample size of 104 + *k,* so again taking the example of 5 predictors you'd need a sample size of 104 + 5 = 109. (p. 222)

I included 12 predictors in a model. Hence, at a minimum, I needed 50 + 8(12) = *N*, or a total of 146 cases. The sample sizes ($N = 399$ and $N = 398$) provided enough power to identify an effect size of at least 0.50 at the 95% confidence interval, and also to generalize results to the remaining districts in the state.

Variables

The dependent variables were the percentages of students who scored proficient or above for each mathematics and language arts state test in Grade 5 during 2010, 2011, and 2012. The independent variables were drawn from 2009 U.S. census data estimates. The 2010 U.S. census data results were not available when the 2010 New Jersey state tests were given, so I had to use the 2009 estimates. The independent variables, selected from those variables found in the extant literature, coalesced around three groups: (a) median household income of a community, (b) education level of a community, and (c) percentage of families in a community headed by only one parent.

Median household income was represented by the following U.S. census variables: (a) median household income, (b) percentage of economically disadvantaged households, (c) percentage of households with income of $200,000 or more, (d) percentage of families in poverty, and (e) percentage of households with income of $30,000 or less. The education level of the community was determined by the percentage of community members with (a) less than a high school diploma, (b) a high school diploma, (c) some college, (d) a bachelor's degree, or (e) an advanced degree. The final independent variable was the percentage of lone parent households in a community.

Data Analysis

Two forms of multiple regression were used to analyze results for each subject area: simultaneous multiple regression (SMR) and then hierarchical linear regression (HLR) to identify statistically significant predictor variables to use in the predictive algorithm. I inspected the skewness of the dependent variables to determine whether the data were normally distributed within the 1.00 to −1.00 ranges. The dependent variables Math11 and Math12 exhibited negative skew of −1.20 and −1.45, respectively. Therefore the data were transformed using a log10 reflection and reducing the skew to −.676 and −.651 with a standard error of .122.

For each subject area in each year (2010–2012), I conducted a series of layered analyses. First, the correlation matrix and scatterplots were examined to help develop more refined models. Then, I loaded all the independent variables into an initial simultaneous multiple regression model. Next, a series of hierarchical linear regression models was built that used the strongest predictor variables from the initial regression models to inform the construction of hierarchical regression models.

My first goal was to identify the combination of statistically significant demographic variables that explained the largest amount of variance in 2010–2012 NJASK5 math and language arts percentages of students proficient or above in order to create an algorithm that could predict those scores. I considered the threat of multicolinearity on the predictive variables in constructing the models. The results from the hierarchical models of best fit that provided the most accurate predictions of the percentages of students who scored proficient or above on each subject area test, each year, are presented.

Each of the final models included two or three demographic variables related to the human capital of the family and/or social capital of the community. These variables were then used to complete the predictive algorithm. To determine the predicted percentage of students proficient or above at the district level, I entered the community-level percentages for the predictive demographic variables identified into the hierarchical models, multiplied by the unstandardized betas for the strongest statistically significant predictor variables identified in the hierarchical models, and then added the constant value for each of the best models into the following algorithm used originally by Maylone (2002):

$$A_i (X_i) + A_{ii} (X_{ii}) + A_{iii} (X_{iii}) \ldots + \text{Constant} = Y$$
A_i = demographic predictor percentage
X_i = unstandardized beta for demographic predictor
Y = predicted percentage of students scoring proficient or above

A predicted percentage proficient or above was calculated for each of the models for each school district in the sample, for each test, and for each year. For example, for the 2012 language arts test, the predictive formula was (% lone parent households in a district × unstandardized beta for lone parent variable) + (% of households with income $200K or more × unstandardized beta for $200K variable) + constant = predicted score. The actual predictive model for language arts 2012 was (% lone parent × −0.594) + (% 200K × 0.542) + 73.71 = predicted percentage.

I first calculated the predicted percentage of students who scored proficient or above for each school district and then subtracted the predicted percentage from the actual reported percentage to obtain a difference. Differences within the standard error for each predictive model were considered to be accurate within the 95% confidence interval, whereas differences larger than the standard error of the model were considered inaccurate. Finally, I calculated the percentage of districts that I predicted accurately for each model. A total of six predictive algorithms were created to represent each year and subject area test from 2010 through 2012.

Results

The best statistically significant ($p < .05$) models were able to accurately predict the percentage of students scoring proficient or above in 64% to 80% of the districts in the sample, on the mathematics and language arts sections of the New Jersey state-mandated tests in Grade 5 for the 2010–2012 school years within the standard measure of error for each model. For example, the predictive model for the 2011 New Jersey mathematics test predicted accurately the percentage of students scoring proficient or above in 76% of the 397 districts in the sample (see Table 7.1).

The statistically significant ($p < .05$) models of best fit accounted for between 47% and 65% of the variance in the percentage of students who scored proficient or above on state-mandated tests. This means that community and family

TABLE 7.1 Statistically significant predictor variables for each model, amount of variance accounted for in each model, and percentage of districts accurately predicted by each model

Year	Mathematics	R^2 for math model and % accurately predicted	Language arts	R^2 for language arts mode and 1% accurately predicted
2010	% Families below poverty	.643	% Advanced degrees	.511
	% Lone parent households	(78%)	% Families below poverty	(64%)
	% $200K households		% $200K households	
2011	% Families below poverty	.467	% Families below poverty	.645
	% Lone parent households	(76%)	% Lone parent households	(76%)
	% Some college		% No HS diploma	
			% $200K households	
2012	% Families below poverty	.516	% Lone parent households	.571
	% Some college	(79%)	% $200K households	(80%)

demographic variables explained between half and two-thirds of variance in the test results for the years 2010 through 2012 in Grade 5. The results suggest that the percentage of students scoring proficient or above at the district level is heavily compromised by out-of-school factors.

Three demographic variables accurately predicted the results in both subject areas for the 2010 and 2011 models in language arts and mathematics, and only two variables were necessary for the 2012 models of best fit. The percentage of families in poverty was the strongest statistically significant predictor variable in five of the models. It was not a predictor in the 2012 language arts model. The percentage of lone parent households in a community was a statistically significant predictor in all of the models except mathematics 2012 and language arts 2010. The percentage of households with incomes of $200,000 or more was a statistically significant predictor in four models. Other statistically significant predictors that presented themselves in at least one model were the percentage of people with some college, percentage of people with advanced degrees, and the percentage of people in the community without a high school diploma.

The standard errors of measure ranged from 7.27 percentage points to 10.55 percentage points for the models. The median standard error of measure was 9.00 and the mean for all models was 8.98 percentage points. I used the standard error of measure as a guide to locate districts in which percentages of students who were rated proficient or above were within the predictions when taking into account the margin of error. I subtracted the predicted percentage from the actual percentage of students rated proficient or above by the state and rated the prediction accurate if the difference fell within the standard measure of error, whether the difference was positive or negative. Doing so allowed me to find all the accurate predictions within the 95% confidence interval. The following are examples from each year for districts in the samples.

Example 1: 2010 Language Arts, Branchburg Township, NJ

For the Branchburg Township school district, the demographic values for the three best predictors (% advanced degrees, % families in poverty, % $200K households) were as follows:

$$a = \% \text{ advanced degrees} \quad = \quad 14.67$$
$$b = \% \text{ families in poverty} \quad = \quad 1.66$$
$$c = \% \text{ \$200K households} \quad = \quad 17.29$$

I entered these values into the predictive algorithm along with the unstandardized betas and the constant:

$$14.67 \, (-.300) + 1.66 \, (-.863) + 17.29 \, (.610) + 70.887 = 75.60$$

The result, 75.60, represents the percentage of students in the Branchburg Township School District predicted to score proficient or above on the 2010 Grade 5 New Jersey state-mandated language arts test. The actual percentage of Grade 5 students in the district who scored proficient or above on the test according to reports from New Jersey education bureaucrats was 76.70. The standard error of measure for the model was 9.20 points. The difference between the predicted percentage and the actual percentage was: 76.70 − 75.60 = 1.10 percentage points. The difference was within the margin of error for the model and considered accurate.

Example 2: 2011 Mathematics, Ventnor City School District, NJ

For the Ventnor City School District, the values for the three out-of-school variables (% families in poverty, % lone parent households, % some college) were as follows:

$$a = \text{\% families in poverty} = 6.22$$
$$b = \text{\% lone parent households} = 40.32$$
$$c = \text{\% some college} = 21.32$$

I entered these values into the predictive algorithm along with the unstandardized betas and the constant:

$$6.22 \, (-.465) + 40.32 \, (-.206) + 21.32 \, (-.666) + 100.402 = 75.00$$

The result, 75.00, represents the percentage of students in the Ventnor City School District predicted to score proficient or above on the 2011 Grade 5 New Jersey state-mandated mathematics test. The actual percentage of Grade 5 students in the district who scored proficient or above on the test was 74.80. The standard error of measure for the model was 8.81 points. The difference between the predicted percentage and the actual percentage was: −0.20 percentage points. The difference was within the margin of error for the model and considered accurate.

Example 3: 2012 Language Arts, Northfield City School District, NJ

The values for the two out-of-school variables from the model of best fit (% lone parent households, % $200K households) were as follows:

$$a = \text{\% lone parent households} = 20.72$$
$$b = \text{\% \$200K households} = 3.51$$

I entered these values into the predictive algorithm along with the unstandardized betas and the constant:

$$20.72 \ (-.594) \ +3.51 \ (.542) + 73.710 = 63.30$$

The result, 63.30, represents the percentage of students in the Northfield City School District predicted to score proficient or above on the 2012 Grade 5 New Jersey state-mandated language arts test. The actual percentage of Grade 5 students in the district who scored proficient or above on the test was 66.40. The standard error of measure for the model was 10.55 points. The difference between the predicted percentage and the actual percentage was −3.10 percentage points. The difference was within the margin of error for the model and considered accurate.

I hypothesize that the models used in this study could be transferred to the individual school level of analysis if student-level demographic data that helps describe the human capital and social capital of the student were available.

Implications and Conclusions

In this chapter I argued, based on the findings from this study and those of earlier studies, that the results from high-stakes state standardized tests are an inappropriate choice for use in education accountability policies aimed at making potentially life-influencing judgments about educators and children. The fact is that the results can be influenced strongly by out-of-school demographic factors related to human and social capital, and can actually be predicted by factors completely outside the control of school personnel. Simply put, the continued use of results from commercially prepared state standardized tests by policymakers and bureaucrats as important or deciding factors in education policies that can result in potentially life-influencing decisions about educators and children constitutes education malpractice.

So What?

The results from this study and those of others (Jones, 2008; Maylone, 2002; Sackey, 2014; Turnamian & Tienken, 2013; Weinberg, 2001; Wilkins, 1999) predicted, with accuracy, the percentages of students scoring proficient or above in various grade levels in Michigan, Virginia, New Jersey, and Connecticut on state tests of math and language arts from 1999 through 2012. The various test-based accountability schemes currently deployed in states rely on instrumental use policies steeped in behaviorism and rational choice theories. Unfortunately, the specific use of students' proficiency rates on state-mandated tests as part of policies to make pivotal decisions about student achievement, student readiness for colleges and careers, or teacher effectiveness at the school-district level is clearly inappropriate given that the results can be predicted for a majority of the districts.

Now What?

Policymakers and education bureaucrats should pledge a moratorium on any accountability policies that rely on results from state standardized tests as important indicators or as the deciding factor to trigger consequences for educators or students. Also, people in policymaking positions or those who influence policymaking should strive to develop accountability policy based on factors that education personnel control. The achievement of the goals attached to such policies should be determined through methods that limit the contamination of factors outside the control of policymakers. The results and those from previous studies demonstrate that the data received from state test results is, in fact, corrupted by family- and community-level demographic factors. They are, in essence, dirty data.

A moratorium on the use of high-stakes test results might provide the think-time and cognitive space to consider accountability models based more on self-determination theory and the vision of assessment to inform versus assessment to punish. I propose looking at alternative models currently in use around the country as well as going back to the future and using examples of successful programs from education's past to drive the policymaking of the future.

The Nebraska STARS and New York Performance Assessment Consortium offer two high-profile examples of accountability systems that strike a balance between state-mandated assessment methods and locally developed initiatives used during the standards-based era that can be scaled up or replicated. For example, if policymakers must include the use of commercially prepared standardized tests in their systems to adhere to a mandate by their federal overlords, they could use them as no-stakes data points.

Commercially prepared standardized tests are one possible tool to efficiently provide information about student attainment of low-level skills. Commercially prepared standardized tests are one of the most economical ways to measure low-level learning. Therefore, an accountability policy could include their use for a very specific and narrow purpose. The results from such tests would not carry any more weight than locally developed methods or teachers' assessments. The results from commercially prepared tests would be used to inform, not punish—just another data point to triangulate the cognitive development of children.

The centerpiece of accountability policy should be classroom assessment, including problem-based and project-based outputs as well as teacher-crafted narratives about students. One need only look back to the epic Eight-Year Study to know that education professionals are capable of developing high-quality assessments in the form of learning activities and more traditional models such as surveys and tests.

Qualitative methods such as interviews and reviews of student work over time could also be part of a comprehensive system. School districts could decide, along with their stakeholders, which outcomes to emphasize; but a nonnegotiable aspect of any accountability system should be to develop a structure that provides information about cognitive, social, and emotional development of students. A secondary level of assessment could come from the state as bureaucrats could identify long-term goals that school personnel could also work toward and develop assessments to inform their practice. Commercially prepared standardized tests could be used, at the choice of the district, to efficiently measure low-level cognitive skills.

In this way, accountability policy would be based more on self-determination theory than on instrumental use theory. There is no necessity for carrots and sticks in a professional environment where reflection and self-actualization are the goals as opposed to the mechanistic improvement of standardized test results.

Of course, the *Standards for Educational and Psychological Testing* (AERA, APA, & NCME, 2014) should be followed if accountability policies include the use of standardized tests. In my opinion, the item from the standards that needs to be included in state accountability policies is Standards for Validity 1.1: "No test permits interpretations that are valid for all purposes or in all situations. Each recommended interpretation for a given use requires validation" (p. 23). In an era in which state bureaucrats use results from state tests to determine student achievement, teacher effectiveness, school administrator effectiveness, and overall school quality, it is important that basic standards of test-result use be followed.

School Administrator Practice

In addition to the potential policy implications of results from the study reported in this chapter, I suggest that the results from the study and studies like this one have potentially important consequences for administrative decision-making. School administrators make decisions daily about allocations of time, money, instruction, student learning, and staffing based on information and influences emanating from the macro- and micro-systems in which they administer (Hoy & Hoy, 2013).

An example of an influence from the micro-system includes policies adopted by a local board of education, whereas an influence from the macro-system is a program like the CCSS initiative, developed in part to address the perception on the part of policymakers that U.S. students lag behind their international peers on international tests of mathematics such as TIMSS and PISA (Tienken & Mullen, 2014). Although the CCSS and state-mandated standardized tests aligned to the CCSS were developed and are being imposed by a distal body, local school administrators must still handle the local implementation.

I incorporated Vroom and Jago's (1988) model of decision effectiveness into the design of this study because decision-making is a prominent function of school administration and local policymaking. Decision effectiveness relies on the premise that access to quality information drives administrator action and can influence the quality and outcomes of those actions. I also drew upon Path-Goal Theory (House, 1996) in that leadership behavior motivates followers to pursue a path toward the identified goal. Inherent in Path-Goal Theory is the underlying assumption that the school administrator is gathering and processing quality information to set appropriate goals and paths and monitor the attainment of those goals. Whether the leader exhibits supporting, participative, achievement-oriented, or directive behaviors, access to and the processing of quality information is important within the Path-Goal Theory.

As decision-makers, school administrators must decide whether to pursue specific policies and practices, and how zealously in each case, based on the information available to them at the time they make a decision. Therefore, research that helps explain the level of effectiveness of a proposed or mandated program or substantiates a policy claim can prove useful to evidence-informed administrative decision-making.

School administrator goal-setting and decisions can be compromised if school administrators do not have access to quality information about the policies and practices they are mandated to implement or choose to pursue. Pertinent, factually correct information is seemingly pushed underground or simply aside in the mainstream information networks such as professional journals, media outlets, and professional organizations, making the decision-making situation even more precarious for school administrators.

Clearly, school administrators who voluntarily use the results from their state tests to make life-influencing decisions about teachers or students should interrogate their reasoning process and cease using the results as the deciding factor in any decisions related to school quality, student achievement, or educator effectiveness. The findings from this study and previous studies demonstrate consistently that the results from state standardized tests are compromised by factors outside the control of teachers and their students. In fact, I propose that the use of those results for student academic track placement, entrance or dismissal from academic programs or cocurricular activities, student promotion decisions, or any other decisions that restrict student access to comprehensive education programs, with a broad and deep macro-curriculum, constitutes school administrator malpractice.

School administrators and their professional associations need to inform themselves about the liabilities and dangers of misusing standardized test results to make important decisions about human beings. Purposeful ignorance is not acceptable leadership behavior. In an era in which a nine-year-old can be deemed unready for college and careers based on the results from one test, school administrators need to reflect upon the policies and practices they control to ensure they are in fact aligned to the information that science on this topic is producing.

Certainly, decision effectiveness (Vroom & Jago, 1988) will be threatened by using dirty data. A keen awareness of the macro-assessment environment by school administrators is necessary to avoid harmful practices brought on by poor decision-making at the micro-policy development level of the school district. Therefore, I call upon school superintendents to review their local policies that rely on results from state standardized tests as the deciding factor or as a factor that can influence decision-making about students and teachers.

Policies that delineate entrance criteria into district and school programs, or placements into academic tracks that depend on those results, should be revised so that the results are rendered nontoxic to decision-making. Superintendents should challenge themselves and the school principals within their jurisdiction to kick the standardized test results habit and thereby outlaw their use for decision-making, as a way to facilitate the development of higher-quality in-house assessment systems on the part of their principals and teachers.

Although school superintendents do not control how state education bureaucrats use results from state-mandated standardized tests, they can control what they have control over at the local level: district-level policy on how test results are used voluntarily by school personnel. Superintendents should work with their boards of education to revise policies that use standardized test scores as the deciding factor in decision-making because those scores are highly contaminated and influenced by out-of-school factors. If educators accept Hoy and Hoy's (2013) view of the school administrator as a decision-maker as a bedrock view of the education administration field, then nothing could be more important than quality information from which to base those decisions.

School administrators also should work with their professional organizations and school board organizations to develop statements that call for the appropriate use of test results in an overall accountability system. Leaders of some professional organizations can no longer remain purposefully ignorant to the appropriate and inappropriate use of standardized test results. Professional organizations have a role to play in ensuring that education policy does not harm the very people it is developed to influence.

Closing Comments

The time for debate is over. It is inappropriate, professionally reckless, and educationally bankrupt for policymakers and educators to continue to bow their heads at the altar of standardized test results. The results from such tests tell us more about the human and social capital of the home and community in which a child is raised than about the academic, social, or emotional intelligence and potential of the child. The sun does not revolve around the earth. The science of testing suggests that results from standardized tests should not be used as the deciding data point (AERA, APA, & NCME, 2014). It is time for action, and school leaders are in a prime position to lead at the community level and within their professional organizations to craft appropriate local accountability policies and advocate for evidence-based uses of standardized test results at state and national levels. School leaders must lead toward accountability policies based on scientific evidence that are not harmful to children and educators.

References

Achieve, Inc. (2004). *Do graduation tests measure up? A closer look at state high school exit exams.* Washington, DC: Author. Retrieved from www.achieve.org/files/TestGraduation-FinalReport.pdf

Aikin, W. M. (1942). *The story of the eight-year study, with conclusions and recommendations.* New York, NY: Harper.

Allensworth, E. M. (2005). Dropout rates after high-stakes testing in elementary school: A study of the contradictory effects of Chicago's efforts to end social promotion. *Educational Evaluation and Policy Analysis, 27*(4), 341–364.

American Educational Research Association, American Psychological Association, & National Council on Measurement in Education. (2014). *Standards for educational and psychological testing.* Washington, DC: AERA.

Amrein, A. L., & Berliner, D. C. (2002). High-stakes testing, uncertainty, and student learning. *Education Policy Analysis Archives, 10*(18). Retrieved from http://epaa.asu.edu/ojs/article/view/297

Amrein-Beardsley, A., & Berliner, D. C. (2003, August). Re-analysis of NAEP math and reading scores in states with and without high-stakes tests: Response to Rosenshine. *Education Policy Analysis Archives, 11*(25). Retrieved from http://epaa.asu.edu/ojs/article/view/253

Andreoni, J., Harbaugh, W., & Versterlund, L. (2003). The carrot or the stick: Rewards, punishments, and cooperation. *American Economic Review, 93*(3), 893–902.

Au, W. (2011). Teaching under the new Taylorism: High-stakes testing and the standardization of the 21st century curriculum. *Journal of Curriculum Studies, 43*(1), 25–45.

Baker, B. D., Oluwole, J. O., & Green, P. C., III. (2013). The legal consequences of mandating high-stakes decisions based on low quality information: Teacher evaluation in the race-to-the-top era. *Education Policy Analysis Archives, 21*(5). Retrieved from http://epaa.asu.edu/ojs/article/view/1298

Bryk, A. S., & Hermanson, K. L. (1993). Educational indicator systems: Observations on their structure, interpretation, and use. *Review of Research in Education, 19*, 451–484.

Coleman, J. S. (1988). Social capital in the creation of human capital. *American Journal of Sociology, 94*, S95–S120.

College Board. (2012). *2012 college-bound seniors: Total group profile report.* New York, NY: Author. Retrieved from http://research.collegeboard.org/programs/sat/data/archived/cb-seniors-2012

Dappen, L., & Isernhagen, J. C. (2005). Nebraska STARS: Assessment for learning. *Planning and Changing, 36*(3–4), 147–156.

Davis-Kean, P. E. (2005). The influence of parent education and family income on child achievement: The indirect role of parental expectations and the home environment. *Journal of Family Psychology, 19*(2), 294–304.

Dawson, D. A. (1991). Family structure and children's health and well-being: Data from the 1988 national health interview survey on child health. *Journal of Marriage and Family, 53*(3), 573–584.

Deci, E. L., & Ryan, R. M. (2012). Motivation, personality, and development within embedded social contexts: An overview of self-determination theory. In R. M. Ryan (Ed.), *Oxford handbook of human motivation* (pp. 85–107). New York, NY: Oxford University Press.

Dee, T. S., & Jacob, B. (2009). The impact of No Child Left Behind on student achievement. *Journal of Policy Analysis and Management, 30*(3), 418–446.

Field, A. (2009). *Discovering statistics using SPSS* (3rd ed.). Thousand Oaks, CA: SAGE Publications.

Freedman, M. K. (2004). The fight for high standards. *Hoover Digest, 3.* Retrieved from www.hoover.org/research/fight-high-standards

Fuller, E. (2014). An examination of Pennsylvania school performance profile scores [Policy brief 2014-1]. University Park, PA: Center for Evaluation and Education Policy Analysis, Pennsylvania State University. Retrieved from http://vamboozled.com/wp-content/uploads/2014/10/Fuller.pdf

Green, S. B. (1991). How many subjects does it take to do a regression analysis? *Multivariate Behavioral Research, 26*(3), 499–510.

Greene, J. P., & Winters, M. A. (2004). *Pushed out or pulled up? Exit exams and dropout rates in public high schools* [Education working paper 5]. New York, NY: Manhattan Institute for Policy Research. Retrieved from www.manhattan-institute.org/html/ewp_05.htm

Haller, E. J., & Kleine, P. F. (2001). *Using educational research: A school administrator's guide.* New York, NY: Longman.

Hanushek, E. A., & Welch, F. (Eds.). (2006). *Handbook of the economics of education.* Amsterdam, The Netherlands: North-Holland/Elsevier.

Harwell, M. R., & LeBeau, B. (2010). Student eligibility for a free lunch as an SES measure in education research. *Educational Researcher, 39*(2), 120–131.

Harwell, M. R., Maeda, Y., & Lee, K. (2004, April). *Replicating and extending White's (1982) meta-analysis of the relationship between SES and student achievement.* Paper presented at the annual meeting of the American Educational Research Association, San Diego, CA.

Heilig, J. V., & Darling-Hammond, L. (2008). Accountability Texas-style: The progress and learning of urban minority students in a high-stakes testing context. *Educational Evaluation and Policy Analysis, 30*(2), 75–110.

Hoover Institution. (2004, February 18). *Task force presents education reform recommendations to Texas House Select Committee on Public School Finance* [Press release]. Retrieved from www.hoover.org/press-releases/task-force-presents-education-reform-recommendations-texas-house-select-committee

House, R. J. (1996). Path-goal theory of leadership: Lessons, legacy, and a reformulated theory. *Leadership Quarterly, 7*(3), 323–352. doi:10.1016/S1048-9843(96)90024-7

Hoy, A. W., & Hoy, W. K. (2013). *Instructional leadership: A research-based guide to learning in schools* (4th ed.). Boston, MA: Allyn & Bacon/Pearson.

Hursh, D. (2008). *High-stakes testing and the decline of teaching and learning: The real crisis in education.* Lanham, MD: Rowman & Littlefield.

Jones, M. (2008, May). *The influence of variables on school report cards regarding the passing rates for students taking the high school proficiency assessment (HSPA) in New Jersey's comprehensive high schools* (Doctoral dissertation). Retrieved from ProQuest LLC. (UMI Microform 3319531)

Koretz, D. (2008). *Measuring up: What educational testing really tells us.* Cambridge, MA: Harvard University Press.

Kridel, C., & Bullough, R. V., Jr. (2007). *Stories of the eight-year study: Reexamining secondary education in America.* Albany, NY: State University Press of New York.

Laitsch, D. (2006). *Assessment, high stakes, and alternative visions: Appropriate use of the right tools to leverage improvement.* Tempe, AZ: Education Policy Unit, Arizona State University. Retrieved from http://epsl.asu.edu/epru/documents/EPSL-0611-222-EPRU.pdf

Lee, J., & Wong, K. K. (2004). The impact of accountability on racial and socioeconomic equity: Considering both school resources and achievement outcomes. *American Educational Research Journal, 41*(4), 797–832.

Maylone, N. (2002). *The relationship of socioeconomic factors and district scores on the Michigan educational assessment program tests: An analysis.* (Unpublished doctoral dissertation). Eastern Michigan University, Ypsilanti, MI.

McGregor, D. (1960). *The human side of enterprise.* New York, NY: McGraw-Hill.

Messick, S. (1994). *Standards-based score interpretation: Establishing valid grounds for valid inferences.* Proceedings of the Joint Conference on Standard Setting for Large-Scale Assessments, sponsored by the National Assessment Governing Board and the National Center for Education Statistics. *ETS Research Report Series, 1994*(2), 291–395.

National Governors Association Center for Best Practices & Council of Chief State School Officers. (2010). *Common Core State Standards: Frequently asked questions.* Washington, DC: NGA & CCSSO. Retrieved from www.corestandards.org/about-the-standards/frequently-asked-questions

New York Performance Assessment Consortium. (2015). *Alternatives to high-stakes testing.* Retrieved from http://performanceassessment.org/consortium/calternatives.html

Nichols, S. L., Glass, G. V், & Berliner, D. C. (2012) High-stakes testing and student achievement: Updated analyses with NAEP data. *Education Policy Analysis Archives, 20*(20). Retrieved from http://epaa.asu.edu/ojs/article/view/1048

No Child Left Behind Act of 2001, 20 U.S.C.A. § 6301 *et seq.* (West, 2003).

Papay, J. P., Murnane, R. J., & Willett, J. B. (2010). The consequences of high school exit examinations on low-performing urban students: Evidence from Massachusetts. *Educational Evaluation and Policy Analysis, 32*(1), 5–23.

Partnership for Assessment of Readiness for College and Careers. (2013). *PARCC fact sheet and FAQs.* Washington, DC: Author. Retrieved from www.parcconline.org/sites/parcc/files/PARCCFactSheetandFAQsBackgrounder_FINAL.pdf

Partnership for Assessment of Readiness for College and Careers. (2014). *PARCC states.* Washington, DC: Author. Retrieved from www.parcconline.org/parcc-states

Penfield, R. D. (2010). Test-based grade retention: Does it stand up to professional standards for fair and appropriate test use? *Educational Researcher, 39*(2), 110–119.

Putnam, R. D. (2000). *Bowling alone: The collapse and revival of American community.* New York, NY: Simon & Schuster.

Reed, E., Scull, J., Slicker, G, & Northern, A. M. (2012). *Defining strong state accountability systems: How can better standards gain traction?* Washington, DC: Thomas B. Fordham Institute.

Rose, S. (2012, August). *Third grade reading policies.* Denver, CO: Education Commission of the States. Retrieved from http://co.chalkbeat.org/wp-content/uploads/sites/2/2012/08/ecsreport.pdf

Russell, M. K., Ramos, M. A., & Miao, J. (2003). *Perceived effects of state-mandated testing programs on teaching and learning: Findings from a national survey of teachers.* Boston, MA: National Board on Educational Testing and Public Policy.

Sackey, A. N. L., Jr. (2014). *The influence of community demographics on student achievement on the Connecticut Mastery Test in mathematics and English language arts in grade 3 through 8* (Unpublished doctoral dissertation). Seton Hall University, South Orange, NJ. Retreived from http://scholarship.shu.edu/cgi/viewcontent.cgi?article=3033&context=dissertations

Santos, F. (2012, February 24). *City teacher data reports are released.* New York, NY: WNYC. Retrieved from WNYC.org: www.wnyc.org/blogs/schoolbook/2012/feb/24/teacher-data-reports-are-released

Sirin, S. R. (2005). Socioeconomic status and academic achievement: A meta-analytic review of research. *Review of Educational Research, 75*(3), 417–453.

Smarick, A. (2014, October 13). *In defense of annual testing.* Washington, DC: Thomas B. Fordham Institute. Retrieved from http://edexcellence.net/articles/in-defense-of-annual-testing

Smarter Balanced Assessment Consortium [SBAC]. (2014a). Frequently asked questions. Olympia, WA: SBAC. Retrieved from www.smarterbalanced.org/resources-events/faqs/#

Smarter Balanced Assessment Consortium [SBAC]. (2014b). Member states. Olympia, WA: SBAC. Retrieved from www.smarterbalanced.org/about/member-states

Stringfield, S. C., & Yakimowski-Srebnick, M. E. (2005). Promise, progress, problems, and paradoxes of three phases of accountability: A longitudinal case study of the Baltimore City Public Schools. *American Educational Research Journal, 42*(1), 43–75.

Tanner, D., & Tanner, L. (2007). *Curriculum development: Theory into practice* (4th ed.). Saddle River, NJ: Pearson.

Tienken, C. H., & Mullen, C. A. (2014). The curious case of international student assessment: Rankings and realities in the innovation economy. In S. Harris & J. Mixon (Eds.), *Building cultural community through global educational leadership* (pp. 146–164). Ypsilanti, MI: NCPEA Press.

Tienken, C. H., Tramaglini, T. W., & Lynch, C. (2013, August). *Predicting state test results in mathematics and language arts using community demographic data.* Paper presented at the National Council of Professors of Educational Administration Conference, Rutherford, NJ.

Turnamian, P. G., & Tienken, C. H. (2013). Use of community wealth demographics to predict statewide test results in Grade 3. In C. A. Mullen & K. E. Lane (Eds.), *Becoming a global voice* (pp. 134–146). Ypsilanti, MI: National Council of Professors of Educational Administration.

U.S. Department of Education. (2012, October). *NCLB/More local freedom: Flexibility and waivers.* Washington, DC: ED. Retrieved from www2.ed.gov/nclb/freedom/local/flexibility/index.html

U.S. Department of Education. (2014, July). *NCLB/More local freedom: ESEA flexibility.* Washington, DC: ED. Retrieved from www2.ed.gov/policy/elsec/guid/esea-flexibility/index.html

Vroom, V. H., & Jago, A. G. (1988). *The new leadership: Managing participation in organizations.* Englewood Cliffs, NJ: Prentice Hall.

Weinberg, B. A. (2001). An incentive model of the effect of parental income on children. *Journal of Political Economy, 109*(2), 266–280.

Wilkins, J. L. M. (1999). Demographic opportunities and school achievement. *Journal of Research in Education, 9*(1), 12–19.

World Bank, The. (2011). *Social capital.* Washington, DC: Author. Retrieved from http://go.worldbank.org/K4LUMW43B0

EDITORS AND CONTRIBUTORS

Editors

Christopher H. Tienken, EdD, is Associate Professor of Education Administration at Seton Hall University in the College of Education and Human Services, Department of Education Management, Policy, and Leadership. A former public school teacher, principal, assistant superintendent, and director of curriculum and instruction, Dr. Tienken is journal editor of the American Association of School Administrators' *Journal of Scholarship and Practice* and the *Kappa Delta Pi Record*. His research interests include school reform issues such as the influence of curriculum quality on student outcomes and the construct validity of high-stakes standardized tests as decision-making tools to determine school effectiveness. His research has been recognized with awards from the Institute of Education Sciences and the National Staff Development Council. Also, he received the Truman Kelley Award for Outstanding Scholarship from Kappa Delta Pi in 2013 and was named the 2014 College of Education and Human Services Researcher of the Year. His book, with coauthor Don Orlich, is titled *The School Reform Landscape: Fraud, Myth, and Lies* (Rowman & Littlefield Education, 2013).

Carol A. Mullen, PhD, is Professor of Educational Leadership at Virginia Tech, Blacksburg. She is a U.S. Fulbright Scholar whose visit in China in 2015 furthered her research in leadership, mentoring, and policy from a social justice perspective. She served as President of the National Council of Professors of Educational Administration and as Department Chair and School Director/Associate Dean at two universities. She is serving as a Plenary Senator for the University Council for Educational Administration and is on the Kappa Delta

Pi Presidential Commission. An award-winning researcher and professor, her coauthored books include *The Leadership Identity Journey: An Artful Reflection* (Rowman & Littlefield, 2014), *Shifting to Fit: The Politics of Black and White Identity in School Leadership* (Information Age, 2014), and, as coeditor, *The SAGE Handbook of Mentoring and Coaching in Education* (Sage, 2012).

Contributors

Christopher Lubienski, PhD, is Professor of Education Policy and Director of the Forum on the Future of Public Education at the University of Illinois. He is also a Fellow with the National Education Policy Center and Sir Walter Murdoch Visiting Professor at Murdoch University in Western Australia. Dr. Lubienski's research focuses on education policy, reform, and the political economy of education, with a particular concern for issues of equity and access. His book *The Public School Advantage: Why Public Schools Outperform Private Schools* (University of Chicago Press, 2014) won the 2015 PROSE Award for Education Theory from the American Publishers Awards for Professional and Scholarly Excellence.

Michael Marder, PhD, is a Professor of Physics at the University of Texas at Austin, specializing in nonlinear dynamics and materials physics. He also is the Executive Director of the UTeach Science Program and codirects the preparation of mathematics and science teachers at the university, as well as oversees more than 6,500 math and science majors preparing to become teachers at 44 UTeach replication sites throughout the United States.

P. S. Myers is a PhD student in the Department of Education Policy, Organization and Leadership at the University of Illinois at Urbana–Champaign. His research interests include the experiences of marginalized populations in educational quasi-markets as well as how market solutions proliferate and function in different contexts.

Mariela A. Rodríguez, PhD, is an Associate Professor in the Department of Educational Leadership and Policy Studies at the University of Texas at San Antonio. Her research agenda focuses on the role of elementary school principals leading schools with additive language programs like two-way immersion education programs. She currently serves on the Executive Committee of the University Council for Educational Administration and is an ex-officio member on the Board of the National Council of Professors of Educational Administration.

Svein Sjøberg, PhD, is Professor Emeritus in science education at Oslo University, Norway. He has worked internationally with science education for national and international authorities like the Organisation for Economic

Co-operation and Development, the United Nations Educational, Scientific and Cultural Organization, the World Bank, and the European Union. Dr. Sjøberg has numerous honorary professorships and doctorates and has won several prizes and awards for his research as well as science communication and outreach. His major current concern is the ethical, social, political, and cultural aspects of education in an international perspective.

Thomas Tramaglini, EdD, is the PreK–12 Chief Academic Officer of the Keansburg School District in Keansburg, New Jersey and an Adjunct Professor in the Graduate School of Education at Rutgers, The State University of New Jersey. Previously, Dr. Tramaglini served in several school and district leadership positions, and was a middle and high school teacher. His research interests and career are devoted to leading public school organizations for equity, access, and excellence. Some of Dr. Tramaglini's honors include the 2012 University Council for Educational Administration's Excellence in Educational Leadership Award and the 2013 New Jersey Outstanding Educator Award

INDEX

Note: Page numbers in **bold** are for figures, those in *italics* are for tables.